AF733166

THE LAW OF MEDICAL NEGLIGENCE IN ENGLAND AND GERMANY

This new work adds to the theoretical understanding and discussion of possible solutions to various conceptual and practical problems that arise within the field of medical negligence—an area whose legal treatment is perceived, both in England and Germany, as containing a number of special difficulties and shortcomings. In addition it seeks to make a contribution to the developing field of comparative law, by employing a detailed and closely focused analytical approach in a tightly defined subject area. These twin aims serve to reveal the similarities and differences between two legal cultures in a particularly clear and striking way.

The book offers an analysis which is neutral as between the English and German approaches. The issues are dealt with thematically so far as possible, so that the respective treatments in each country of a given matter, eg the standard of care owed by medical practitioners, are discussed side-by-side. The book thus avoids the 'country-report' style, whereby the systems are presented largely separately from each other. What is of particular interest is how, notwithstanding their common starting point in terms of the application of the fault-principle under private law, the detailed rules in the two countries differ markedly. This is true both in the divergent way that claims are structured and argued, and also quite often as regards their substantive outcome. It will be of interest to comparative lawyers, tort and medical lawyers, and practising lawyers working in these areas.

The Law of Medical Negligence in England and Germany

A Comparative Analysis

MARC STAUCH

·HART·
PUBLISHING

OXFORD AND PORTLAND, OREGON
2008

Published in North America (US and Canada) by
Hart Publishing
c/o International Specialized Book Services
920 NE 58th Avenue, Suite 300
Portland, OR 97213-3786
USA
Tel: +1 503 287 3093 or toll-free: (1) 800 944 6190
Fax: +1 503 280 8832
E-mail: orders@isbs.com
Website: http://www.isbs.com

© Marc Stauch 2008

Marc Stauch has asserted his right under the Copyright, Designs and Patents Act 1988, to be identified as the author of this work.

All rights reserved. No part of this publication may be reproduced, stored in a retrieval system, or transmitted, in any form or by any means, without the prior permission of Hart Publishing, or as expressly permitted by law or under the terms agreed with the appropriate reprographic rights organisation. Enquiries concerning reproduction which may not be covered by the above should be addressed to Hart Publishing at the address below.

Hart Publishing, 16C Worcester Place, OX1 2JW
Telephone: +44 (0)1865 517530 Fax: +44 (0)1865 510710
E-mail: mail@hartpub.co.uk
Website: http://www.hartpub.co.uk

British Library Cataloguing in Publication Data
Data Available

ISBN: 978-1-84113-646-2

Typeset by Hope Services, Abingdon
Printed and bound in Great Britain by
TJ International Ltd, Padstow, Cornwall

PREFACE

This book is a slightly revised version of my thesis of the same title, which I submitted in December 2007 towards a doctorate from the University of Göttingen. At the same time it represents the principal harvest of some five years that I have spent in German academia, during which time I had the chance to assimilate German legal materials on medical negligence and reflect upon how the treatment of such claims differs from the English approach with which I was previously familiar. Though the difficulties for a mature legal scholar in moving to a foreign academic and legal environment should not be underestimated—the absence of secure bearings within a new and strange system; one's own lack of academic status; not least the need to master another legal language—nor can the ultimate benefit for one's legal understanding be denied. At least my hope is that this work may be found to bear out such a claim.

I should like to record my gratitude to my doctoral supervisor, Professor Christiane Wendehorst, for her patient and flexible support during the years that I was writing my thesis, and for correcting a number of infelicities in the material. I am also grateful to the Law Faculty at the University of Göttingen for allowing the publication of the work to proceed in parallel with the formal process leading to the award of a doctorate.

While writing this thesis, I held a teaching and research position at the Centre for British Studies, an interdisciplinary institute at the Humboldt University, Berlin. I should like to thank my colleagues at the Centre for their help and encouragement while I was there, especially Professor Gerhard Dannemann and Christian W. Handke (now of the Erasmus University in Rotterdam).

Finally, special thanks are due to my parents, Günther and Jane Stauch, and to my wife, Dr Christiane Trüe, for their love and support over the years; Christiane also provided me with valuable help in proofing the work and correcting its German summary.

TABLE OF CONTENTS

TABLE OF CASES

English cases

US and Commonwealth cases

German cases

TABLE OF STATUTES

Other

European Union

Former German Democratic Republic

TABLE OF ABBREVIATIONS

AC	Appeal Cases (Law Reports)
ALJR	Australian Law Journal Reports
AMG	Arzneimittelgesetz (Pharmaceutical Products Law)
All ER	All England Law Reports
ALR	Australian Law Reports
BGB	Bürgerliches Gesetzbuch (Civil Code)
BGH	Bundesgerichtshof (Federal Supreme Court)
BGHZ	Entscheidungen des Bundesgerichtshofs in Zivilsachen (Federal Supreme Court Civil Decisions)
BMJ	British Medical Journal
BMLR	Butterworths Medico-Legal Reports
BVerfG	Bundesverfassungsgericht (Federal Constitutional Court)
CA	Court of Appeal
Cal App	California Appellate Court Opinions
CLJ	Cambridge Law Journal
Cr App R	Criminal Appeal Reports
DLR	Dominion Law Reports
EWCA Civ	England and Wales Court of Appeal, Civil
EWCA Crim	England and Wales Court of Appeal, Criminal
EWHC	England and Wales High Court
Exch	Welsby, Hurlstone and Gordon's Exchequer Reports
F	Federal Reporter
FLR	Family Law Reports
GG	Grundgesetz (Constitution)
H & C	Hurlstone and Coltman's Exchequer Reports
HL	House of Lords
ICLQ	International and Comparative Law Quarterly
KB	King's Bench (Law Reports)
KVG	Krankenversicherungsgesetz (Health Insurance Law)
Lloyd's Rep Med	Lloyd's Law Reports, Medical
LQR	Law Quarterly Review
LR	Law Reports
Med LR	Medical Law Reports
MLR	Modern Law Review
NBR	New Brunswick Reports
NE	North Eastern Reporter

NJW	Neue Juristische Wochenschrift
NLJ	New Law Journal
NStZ	Neue Zeitschrift für Strafrecht
NY	New York Reports
OJLS	Oxford Journal of Legal Studies
OLG	Oberlandesgericht (State Appellate Court)
P	Pacific Reporter
PC	Privy Council
PIQR	Personal Injuries and Quantum Reports
Price	Price's Exchequer Reports
QB	Queen's Bench (Law reports)
QBD	Queen's Bench Division
RG	Reichsgericht (Imperial Court)
RGSt	Entscheidungen des Reichsgerichts in Strafsachen (Imperial Court Criminal Decisions)
RGZ	Entscheidungen des Reichsgerichts in Zivilsachen (Imperial Court Civil Decisions)
RTR	Road Traffic Reports
SC	Session Cases
SCR	Canada Supreme Court Reports
SGB	Sozialgesetzbuch (Social Security Code)
SJ	Solicitor's Journal
StGB	Strafgesetzbuch (Criminal Code)
StPO	Strafprozessordnung (Code of Criminal Procedure)
UKHL	United Kingdom House of Lords
VersR	Versicherungsrecht
WLR	Weekly Law Reports
ZPO	Zivilprozessordnung (Code of Civil Procedure)

1

The Social and Legal Background

I. Introduction

THIS WORK AIMS to compare the legal rules in England and Germany that allow patients to seek compensation, in the form of damages, for unplanned injury suffered in the course of their medical treatment.[1] More specifically, our interest is in cases where the patient alleges the injury in question could and should have been avoided by proper conduct on the part of the doctor or other members of the treating team. Broadly, and without prejudice to the detailed legal rules that constitute and substantiate such actions in the two jurisdictions under study, we shall refer to these as 'medical malpractice claims'.

At the outset, it is helpful to distinguish the two forms of injury that may be the subject of such a claim. In the first place, medical treatment usually requires invasion of the patient's body, and it is a commonplace that such interventions carry risks of causing the patient 'iatrogenic injury', ie harm that is additional to his underlying illness. Indeed modern therapies have become increasingly aggressive in their attempts to cure previously incurable conditions; as the Pearson Report in England noted in the 1970s, 'this trend of greater risks for greater gain is likely to continue'.[2] Secondly, even in the absence of iatrogenic injury, the patient may remain disappointed in his expectations of the amelioration of his illness. Though at first sight it may seem odd to regard the progress of a natural condition as 'injury', it is clear that in principle the law is prepared to categorise it in these terms. Since treatment is undertaken for a positive purpose (involving the hope of achieving a given benefit, ideally a cure), its failure can legitimately be regarded as harm—the patient finds himself in a state of health less than that which (so at least he believes) ought to have been achieved.[3]

[1] Ie excluded from the discussion are 'injuries' that, from the outset were an unavoidable and intended part of the treatment, and were accepted as such by the patient, eg the amputation of a diseased limb.

[2] Pearson, *Report of the Royal Commission on Compensation for Personal Injury*, Cmnd 7054 (London, HMSO, 1978) vol 1, para 1349.

[3] For a discussion of this point in the context of the need under German law for injury to body or health, see S Heidelk, *Gesundheitsverletzung und Gesundheitsschaden: Ärztliche Verantwortung im Kontext des § 280 Abs. 1 BGB* (Berlin, Duncker & Humblot, 2005) 62 ff.

Both England and Germany have seen a sharp rise in the number of medical malpractice claims against medical professionals in recent years. A recent study in England suggests that some 6,000 claims will be commenced each year by patients (or their surviving relatives).[4] This compares with the 500 per year estimated by the Pearson Report in the mid-1970s.[5] In Germany, where the increase in medical malpractice litigation began earlier, the numbers are significantly higher; there were already around 6,000 claims per annum by the end of the 1970s, and today the figure is estimated to lie somewhere between 20,000 and 35,000.[6] By comparison, before the 1960s claims in both countries appear to have been limited to a handful per year.

Admittedly, these figures must be read in the context of a general upsurge in litigation in modern Western societies: doctors are by no means alone in attracting legal action from dissatisfied recipients of their services. Factors cited to explain this trend include the growth of a more atomised society where individuals see themselves as rights-holders against other persons, together with a decline in deference due to higher levels of education among the general population. Even so, given the very low base-line of claims 50 years ago, there is reason to think that the medical profession has been disproportionately implicated. In this regard, it seems likely that two further factors of importance have been the great advances in medical technology over the last century, together with changes away from the traditional 'doctor-patient' relationship towards mass systems of healthcare delivery supervised by the state itself.

1. The Treatment Context

It is easy to forget, so used are we to media reports celebrating the latest triumphs of modern medicine, that until quite recently engaging the services of a physician was a hazardous exercise.[7] There were serious limitations in the medical knowledge of even the best doctors as to the nature of many illnesses and how to treat them; treatment itself was hampered—in cases where surgical intervention came into question—by the lack of anaesthetic techniques and hygienic facilities. In

[4] R Lewis, A Morris and K Oliphant, 'Tort Personal Injury Statistics: Is there a Compensation Culture in the United Kingdom?' [2006] *Journal of Personal Injury Law* 87 at 92 ff; see also the Government Chief Medical Officer's Report, *Making Amends: A consultation paper setting out proposals for reforming the approach to clinical negligence in the NHS* (London, Department of Health, 2003) 58.

[5] Pearson, *Report of the Royal Commission* (n 2 above) vol 1, para 1318.

[6] C Katzenmeier, *Arzthaftung* (Tübingen, Mohr Siebeck, 2002) 41. As with the figures cited for England, these numbers relate to the total number of actions begun, not the (far smaller) number that ultimately go to judgment; the majority of claims in both countries will be abandoned or settled: see further the discussion in ch 5 pt II.

[7] According to a remark ascribed to the Harvard Professor of Medicine, Laurence Henderson, 'it was only after 1910 or 1912 that a random patient with a random condition choosing a physician at random had more than one chance in two of benefiting from the encounter' (cited in M Moran, *Governing the Health Care State: a comparative study of the United Kingdom, the United States, and Germany* (Manchester, Manchester University Press, 1999) 175).

these circumstances, it was the ethical and personal dimension of the doctor-patient relationship that received most attention—physicians, aware of their limits, should act as comforters, and minister to the patient's emotional needs. Ideally—if not always in practice—they should refrain from speculative and risky interventions: *primum non nocere* ('first, do no harm'), as the Hippocratic Oath enjoined. For their part, patients were expected to defer uncritically and unconditionally to the doctor's judgement and advice. Their hope of a cure was often no doubt a slender one, but they had little alternative.

However, from around the middle of the nineteenth century, the above picture began to change rapidly in modern industrialising states such as England and Germany. Breakthroughs in the understanding of diseases, the development of antiseptics and anaesthetics, and the discovery of the X-ray as a diagnostic tool all dramatically increased the doctor's scope for successfully recognising and treating illness in his patient. During the twentieth century further developments continued apace: a major new advance was the discovery of antibiotics; more recently, the treatment and palliation of chronic long-term conditions has benefited from the development of modern pharmaceutical products.

The improvement in medical care coincided with the emergence of modern Western states, with their impulse towards social regulation and welfare provision. Traditionally, access to medical services had been a haphazard affair. Only those who could afford to pay the doctor's fees could be sure of receiving treatment; those who could not were reliant on charitable initiatives of varying quality and availability. Once, however, medicine began to prove its efficacy, especially in tackling the scourge of contagious disease, it was natural that the state should take an interest in its promotion, and in extending access to treatment to the population at large. In Germany, state involvement in healthcare began with one of Bismarck's landmark social reforms of the 1880s, which established a system of public health insurance funds (*Krankenkassen*) for workers and their families, financed partly by the employer and in part by deductions from the worker's salary (paid directly by the employer to the relevant fund).[8] In England a similar development occurred around 60 years later with the setting up in 1948 of the National Health Service (NHS)—a key achievement of Clement Atlee's post-war Labour Government.[9]

These schemes retain their essential features to this day. As a whole, the English system, which is funded directly by taxation, is more centralised than that in Germany. Health authorities, answerable to the NHS Executive (and ultimately the Department of Health), are responsible for organising and funding treatment services in their respective geographical regions.[10] In Germany, the financing of

[8] *Krankenversicherungsgesetz* (KVG) 1883.

[9] National Health Service Act 1948.

[10] In recent years, in an effort to introduce greater choice and competition into the system, the delivery of treatment has been hived off from the health authorities (which remain responsible for its financing) into separate NHS trusts, normally made up of a number of hospitals or primary care practices.

treatment remains a matter for the insurance funds, contracting with doctors and hospitals to provide healthcare. The hospitals may be either public institutions (run by a given municipality or other public body) or private and/or charitable in nature.[11] Notwithstanding this different basis of organisation, both overall schemes provide for mass coverage: their most important common feature is of guaranteeing treatment on the basis of medical need and (more or less) free at the point of delivery. While the possibility that individuals may prefer to arrange privately for treatment is left open, the large majority of the population in both countries will have its medical care paid for by the state in this way.[12]

Against this background, it is unsurprising that public perceptions as to what medicine can achieve have increased, and with them the expectations of patients as to what should be accomplished in their particular case; what was formerly bad luck or fate is now often ascribed to fault. Moreover, given the role of the state in healthcare provision, where something goes wrong, the aggrieved citizen may be disposed to regard himself as the victim not only of an individual wrong (perpetrated by a given doctor), but of a social injustice—in failing to receive his share of a public good. This tendency is encouraged by the mode of delivery of much modern-day healthcare in which teams of specialist doctors and nurses offer high-tech but depersonalised treatment in an institutionalised hospital setting.[13]

2. The Regulation of Medical Practice

Doctors in both England and Germany are subject to concurrent bodies of rules, designed in a broad sense to secure good practice and to protect patients from suffering harm at their hands. Historically, the most significant of these were not law in the formal sense, but stemmed from the doctors' professional licensing bodies. In the past, this was instrumental in securing registered medical practitioners a monopoly over the supply of medical services.[14] Today, the relevant bodies and rules retain an important disciplinary and preventative function: incompetent or morally suspect doctors who pose a danger to the public should be removed from practice (or have limiting conditions imposed upon it, eg be subject to supervision by another doctor). In this regard, the General Medical Council in England has power, pursuant to legislation, to erase the doctor's name from the medical register in serious cases of professional misconduct. This is subject to a right of appeal by the doctor to a court of law.[15] In Germany, similar functions are divided

[11] For a comparative examination of the English and German (and US) healthcare systems, see Moran, *Governing the Health Care State* (n 7 above).

[12] In both countries around 10–15% of the population carries private health insurance of some form.

[13] See the remarks on this in Pearson, *Report of the Royal Commission* (n 2 above) vol 1, 1320–22; see also Katzenmeier, *Arzthaftung* (n 6 above) 11 ff.

[14] J Healy, *Medical Negligence: Common Law Perspectives* (London, Sweet & Maxwell, 1999) 11 ff.

[15] Medical Act 1983 s 36. More recently, the GMC has also acquired the power to discipline seriously deficient conduct under the Medical (Professional Performance) Act 1995.

between the *Ärztekammern* at state level, and the approbation (licensing) authorities: infractions of the codes of conduct of the *Ärztekammern*, known as *Standesrecht*, are dealt with by a system of professional tribunals (*Berufsgerichte*).[16]

More recently, criminal law, with its deterrent and punitive functions, has become increasingly important in the regulation of the medical profession. This is relevant inter alia where the doctor fails to gain the patient's consent, reflecting the fact that, both in England and Germany, the non-consensual treatment of a competent adult—even that objectively benefiting him—is unlawful. In England, the doctor may in such a case be liable for criminal assault contrary to the Offences Against The Person Act 1861. In Germany, he is likely to be charged with unlawful bodily injury (*Körperverletzung*) under § 223 of the Criminal Code (*Strafgesetzbuch* (StGB)).[17] Criminal sanctions will also apply to procedures that are ethically controversial and/or therapeutically dubious and remain unlawful (notwithstanding the patient's consent)—either absolutely or failing the fulfillment of further special conditions. This includes such matters as embryo research, abortion and euthanasia; and also risky irreversible procedures like live organ donation.[18]

Nonetheless, as regards the main concern of this work—unplanned injury arising from consensual and therapeutically indicated treatment—the criminal law occupies a more peripheral role. This is unambiguously true for England, where criminal liability is reserved for egregious lapses that result in the patient's death: in such circumstances the doctor may be convicted of 'gross negligence' manslaughter.[19] By contrast in Germany, criminal proceedings appear to be more frequent: indeed it has been estimated that some 3,000 criminal investigations against doctors are begun each year, of which around 10 per cent result in prosecution.[20] This follows from two features of German law—the first specific to medical malpractice, the second, more general. First, as will be discussed in detail in chapter four, it is quite common for a patient's ostensible consent to be impugned retrospectively on the basis of inadequate information disclosure—opening the way to a charge of *Körperverletzung* under § 223 StGB.[21] Secondly, German law also knows a crime of 'negligent bodily injury' (*fahrlässige Körperverletzung*),

[16] See E Deutsch and A Spickhoff, *Medizinrecht*, 5th edn (Berlin, Springer, 2003) para 9. In the case of a *Kassenarzt* (ie a doctor licensed to treat publicly insured patients), their entitlement so to practise may be removed by the relevant authority under § 95, Book V *Sozialgesetzbuch* (SGB).

[17] See further the discussion in ch 4, pt II. As noted there, in England a prosecution against a bona fide doctor will in practice not be brought—this not being regarded as in the public interest.

[18] For a discussion of the law in these areas see generally, for England, A Grubb (ed), *Principles of Medical Law*, 2nd edn (Oxford, Oxford University Press, 2004) chs 10 ff and for Germany, A Laufs and W Uhlenbruck (eds), *Handbuch des Arztrechts*, 3rd edn (Munich, Beck, 2002) chs 22–23.

[19] See *R v Adomoko* [1994] 3 All ER 79, (1994) 5 Med LR 27 (HL); *R v Amrit Misra* [2004] EWCA Crim 2375.

[20] K Ulsenheimer, 'Die Entwicklung des Arztstrafrechts in der Praxis der letzten 20 Jahre' in A Laufs (ed), *Die Entwicklung der Arzthaftung* (Berlin, Springer, 1997) 27 ff. In about half, a conviction will follow: thus around 100–150 doctors are found guilty of a criminal offence each year. In nearly all cases the result will be a fine.

[21] See ch 4, pt II 2.

which has no common law equivalent and applies to lower-level unintentional injuries.[22] This means that in any case involving injury allegedly stemming from medical malpractice (and even where consent is not impugned) the patient has the option of reporting the doctor to the police.[23]

Be that as it may, and notwithstanding the seriousness of criminal law and/or professional sanctions from the doctor's point of view—including the loss of his livelihood or even liberty—the rules in question do not (and are not designed to) offer a remedy to the injured patient. Instead, to obtain compensation for harm allegedly suffered at the hands of a delinquent doctor the patient must turn to the private law.

II. The Framework of Private Law

1. Comparative Background

Private law (*Privatrecht*)[24] encompasses the legal rules that apply between individual actors in civil society. The law in question operates in a bilateral way—conferring rights on one party against the other party (and the correlative duty on the other party), primarily to some course of conduct or tangible outcome. Insofar as this is not forthcoming, this will convert after the event into a right to compensation. In this context, both jurisdictions—in common with other modern legal systems—distinguish broadly between two main institutions of rules, namely of tort or delict (*Deliktsrecht, unerlaubte Handlungen*); and contract (*Vertragsrecht*).[25] Generally, tort law plays a wider, but also more negative role in the social order in protecting the status quo: in tort what is typically compensated is a setback to a person's existing interests. By contrast, contract law governs agreements between agents aimed at achieving positive results and has, as its focus of compensation, the claimant's disappointed expectations. As Tony Weir has written,

> [h]uman good, for which the law exists, depends upon the maintenance and development of human goods—life, health, property, and wealth . . . To ensure their maintenance we have the law of tort, and to promote their development we have the law

[22] Under § 229 of the StGB. In the event that the patient dies, a charge may lie for *fahrlässige Tötung* under § 222 StGB.

[23] In practice, proceedings are normally discontinued for want of evidence, or stayed under § 153 *Strafprozessordnung* (StPO) for lack of public interest once a settlement is reached in the patient's private suit. Ulsenheimer, 'Die Entwicklung des Arztstrafrechts' (n 20 above) 33–4 notes the concern that patients may use the threat of criminal proceedings to pressurise doctors into settling civil claims.

[24] In one usage, the term 'civil law' (*Zivilrecht*) is broadly synonymous with 'private law'. However, in both England and Germany, this may also refer to codified systems by way of contrast to 'common law'. To avoid confusion, the term 'private law' is generally preferred in this work.

[25] For the sake of simplicity, the claims of restitution (*ungerechtfertigte Bereicherung*) to be a third branch of private law are ignored. Restitution (obliging the repayment of unearned benefits) is not relevant to medical malpractice claims.

of contract. Contract is productive, tort law protective. In other words, tortfeasors are typically liable for making things worse, contractors for not making them better.[26]

With respect to claims for medical malpractice, involving the alleged default of a doctor or hospital, neither English nor German law has any distinct set of rules (eg in the form of a special statute); rather they fall within the general framework of private law just outlined. In that regard it is apparent that such claims have both a contractual and a tortious dimension. The first stems from the classical, two-party quality of the doctor-patient relationship, in which the patient sought the doctor out in the hope that the latter might do something positive for him, ie cure or palliate his illness. For its part, tort is in point, given that the doctor, to secure this objective, must interfere directly with the patient's body and in the process may harm the latter's negative interests (by causing iatrogenic injury).

As we shall see shortly, a significant difference—at least at first sight—between English and German medical malpractice law lies in their contrasting positioning of such claims in tort and contract, respectively. However, first a general divergence in English and German legal methodology requires our attention. This concerns the source of the relevant rules: in particular, whereas England is a common law jurisdiction, Germany has a civil law system. Thus, while in the former country, legal rules have traditionally been fashioned by the courts through decisions reached in particular cases, in Germany they have been incorporated into legislative codes, which aim to present the rules in an orderly and systematic way. In the case of private law, the relevant code is the *Bürgerliches Gesetzbuch* (BGB) (Civil Code), which was drafted in the last quarter of the nineteenth century and entered into force in 1900.

In fact, there has been an increasing perception among legal scholars that the differences between the two approaches are less substantial than may first appear.[27] Ultimately, any legal rule—be it contained in a code, statute, or judicial decision—must be subject to further interpretation in the course of its application to settle a given dispute. This is required to define the concepts contained in the rule, and to determine its application in unforeseen situations (including where the surrounding context has changed), and is perforce the task of the courts. Accordingly, the distinction largely reduces to two matters: first the greater sense of architecture in the civil law (as opposed to the ad hoc structure of the common law); and secondly, the different influence on the law's development exercised by courts, practising lawyers, and academics. Under the common law the prime movers are the courts and the practitioners whose arguments assist them; by

[26] T Weir, 'Chapter 12: Complex Liabilities' in A Tunc (ed), *International Encyclopaedia of Comparative Law*, vol XI, *Torts* (Tübingen, Mohr, 1976) para 6.

[27] See generally K Zweigert and H Kötz, *An Introduction to Comparative Law* (trans T Weir) (Oxford, Clarendon Press, 1998) 256 ff; DN MacCormick and R Summers, *Interpreting Precedents: a Comparative Study* (Aldershot, Dartmouth Publishing, 1997) 1 ff; BS Markesinis (ed), *The Gradual Convergence: Foreign Ideas, Foreign Influences and English Law on the Eve of the 21st Century* (Oxford, Clarendon Press, 1994); R Zimmermann and N Jansen, '*Quieta Movere*—Interpretative Change in a Codified System' in P Cane and J Stapleton (eds), *The Law of Obligations—Essays in Celebration of John Fleming* (Oxford, Oxford University Press, 1998) 285 ff.

contrast under the civil law, greater prominence is accorded to the academics (responsible for systematising the codes, and who remain influential in their interpretation).[28]

There is, however, a further reason in the context of medical malpractice claims why the common law/civil law divide is of limited significance. This is because, in Germany too, the rules that govern such claims are essentially judge-made, with the courts having to develop and apply the (in this area) highly abstract formulations of the BGB in a concrete manner. A plausible systemic reason for this, suggested by HLA Hart, is that fact-situations raising potential liability for accidental harm are too varied to be made the subject of detailed ex ante rules:

> [O]wing to the immense variety of possible cases where care is called for, we cannot ab initio foresee what combinations of circumstances will arise nor foresee what interests will have to be sacrificed or to what extent, if precaution against harm is to be taken . . . our aim of securing people against harm is indeterminate till we put it in conjunction with, or test it against, possibilities which only experience will bring before us[29]

In this context, § 823 I BGB, the German Civil Code's main delictual provision, provides for compensation in case of certain types of unlawful injury 'arising from' conduct that is 'willful or negligent' in nature. Similarly, as regards contractual obligations, § 280 I (in conjunction with § 276 I) BGB, states that the contractor is answerable for negligent performance. For its part, 'negligence' (*Fahrlässigkeit*) is defined in § 276 II BGB as the failure to observe the socially required level of care (*die im Verkehr erforderliche Sorgfalt*). However, that is also where the Code ends: it is not further specified, for example, how negligent conduct is to be assessed in the case of a doctor; nor when the injury suffered by the patient is to be regarded as unlawfully resulting from the same, etc. Instead, these questions have been left to the courts, in particular to the *Bundesgerichtshof* (BGH)—the Federal Supreme Court, which is the final appeal court in matters of private and criminal law. Admittedly, there was, in the early 1980s, some interest in codifying medical malpractice law as a separate chapter within the BGB, culminating in a proposal by Deutsch and Geiger, which would have developed the rules from the case law into 12 new codal paragraphs. However, this ran into objections, based on the concern that the law would thereby become unduly rigid and ossified, and the idea was ultimately dropped.[30]

[28] See especially S Vogenauer, 'An Empire of Light? Learning and Lawmaking in the History of German Law' (2005) 64 *CLJ* 481 and 'An Empire of Light? II: Learning and Lawmaking in Germany Today' (2006) *OJLS* 627. In this regard the case law of the German courts has less formal claim to authority than in England (reflected in less strict rules of precedent); the courts 'interpret' the codes and such interpretations are—in theory, albeit not in practice—on a par with divergent interpretations that may be offered by academic commentators.

[29] HLA Hart, *The Concept of Law*, 2nd edn (Oxford, Clarendon Press, 1994) 133.

[30] E Deutsch and M Geiger, 'Medizinischer Behandlungsvertrag—Empfiehlt sich eine besondere Regelung der zivilrechtlichen Beziehung zwischen dem Patienten und dem Arzt im BGB?' in Bundesminister für Justiz (ed), *Gutachten und Vorschläge zur Überarbeitung des Schuldrechts* (Cologne, BMJ, 1981) 1049 ff; for discussion, see Katzenmeier, *Arzthaftung* (n 6 above) 85 ff.

As we shall see in the course of this work, the BGH's Sixth Senate, which deals with medical malpractice actions, has developed an intricate jurisprudence in this area, which is the rival of anything produced by Common law courts (indeed in terms of complexity it surpasses the latter). Here the sheer number of medical malpractice claims going all the way to the BGH should also be mentioned: over the last 40 years the Court has handed down some 10–20 decisions in this area per year; this compares with the 10 or so such cases that have exercised the House of Lords during the entire same period.[31]

2. Medical Malpractice in Tort and Contract

As noted above, a key distinction on the face of things between the English and German approaches to medical malpractice claims lies in the different importance accorded to contract and tort. Whereas English law has tended to deal with such claims in tort, in German law a contractual solution has been favoured. Nonetheless, as we shall see, this makes little difference in practice; rather the law in both countries has put the emphasis on approximating the protection available to the patient under both legal institutions, as well as ensuring that the latter has a solid defendant to sue.

(a) England: the Primacy of Tort

In positioning the doctor's duties to their patient in tort law, the English courts have fastened upon his assumption of responsibility for the latter's welfare, coupled with the representation of specialist knowledge and skill. As Lord Hewart CJ stated in *R v Bateman*,

> [i]f a person holds himself out as possessing special skill and knowledge, and he is consulted, as possessing such skill and knowledge, by or on behalf of a patient, he owes a duty to the patient to use due caution in undertaking the treatment. If he accepts the responsibility and undertakes the treatment and the patient submits to his discretion and treatment accordingly, he owes a duty to the patient . . . No contractual relation is necessary, nor is it necessary that the service be rendered for reward.[32]

The pre-eminence of tort has been reinforced, since 1948, with the coming into being of the NHS scheme. Here, the fact that treatment on the NHS is free at the point of delivery has been held to militate against the existence of a contract.[33] This

[31] This disparity rests only in part on the greater number of medical malpractice claims originating in Germany. Above all it has to do with the lesser prestige of lower court decisions in Germany, as well as differences in civil procedure making appeals easier and cheaper than in England. In fact latterly, following changes in 2002 to the German civil procedure rules, the number of BGH decisions in this area has fallen.

[32] *R v Bateman* (1925) 19 Cr App R 8 (CA) 12–13.

[33] *Appleby v Sleep* [1968] 2 All ER 265 (Divisional Court).

follows from the strict application of consideration in English contract law (ie the idea that there must be an exchange of benefits between contracting parties).[34]

It remains true, as regards the minority of patients who are privately insured (currently around 10 per cent of the UK population), that there will be such consideration, and hence a contract. However, this does not secure the private patient any advantage over his NHS counterpart; rather, the rights under the contract will merely duplicate those he already enjoys under tort law. This parity of protection is apparent at various levels. An initial point of importance is that in tort law, too, the courts have imposed a positive duty of care on the doctor, the effect of which is to protect the patient's expectation interest (ie allowing him to sue where he fails to benefit from defective treatment).[35] Secondly, as we shall see in chapter two, the rules governing the further legal elements that the patient must establish in order to succeed in his claim are the same.

Generally, where NHS treatment goes wrong, the defendant of choice will be the relevant NHS trust (previously, the health authority), which was responsible for delivering the treatment and will be vicariously liable for the acts of the individual doctor or nurse who was actually negligent. In particular, the trust will have 'deeper pockets' to meet the high awards that are often a feature of such cases.[36] Sometimes, too, it may be liable directly for negligence at an organisational level, eg by putting inexperienced and unsupervised staff in charge of complex operations.[37] However, where the patient holds a particular doctor accountable (and wishes this to be reflected in individual liability), he may proceed against the latter as well: in such a case, the NHS will indemnify the doctor, ie bear out of central funds the award for damages against the latter.[38] As regards patients in the private sector, the patient may proceed against both the individual doctor (directly responsible for the injury) and his employer, the private hospital (vicariously so). Here the principle of joint and several liability means the latter will bear the award in the event of the doctor's impecuniosity. In most cases, both defendants will be covered by liability insurance.[39]

[34] See G Treitel, *The Law of Contract*, 11th edn (London, Sweet & Maxwell, 2003) 67 ff. In *Reynolds v Health First Medical Group* [2000] Lloyd's Rep Med 240 (Hitchin CC), the claimant attempted to argue that registering with a GP amounted to consideration, in view of the value to the GP of this act (since the latter's remuneration under his own contract with the Health Authority was calculated on the basis of the number of patients on his list). However, this was rejected by the court.

[35] See pt III 1 (a) below.

[36] Damages, calculated on the full-restitution basis in tort law, may run into hundreds of thousands of pounds. Indeed, in the worst cases of catastrophic injury to a young person, who then requires ongoing care for the rest of his life, awards of several million pounds are possible: see the CMO's Report, (n 4 above) 73–4.

[37] *Wilsher v Essex Area Health Authority* [1987] QB 730 (CA).

[38] In the case of general practitioners who are not NHS employees, the patient's damages will normally be borne by the doctor's insurer: see M Brazier, *Medicine, Patients and the Law*, 3rd edn (London, Penguin Books, 2003) 177 ff.

[39] Grubb, *Principles of Medical Law* (n 18 above) para 8.02.

(b) Germany: the Primacy of Contract

In Germany, the patient will almost invariably be in a contract with the doctor/treating side. Since, in contrast to the position under English law, consideration is not required as an element in contract law, it is irrelevant whether the patient has private healthcare insurance or is (one of the large majority) treated via a public insurance fund: here the existence of a treatment contract between the latter type of patient and the doctor/hospital is confirmed by § 76 IV in Book V of the *Sozialgesetzbuch* (SGB).[40] Indeed, a contractual relationship will arise in cases where treatment is entirely gratuitous (eg it takes place between doctors who are friends or colleagues).[41] All that is required is that the doctor indicates willingness to treat, and the patient to be treated. Similarly, a contractual or quasi-contractual relationship applies in respect of the treatment of children and incompetent adults—either through a contract concluded by a proxy, or, in relation to the temporarily incompetent (eg an unconscious patient brought into casualty), through the operation of the principles of *negotiorum gestio* (*Geschäftsführung ohne Auftrag*) under §§ 677 ff BGB.[42]

Nevertheless, until recently tort law continued to have an important, indeed arguably the dominant, role in medical malpractice actions.[43] This was because a distinctive feature of German contract law was its categorical exclusion of non-pecuniary loss, including for pain and suffering (*Schmerzensgeld*). Instead, to recover under this head, an injured patient had to rely on a concurrent claim in tort law.[44] However, following reforms made to the BGB in 2002, the position has changed so that in appropriate cases contractual damages may also include such non-material losses. In particular, (new) § 253 II BGB provides that damages for pain and suffering are available (both in contract and tort) in case of injury to a claimant's body, health, liberty or sexual self-determination. In the wake of this change, it has been argued that contract law will become the dominant institution, with patients more likely to base their claim on a breach of contract alone.[45]

In fact, the relevant rules determining whom the patient may proceed against in contract are quite complex. First, as regards patients treated outside hospital in doctors' practices, the relevant treatment contract will be with the particular doctor. By contrast, patients receiving hospital care, either as outpatients (*ambulante Behandlung*) or inpatients (*stationäre Behandlung*) will usually have a contract with the hospital authority (*Krankenhausträger*) as opposed to the treating doctor(s). This (a so-called *totaler Krankenhausvertrag*) is invariably the position with regard to publicly insured patients, and normally also applies to the privately

[40] See Deutsch and Spickhoff, *Medizinrecht* (n 16 above) para 63.

[41] BGH, 7 June 1977, NJW 1977, 2120; Deutsch and Spickhoff, *Medizinrecht* (n 16 above) para 64.

[42] See Deutsch and Spickhoff, *Medizinrecht* (n 16 above) paras 72–4.

[43] Katzenmeier, *Arzthaftung* (n 6 above) 83–4.

[44] As formerly provided for under (ex) §§ 253 and 847 BGB.

[45] Deutsch and Spickhoff, *Medizinrecht* (n 16 above) para 128. Where the patient dies, tort will remain the basis for claims by relatives for loss of dependency under § 844 BGB.

insured. However, a private patient may sometimes enter additionally into a contract with a particular doctor. If so, there is a further distinction according to whether the latter's contractual obligations duplicate those of the hospital (*Krankenhausvertrag mit Arzt-Zusatzvertrag*), or the obligations are split—with the doctor alone responsible for the treatment and the hospital for ancillary matters, such as the provision of facilities and nursing care (*gespaltener Arzt-Krankenhaus-Vertrag*).[46]

As in England, an important factor, given the high sums in damages often at stake, will be the defendant's (or defendants') putative solvency.[47] However, this will rarely if ever be in doubt. With respect to doctors who provide treatment outside hospital (or treat within hospital pursuant to a split doctor-hospital contract), the rules of their professional associations oblige them to carry liability insurance.[48] In the case of hospital treatment, the effect of the contractual rules, as we have seen, is to focus liability on the hospital authority. The latter will in this context be vicariously liable for the defaults of its employees under § 278 BGB. The Authority may also be directly liable either for organisational failures, or for the conduct of doctors occupying managerial positions (pursuant to §§ 31 and 89 BGB).[49] For its part, tort law will continue to play a residual—primarily symbolic—role in cases governed by a *totaler Krankenhausvertrag*, where the patient wishes to target a particular doctor by joining him in proceedings.[50]

III. The Scope of the Patient's Protected Interests

In the treatment context it is apparent that the patient has an interest in diverse matters over which the doctor, by his conduct, has varying degrees of influence. These include maintaining his bodily integrity (to the extent that he does not waive this), participating in the treatment by informed choice, achieving a restoration of health so far as possible, and avoiding unnecessary injury and/or loss. At the same time, it is not every setback to every de facto interest that will qualify for

[46] See K Geiß and H-P Greiner, *Arzthaftpflichtrecht*, 5th edn (Munich, Beck, 2006) paras A21 ff.

[47] As in England, damages are awarded on a full-restitution basis: § 249 I BGB. Their method of calculation, as well as the size of awards in medical malpractice cases, is comparable to the position in England: see WVH Rogers, 'Country Report—United Kingdom: England' in M Faure and H Koziol (eds), *Cases on Medical Malpractice in a Comparative Perspective* (Vienna, Springer, 2001) 232 and 244. For a comparative treatment of the law of damages in English and German law, see W van Gerven J Lever and P Larouche, *Tort Law: Common Law of Europe Casebooks* (Oxford, Hart Publishing, 2000) 739 ff.

[48] See further Katzenmeier, *Arzthaftung* (n 6 above) 194 ff.

[49] BGH, 30 November 1982, NJW 1983, 1374.

[50] This appears to occur quite often in practice; an exception applies to doctors who enjoy the status of officials (such as professors in university clinics): here § 839 I BGB relieves them of individual liability for negligence provided there is another solvent defendant whom the patient can proceed against (ie the clinic).

compensation. Rather, the patient must show at the outset of his claim that the doctor was under a legal duty to safeguard the interest in question.

As discussed above, in England the majority of patients, in bringing an action, will be reliant on tort law; in Germany by contrast, the primary source of the doctor's obligations is contractual. Nonetheless, as we shall see below, the interests recognised in each country as meriting legal protection (and the correlative duties upon the doctor/hospital) are for the most part very similar. In both countries a form of hierarchy may be discerned, with certain central types of interest accorded greater protection by the law than other interests deemed of more contingent importance.

1. The Position in England

(a) Bodily Integrity and Health

The protection of the patient's fundamental interests in bodily integrity and health, which are at stake in the large majority of medical malpractice claims, finds a ready place in the law of tort. As suggested earlier, such interests conceived of in negative terms (freedom *from* bodily invasion and injury) lie at the heart of this branch of private law. However, as a result of the ad hoc development of the common law, the protection at issue has been divided between two discrete torts, namely battery and negligence. Whilst the former embodies protection from intentional invasions of a person's bodily integrity, negligence will cover situations in which injury occurred in an unintended or accidental manner.[51]

In battery the relevant invasion, which includes unwanted and inappropriate touching, is actionable per se. This means that (in contrast to cases of negligence, where causation of damage is an essential element to any claim) the claimant will succeed without needing to show further injury.[52] In this regard, the tort may be seen as protective not just of bodily integrity, but of autonomy: the individual's right to decide for himself what sort of physical interferences he is willing to put up with, including those which do him no tangible harm, or may even do good. In the context of medical care, this is highly relevant in terms of the requirement that the doctor obtain valid consent from the patient. In that context, we shall encounter the tort again in chapter four, when looking at actions by patients based on inadequate information disclosure by the doctor prior to commencing treatment.[53]

Assuming, though (as is in practice far more common), that the patient is seeking compensation for consented to, but poorly executed, medical treatment, it is the tort of negligence that will offer the appropriate cause of action. The latter tort has over the last century become the most commonly pleaded tort in English law,

[51] See *Letang v Cooper* [1965] QB 232 (CA).

[52] However, in the absence of further injury the claimant will only be entitled to nominal damages.

[53] See ch 4 pt II 1. Admittedly, as discussed there, the role of battery in medical injury cases is peripheral, with the courts tending to reject its application in cases of bona fide treatment.

and focuses upon unintended harm. In particular, it offers redress in the form of monetary compensation for careless conduct that damages one of the claimant's protected interests: in negligence parlance, the feature of legal protection is captured by saying that the defendant owed the claimant a 'duty of care'.

In relation to medical negligence claims based upon physical injury to the patient's bodily health there will ordinarily be no doubt that the patient's interest in not being so injured is protected. Indeed, cases establishing the doctor's duty of care in such circumstances long pre-date the general test for a duty of care in negligence, proposed by Lord Atkin in *Donoghue v Stevenson*.[54] On the other hand, one category of claim that used to raise a degree of theoretical difficulty concerned children injured by doctors *in utero* or during birth, at a time when they as yet have no legal personality. In the event, Parliament has intervened to make clear that the legal duty owed to the child (by a doctor or others) pre-dates its birth. Accordingly, where a child is born disabled, which—absent medical negligence—would have been healthy, it will have a claim.[55]

Significantly, as noted earlier, the general protection available in negligence here also encompasses the patient's expectation interest in a cure or palliation of his condition. This is because—in contrast to the ordinary citizen who is not generally required to safeguard others from independent risks—the law places the doctor under a positive duty of care. This is based on his special relationship with the patient, and arises as soon as he 'assumes responsibility' by indicating a willingness to treat. In the case of a hospital, a similar, positive duty of care will come into being when it permits the patient to enter its casualty department.[56]

As to the position of those patients treated in the private sector, in addition to the rules of negligence, there will be a contract between them and the doctor. Accordingly, if the patient is injured during the course of the treatment, he may bring a concurrent claim for breach of contract (alleging that the error constitutes a breach of the doctor's contractually assumed duties). Nonetheless, insofar as the claim relates to duty to preserve and/or promote the patient's bodily health, the contract will duplicate the protection already afforded by tort law.[57]

[54] *Donoghue v Stevenson* [1932] AC 562 (HL). An early decision imposing a duty on a doctor to exercise skill in treating his patient, regardless of whether there was a contract, is *Pippin v Sheppard* (1822) 11 Price 400.

[55] Civil Liability (Congenital Disabilities) Act 1976; at common law too, this was held to be the position in *Burton v Islington Health Authority* [1992] 3 All ER 833 (CA). By contrast a child whose disability arose prior to the doctor's intervention has no claim on the basis that the latter ought to have advised its mother to undergo an abortion, preventing its existence (a so-called 'wrongful life' claim): see *McKay v Essex Area Health Authority* [1982] 1 QB 1166 (CA).

[56] *Barnett v Chelsea and Kensington Hospital Management Committee* [1969] 1 QB 428 (QBD). See Grubb, *Principles of Medical Law* (n18 above) paras 5.31 ff for a discussion of borderline cases where it is uncertain how far a positive duty of care will arise—eg where a doctor is asked to act as a 'Good Samaritan' rescuer in an emergency.

[57] See Grubb, *Principles of Medical Law* (n 18 above) para 5.21.

(b) Other Interests

Occasionally, a patient may allege that the doctor's carelessness led him to suffer not bodily injury, but non-physical harm of some kind, and in such cases the question of liability is more problematic. In particular, in line with their general approach in negligence law, the courts will often impose additional requirements in order for a duty of care to arise. This reflects a policy decision that the category of interest allegedly invaded merits a lesser degree of protection from accidentally caused harm.[58] It is apparent in this context that a doctor will not ordinarily owe a duty to safeguard the patient's purely financial interests. Thus in one case a doctor was not liable for failing to advise the patient (whom he was treating for injuries sustained in a road accident) to sue the person who caused the accident.[59]

The same restrictive approach has been applied to claims brought by secondary victims for psychiatric harm (formerly termed 'nervous shock'), suffered as a result of witnessing an event in which other persons are injured or killed. Here there is a requirement that the immediate victim be someone with whom the claimant has close ties of love and affection. Furthermore, the event must be of a sudden and shocking nature: a dawning awareness that a given situation is becoming increasingly grave is insufficient.[60] Admittedly, this form of claim is in any event more likely to be brought by a non-patient than the patient himself (typically a relative traumatised by an incident connected to the patient's negligent treatment).[61]

In the doctor-patient context, the most significant category of claim in respect of non-physical injury is for maintenance costs arising from the birth of an unwanted child. This comes into question following the failure of a doctor to prevent the claimant woman (or couple) from conceiving and/or bearing the child, either through mistaken contraceptive advice or treatment (a 'wrongful conception' claim), or the omission to advise or carry out a termination (a claim for 'wrongful birth').[62] In the past such claims had been allowed in England in a number of decisions by the lower courts. For example, in *Thake v Maurice* the Court of Appeal awarded damages to a couple in respect of the maintenance costs stemming from the birth of a child following the husband's negligently performed vasectomy.[63] In one High Court decision the parents even received damages to take account of the costs of paying for the child's future private schooling.[64]

[58] See generally, JG Fleming, *The Law of Torts*, 8th edn (Sydney, The Law Book Co Ltd, 1992) 135 ff.

[59] *Stevens v Bermondsey and Southwark Group Hospital Management Committee* (1963) 107 SJ 478 (QBD).

[60] *Sion v Hampstead Health Authority* (1994) 5 Med LR 170 (CA).

[61] See eg *North Glamorgan NHS Trust v Walters* [2002] EWCA 1792. For a discussion as to when a doctor will owe a duty of care to third parties (ie non-patients), see Grubb, *Principles of Medical Law* (n 18 above) paras 5.48 ff.

[62] See Grubb, *Principles of Medical Law* (n 18 above) paras 12.82 ff. The terminology in this area is in fact not completely settled (some commentators using 'wrongful birth' only for actions by parents with disabled children). Both types of claim should be distinguished from ones for 'wrongful life' by the child: see n 55 above.

[63] *Thake v Maurice* [1986] QB 644 (CA).

[64] *Benarr v Kettering Health Authority* (1988) 138 NLJ 179 (QBD).

Nonetheless, in *McFarlane v Tayside Health Board*,[65] the first such case to reach the House of Lords, this category of negligence action was rejected, at least where the child is born healthy. Their Lordships justified this step, inter alia, by reference to the impossibility of separating out the advantages and disadvantages of having a healthy child (so as to assess damages).[66] Another, important factor was the perceived unfairness of compensating parents of unwanted healthy children against the backdrop of involuntary childlessness in society or parents with disabled children. In his speech, Lord Steyn distinguished here between considerations of corrective and distributive justice:

> It is possible to view the case simply from the perspective of corrective justice. It requires somebody who has harmed another without justification to indemnify the other. On this approach the parents' claim must succeed . . . But one may also approach the case from the vantage point of distributive justice. It requires a focus on the just distribution of burdens and losses among members of a society. If the matter is approached in this way, it may become relevant to ask commuters on the Underground the following question: 'Should the parents of an unwanted but healthy child be able to sue the doctor or hospital for compensation equivalent to the cost of bringing up the child for the years of his or her minority, ie until about 18 years?' My Lords, I am firmly of the view that an overwhelming number of ordinary men and women would answer the question with an emphatic 'No'.[67]

Accordingly, the House of Lords limited damages to the mother's pain and suffering and loss of earnings during or immediately following pregnancy and childbirth. Subsequently, in *Rees v Darlington Memorial Hospital*, a seven-man House of Lords reaffirmed its decision in *McFarlane*, subject to one gloss, namely that the parents would also be entitled to a conventional '*solatium*' (of £15,000) to reflect the wrongful thwarting of their reproductive autonomy.[68]

The above at any rate reflects the position where the child is born healthy. By contrast, that in respect of disabled children remains to be clarified. Thus, although the parents will there receive the *solatium* plus some damages to reflect the additional costs (stemming from the disability) of bringing up the child, should they also be entitled to receive compensation for its general maintenance? The Court of Appeal, in *Parkinson v St James and Seacroft University Hospital NHS Trust*,[69] answered this in the affirmative, as an exception to the exclusionary rule in *McFarlane*. However, in the *Rees* case, where the question was obiter,[70] their Lordships were divided: three expressed the opinion that such compensation should be awarded; two were of the view it should not; and the other two left the

[65] *McFarlane v Tayside Health Board* [2000] 2 AC 59 (HL).

[66] *McFarlane* [2000] 2 AC 59 (HL) 83 (Lord Steyn); 97 (Lord Hope); and 111 (Lord Millet).

[67] *McFarlane* [2000] 2 AC 59 (HL) 82.

[68] *Rees v Darlington Memorial Hospital* [2003] UKHL 52.

[69] *Parkinson v St James and Seacroft University Hospital NHS Trust* [2001] EWCA Civ 530.

[70] At issue in *Rees* was whether—as an exception to the rule in *McFarlane*—maintenance costs could be recovered where the *mother* of a (healthy) child was disabled. Their Lordships (by a narrow 4:3 majority) rejected the claim.

issue open.[71] As Lord Scott pointed out in his speech, a distinction between direct and incidental disability may here be significant, ie whether the negligently performed measure was expressly intended to prevent the birth of a disabled child. In the latter case he implies that the argument for full compensation would be stronger.[72]

A further issue in relation to wrongful conception/birth concerns the situation of private patients. In principle, the object of their contract with the doctor may be wider (resulting in more extensive protection of their interests compared to under negligence) if, on its proper interpretation, the contract was aimed at safeguarding their finances. In this context, the possibility of a contractual claim for maintenance costs following a wrongful conception was mooted by Lord Slynn in *McFarlane*, who suggested in his speech that

> if a client wishes to recover such costs [for maintenance], he or she must do so by an appropriate contract.[73]

However, in the *Rees* case, Lord Scott took the view that it would make no difference if the parents in a wrongful conception or birth case sued in tort or contract: given the close link between such costs and the life of the child, these did not amount to a detriment or loss sounding in law.[74]

2. The Position in Germany

(a) Bodily Integrity and Health

As discussed above, in German medical malpractice law, the patient will nearly always be in a contractual relationship with the doctor and/or hospital. Here, so far as the patient is claiming in respect of injury to his body or health, there will be no difficulty in finding that the relevant interest was legally protected: normally the latter will form the central purpose of the contract. Thus where the treatment goes wrong (whether by causing iatrogenic injury or failing to provide the hoped-for beneficial outcome) the patient, in principle, has a claim for breach of contract (*positive Vertragsverletzung*) against the doctor and/or the hospital.[75] As in England the protection afforded will also extend to the unborn child. Thus the

[71] In favour were Lords Steyn [2003] UKHL 52 (para 35), Hope (para 57) and Hutton (para 91); against were Lords Bingham (para 9) and Nicholls (para 18); the issue was left open by Lords Millett (para 112) and Scott (para 145).

[72] *Rees v Darlington Memorial Hospital* [2003] UKHL 52, para 145 (Lord Scott).

[73] *McFarlane v Tayside Health Board* [2000] 2 AC 59 (HL) 76. The question arose in *Thompson v Sheffield Fertility Clinic* (QBD, unreported, 24 November 2001), but the case was settled prior to it being resolved; see A Grubb, 'Infertility Treatment: Multiple Birth and Damages for the Birth of a Healthy Baby—*Thompson v Sheffield Fertility Clinic*' (2001) 9 *Medical Law Review* 170.

[74] *Rees v Darlington Memorial Hospital* [2003] UKHL 52, paras 130 ff. See also Grubb, 'Infertility Treatment' (n 74 above) 172.

[75] Under § 280 I BGB. This provision was passed in 2002 and codified principles that had previously been developed by the courts.

child may (after its birth) recover damages for injuries resulting from negligent treatment, where it would otherwise have been healthy.[76]

As noted earlier, until 2002 the reparation granted in German law for the infringement of a person's contractual interests was limited in a key respect, in that damages were not awarded for pain and suffering. Instead, to recover for these, the patient was required to maintain a concurrent claim in tort law. In this regard, the patient would rely upon § 823 I BGB (together with ex § 847 BGB), which provided for liability—including for non-pecuniary loss—in case of injury through *unerlaubte Handlungen* (broadly, socially disallowed conduct). According to § 823 I,

> a person who wilfully or negligently injures the life, body, health, freedom, property, or other right of another contrary to law is bound to compensate him for any damage arising therefrom.[77]

In practice the differential approach to heads of damage encouraged the courts to adopt a uniform solution, approximating the contractual and tortious rules for medical malpractice claims, at least those concerning bodily injury. It would, after all, have been unsatisfactory for different aspects of the claim to be subject to a different outcome (eg the aspect centering on pecuniary losses succeeding, but not that for pain and suffering).[78]

This unity of protection is apparent, inter alia, in 'failure to benefit' cases following misdiagnosis. Thus, as in England, the doctor will owe a positive duty of care to the patient in tort under § 823 I BGB, as well as in contract, to safeguard him from the dangers arising from his illness: a so-called *Garantenstellung*. In this context, the BGH commented in a decision of 20 September 1988 as follows:

> The defendant owed the claimant a duty both in contract and tort to provide appropriate medical care. These duties, deriving respectively from the treatment contract and from the positive assumption in tort of the task of treating the claimant, were in effect identical . . . Insofar as he breached the said duties . . . the defendant is liable both contractually and tortiously for the deleterious effect this had upon the claimant's body and health; that includes where the effect was to hinder the claimant's prospects of a cure (relative to the position if the treatment had been carried out properly).[79]

(b) Other Interests

As regards the patient's other, less central interests (in being safeguarded from non-physical forms of injury), we find that, as in England, the legal position is

[76] BGH, 20 December 1952, NJW 1953, 417; BGH, 6 December 1988, NJW 1989, 1538. By contrast, as in England, a 'wrongful life' claim by the child (see n 55 above) will not be entertained: BGH, 18 January 1983, NJW, 1371.

[77] As translated in BS Markesinis and H Unberath, *The German Law of Torts*, 3rd edn (Oxford, Hart Publishing, 2002) 14.

[78] See D Giesen, *Arzthaftung*, 4th edn (Tübingen, Mohr, 1995) para 4; Katzenmeier, *Arzthaftung* (n 6 above) 79–81.

[79] BGH, 20 September 1988, NJW 1989, 767 (768). (All translations from German cases are by the author, unless otherwise indicated.)

more complex. Thus, with respect to claims for pure economic loss, the patient may be protected against suffering such loss in contract law, but only so far as this can be construed, either expressly or impliedly, to have been one of the aims of the treatment contract. In this regard, it has been held that doctors owe a subsidiary obligation to privately insured patients to advise them insofar as the costs of a given treatment may not be covered by the terms of their insurance. However, in other cases, failing specific knowledge, it is unlikely that the doctor would be expected to consider the patient's financial interest.[80] For its part, tort law will here offer no protection, as pure economic loss is not enumerated as a protected interest within § 823 I BGB.[81]

By contrast, as regards claims brought by secondary victims of psychiatric injury, tort law will provide the primary source of protection. Such injury—where it takes the form of a recognised illness—has been interpreted as lying within the protective ambit of § 823 I BGB. Indeed, here the rules as to recovery tend to be less restrictive than in England—thus it may sometimes be sufficient that the claimant heard about the shocking event, as opposed to witnessing it directly.[82] As noted, though, in discussing the relevant English law, such a claim will rarely be in issue in a standard doctor-patient scenario (as opposed to where relatives sue in respect of a patient harmed by the doctor's negligence).[83]

As in England, the non-standard injury claim most immediately relevant in the doctor-patient context concerns maintenance costs for children following wrongful conception or birth.[84] This has developed into a complex and controversial area of German law, not least because of the interaction of private law with underlying principles of constitutional law.[85] As a starting point, the parents' interest will not be covered by tort law, as such costs constitute pure economic loss, which is outside the ambit of § 823 I BGB. Admittedly, it has sometimes been argued that thwarting the parents' desire not to reproduce should be seen as an injury to their 'personality' right (a residual protected interest under § 823 I), which would then generate tort

[80] Geiß and Greiner, *Arzthaftpflichtrecht* (n 46 above) para A96.

[81] German tort law does in some instances permit recovery for pure economic loss, notably where this occurs through the breach of a protective statute (under § 823 II BGB) or maliciously (under § 826 BGB). Occasionally, too, the courts have conferred protection under § 823 I BGB by invoking a 'right to an operating business' as a residual protected interest (*sonstiges Recht*) under that paragraph: see generally Markesinis and Unberath, *The German Law of Torts* (n 77 above) 71 ff. However, none of these possibilities will normally be relevant in the context of a medical malpractice claim.

[82] Geiß and Greiner, *Arzthaftpflichtrecht* (n 46 above) para A94; Markesinis and Unberath, *The German Law of Torts* (n 77 above) 122.

[83] As to the circumstances in German law in which non-patients may have legal redress against doctors, see J von Gerlach, 'Die Haftung des Arztes für Fernwirkungsschäden' in E Deutsch (ed), *Festschrift für Steffen* (Berlin, de Gruyter, 1995) 147 ff.

[84] As noted in discussing the English law, the first term is used for cases where the doctor's error occurs prior to conception, whilst 'wrongful birth' applies to the failure to halt an existing pregnancy.

[85] A detailed discussion from a comparative German-English perspective (albeit prior to *McFarlane v Tayside*) is provided by S Hauberichs, *Haftung für neues Leben im deutschen und englischen Recht* (Berlin, Springer, 1998); for a recent account of the German law, see U Riedel, *Kind als Schaden* (Frankfurt am Main, Mabuse-Verlag, 2003). See also the discussion in Markesinis and Unberath, *The German Law of Torts* (n 77 above) 156 ff, providing translations of a number of the key decisions.

compensation.[86] However, the courts have not found it necessary to go down this road. Instead, the patient (and subsequent parent)'s contract for treatment will be regarded as forming the primary—and potentially sufficient—basis for a claim.

In deciding, though, whether actually to allow recovery in a given case, the BGH has gone on to invoke scope of duty considerations (*Schutzzweck der Norm*), deriving from the patient's reason for having treatment.[87] Here, where the procedure in question was a sterilisation (ie the claim is for 'wrongful conception'), a distinction has been drawn according to whether this was to avoid a specific risk associated with pregnancy/birth, or for general family-planning purposes. As regards the former type of case, eg where the sterilisation was to avoid the risk of a congenitally disabled child, recovery will be allowed only if the child is then born disabled, not if it is healthy (ie the risk did not materialise). Similarly, recovery for the child's maintenance will be excluded in cases where the purpose of the procedure was to protect the mother from health risks associated with pregnancy.[88] By contrast, in respect of sterilisations for general family-planning purposes, the BGH has been prepared to allow recovery, especially where the parents had been motivated by financial concerns.[89]

In the past, the award of compensation in such cases sometimes attracted resistance from the lower courts, which were unhappy with the idea that a child's birth should sound in damages.[90] Moreover, for a while it also excited doubts at the level of constitutional law. In particular, in a 1993 decision, the *Bundesverfassungsgericht* (Federal Constitutional Court) suggested in an obiter dictum that maintenance awards, categorising the child's existence as 'damage', were incompatible with the protection of its dignity and life under Articles 1 I and 2 II of the *Grundgesetz* (German Constitution).[91] Nevertheless, the BGH, in its next decision on the issue, stood by its previous line of authority. While agreeing that it would be unacceptable to regard the child's life itself as 'damage', it denied its approach had this effect. As it commented,

> where a contract with a doctor was intended to prevent the parents being burdened with maintenance costs, and this burden is incurred as a direct result of a breach of contract, the protective purpose of the contract and the purpose of damages as equalisation of burdens demand that it be seen as economic loss. . . . this balancing of losses cannot result in a 'negative value judgement' of the child as a person.[92]

[86] See the discussion in Hauberichs, *Haftung für neues Leben* (n 85 above) 150–53.

[87] BGH, 15 February 2000, NJW 2000, 1782. Geiß and Greiner, *Arzthaftpflichtrecht* (n 46 above) para A96.

[88] *Ibid.* For an English case decided on similar lines (prior to the general exclusionary approach adopted in *McFarlane*), see *R v Croydon Health Authority* (1997) 40 BMLR 40 (CA).

[89] BGH, 18 March 1980, NJW 1980, 1450; BGH, 19 June 1984, NJW 1984, 2625.

[90] See eg OLG Frankfurt, 1 December 1982, NJW 1983, 341 (reversed by BGH, 19 June 1984, NJW 1984, 2625).

[91] BVerfG, 28 May 1993, NJW 1993, 1751. The decision was mainly concerned with the constitutionality of new statutory provisions regulating abortion in the reunified Germany.

[92] BGH, 16 November 1993, NJW 1994, 788 (792) (as translated in Markesinis and Unberath, *The German Law of Torts* (n 77 above) 169). The case was brought by the parents of a disabled child who conceived it after faulty genetic counselling—sought after they had one child with the disability—to the effect that they were not at an increased risk of having another disabled child.

This decision, and the constitutional propriety of the BGH's reasoning, was subsequently upheld by a second decision of the *Bundesverfassungsgericht.*[93]

Moving on to cases of 'wrongful birth' arising from a faultily performed termination (or the failure to advise the parent(s) of the medical desirability of the same), the starting point will again be the purpose of the contract between the future parent(s) and the doctor. Here, insofar as general treatment was at issue, rather than a measure directed consciously at preventing the child's birth, liability will be denied. Thus, in a decision from 2004, the BGH rejected the liability of a doctor to pay maintenance costs in respect of a child born severely disabled after the non-diagnosis of the mother's rubella. The latter had consulted the doctor's practice in respect of treatment for a rash (which the locum attributed to an allergy), and though she had mentioned her pregnancy, this was not enough to extend the ambit of the contract to cover the costs bound up with the disabled child.[94]

Nonetheless in other situations (where the parties' interaction *was* concerned with the pregnancy and its continuation), a further complication emerges in the form of the German criminal law provisions on abortion. It is indeed here that the constitutional doubts raised by the *Bundesverfassungsgericht* in its 1993 decision[95] have had their impact. Following that decision, the BGH has held that maintenance costs for wrongful birth will only be recoverable if the failed or hypothetical abortion was (or would have been) legally justified under § 218a II of the *Strafgesetzbuch* (Criminal Code), due to the risk of pregnancy to the woman's life, or serious risk to her health.[96] In other cases, eg where a termination was indicated on social grounds—where it would not be justified, but merely 'not punishable' under § 218a I StGB—the award of damages is regarded as inconsistent with the constitutional protection of the unborn child. In this context, it should be noted that in Germany foetal disability per se is not a ground legally justifying abortion. Rather, to recover maintenance costs in such a case (where the doctor failed to advise/carry out a termination), the woman would need to show that the prospect of bearing a disabled child—as judged at the time of the doctor's failure—would have put such a strain on her own health as to bring her within § 218a II StGB.[97]

In the result, it is evident that—with the single (albeit important) exception of cases of failed sterilisations carried out for family-planning purposes—German law in the area of wrongful conception/birth is no more sympathetic to the parents' financial interests than the relevant English law (after the *McFarlane*

[93] BVerfG, 12 November 1997, NJW 1998, 519. (This was a judgment by the Court's First Senate in contrast to the earlier 1993 decision, which was reached by the more conservative Second Senate.)

[94] BGH, 21 December 2004, NJW 2005, 891.

[95] See n 91 above.

[96] BGH, 28 March 1995, NJW 1995, 1609.

[97] BGH, 18 June 2002, NJW 2002, 2636. In general the courts have been hesitant to accept this argument; for example in BGH, 21 December 2004, NJW 2005, 891—the rubella case referred to earlier, rejected on *Schutzzweck* grounds—the court left it open whether an abortion would have come within § 218a II StGB; see also BGH, 31 January 2006, NJW 2006, 1660.

decision). Indeed, in the category of wrongful birth, including those cases that concern the birth of a disabled child, it is less favourable.

IV. Preliminary Conclusions and Following Structure

As will have become apparent from the foregoing discussion, the overall social context in which the practice of medicine occurs and medical malpractice claims arise is closely comparable in England and Germany. Moreover, notwithstanding certain structural differences—in particular, the differing emphasis in the positioning of such claims on tort and contract, respectively—the broader legal setting also has much in common. This includes the point that it is the courts that have assumed the task of developing the detailed sub-rules and interpreting the salient concepts that apply in this field. By and large the overall putative protection conferred by private law—the forms of interest of the patient that are protected (through allowing an ex post facto private law action against the doctor)—is also very similar. Thus in both countries it is physical harm to the patient, either in the form of iatrogenic injury or through the progress of the patient's condition following a failure to provide proper treatment, that is at the forefront of such protection. In this context, as we saw, a form of merger of tortious and contractual rules has occurred, in which the two institutions have ceded their opposition to each other.

In summary, it may be said that the stage on which medical malpractice claims play out has been set in a similar manner in both countries. Nevertheless, as we shall find in the next three chapters, at a more detailed level there are interesting and significant differences in the rules developed by the courts in England and Germany for deciding whether a particular claim is justified. We begin, in chapter two with the most common type of allegation brought by patients, namely that the harm they suffered was attributable to faulty treatment from the doctor (a 'treatment malpractice' claim). Our focus there is upon the formal legal concepts and rules employed by English and German courts: in particular those that determine, first, when medical treatment qualifies as 'faulty'; and, secondly, when the patient's injury will be held to have resulted from such fault.

For the purposes of exposition in chapter two, it will be assumed that the background facts in relation to a given claim are not in dispute. The parties agree on the issues of how the patient presented to the doctor, and what the latter did in response. There is also agreement on the hypothetical question (relevant in attributing the injury to the doctor) of how the patient would have fared if the doctor had acted otherwise.[98] However, such an assumption is in practice generally misplaced: the parties are often bitterly divided on such issues—indeed frequently it is this, rather than any dispute as to the applicable legal rules, which leads to the

[98] Ie the issue of factual causation: see ch 2 pt III 1.

case coming to court. As will be discussed in chapter three, there are special reasons why treatment malpractice claims so often give rise to evidential disputes. The chapter proceeds to look at the distinctive English and German approaches to resolving these—deriving from divergent starting points in matters of civil procedure and proof.

By contrast in chapter four, we shall consider an alternative form of medical malpractice claim that a doctor will sometimes face, namely in respect of 'disclosure malpractice'.[99] This presents itself as an additional means for the patient to press his entitlement to redress for medical injury. In particular, where the injury is iatrogenic in nature, the doctor may seek to ascribe it to an inherent risk of the therapy (as opposed to negligence in its performance). However, insofar as the patient was not told of the risk beforehand, he may here respond by arguing that he ought to have been. Claims of this form, which focus on the doctor's anterior failure to respect the patient's decision-making autonomy, are of increasing importance in England and Germany. Moreover, the legal rules in the two jurisdictions here show a number of striking divergences, both as to the level of risk disclosure required and the legal effect in cases where it is lacking.

Whereas the focus in chapters two through to four is largely upon the positive law of England and Germany, in chapter five we shall move on to consider the options for law reform in relation to medical malpractice. Proposals for reform have been put forward frequently in both countries over the years, which betrays something of the dissatisfaction with the effects of the private law rules of liability in this area. At the same time, the diversity of the proposals in question bears testimony to the complexity of the issues—how to do greater justice to the interests of patients, doctors, and society at large, while remaining mindful of the potential costs and burdens that reforms may bring. The law reform issue has particular salience in the light of recent English legislation, the NHS Redress Act 2006, whose effect will be to remove a portion of medical malpractice claims from the aegis of private law, and regulate them by means of a centrally administered compensation scheme.

Finally, chapter six will present some overall conclusions, in terms of the insights gained into medical malpractice law through this comparative study of the English and German systems. In addition, some tentative suggestions will be made as to what lessons may be drawn from a micro-comparative survey of this kind (which seeks to examine in some detail the applicable legal rules in relation to a circumscribed field of law, and limited to two countries) for the broader comparative law enterprise.

[99] The terminology of 'treatment-' and 'disclosure malpractice' for these different forms of claim is borrowed from D Giesen, *International Medical Malpractice Law* (Tübingen, Mohr, 1988).

2

Treatment Malpractice—The Substantive Law

I. Introduction

IN THIS CHAPTER, and chapter three, we address claims in respect of treatment errors (*Behandlungsfehler*). The focus of the current chapter is upon the substantive elements that patients, in England and Germany, must establish in order to ground such a claim, whereas in chapter three we look at the proof aspects of determining when the relevant elements are factually present. Such claims involve an allegation by the patient that he has suffered avoidable harm (either iatrogenic injury or the failure to achieve an expected benefit) as a result of faulty treatment by the doctor and/or hospital. In this context, 'treatment' should be understood broadly as including the process of diagnosis, as well as general medical and nursing care of a post-operative nature. Thus it encompasses not only invasive, but also non-invasive aspects of medicine, such as the doctor's taking of a medical history and providing therapeutic advice (eg as to the patient seeking a specialist opinion), etc.[1] Excluded, on the other hand, are cases where the doctor's fault is alleged to lie in the non-disclosure, prior to treatment, of the risks attaching to the same: the rules relating to such disclosure—which bear upon the patient's informed consent—are the subject of chapter four.

As we saw in chapter one, the law in England primarily deals with medical malpractice claims in the tort of negligence; by contrast, in Germany the predominant legal framework is contract law. Nonetheless, there is an underlying similarity in both countries in respect of the elements that constitute a valid claim. Assuming, at the outset, that the injury engages one of the patient's legally protected interests, he must go on to show two things: first that there was some faulty conduct on the doctor's part—the 'malpractice' aspect; and secondly, that there is a causal link between this and the harm—principally that the harm would not have occurred if

[1] For a catalogue of the different types of factual situation in which treatment errors are typically pleaded in both England and Germany, see M Jones, *Medical Negligence*, 3rd edn (London, Sweet & Maxwell, 2003) paras 4-003 ff; D Giesen, *Arzthaftung*, 4th edn (Tübingen, Mohr, 1995) paras 110 ff.

the doctor had acted properly.[2] We have considered the scope of the patient's protected interests under English and German private law in chapter one.[3] Here our concern will be with the latter two elements.

II. Establishing Malpractice

1. A Fault-Based Approach to Liability

As discussed in chapter one, in both jurisdictions medical malpractice claims fall within the general ambit of private law. Central to the latter, and permeating the law in both England and Germany, is the operation of the fault principle: 'no liability without fault'. This principle may be seen as giving effect to the underlying principle of corrective justice, evening out wrongs between two parties that occur through the misuse by one of their freedom in failing (in the case of unintended harm) adequately to consider the risk to the other. In so doing it seeks a reasonable accommodation of the parties' interests: the defendant's in the pursuit of their ends; and the claimant's in not suffering unjustified loss.[4] At the same time, the principle's effect is to divide harms in the world into two kinds: those attributable to faulty human agency—warranting compensation—and those that are not. In the latter case, ie where the harm has a natural cause or stems from non-faulty agency, it will be regarded simply as 'fateful' and for the victim to bear (subject to such assistance he may receive from social security).[5]

In the course of the nineteenth century especially, the fault principle gained steadily in influence and prestige. Under the common law, the rise of negligence as the principal avenue of redress for unintended injury (replacing older, stricter forms of liability) may be seen to reflect a concern to preserve freedom of action in a more complex, man-made environment—where it was harder for actors to be sure in advance that even apparently innocuous conduct might not damage another person's interests in some unforeseen way.[6] In Germany, too, there was

[2] This is the order in which the common law approaches the issues. Admittedly, the German law of obligations has traditionally followed a different structure. There, doctrinally, causation falls to be dealt with first, to decide if there is a prima facie cause of action (*Tatbestandsmäßigkeit*), before examining the defendant's culpability (itself divided into elements of unlawfulness and fault): see especially D Medicus, *Schuldrecht I*, 17th edn (Munich, Beck, 2006) para 301; see also M Stauch, 'Approaches to Fault in German Tort Law' (2005) 13 *Torts Law Journal* 242. However, as regards treatment malpractice, many German authors approach the issues in the same way as the common law: see eg Giesen, *Arzthaftung* (n 1 above); K Geiß and H-P Greiner, *Arzthaftpflichtrecht*, 5th edn (Munich, Beck, 2006); M Gehrlein, *Umriss der Arzthaftpflicht*, 2nd edn (Munich, Verlag Franz Vahlen, 2006); to facilitate a comparative analysis, that structure is used here.

[3] See ch 1 pt III.

[4] See EJ Weinrib, *The Idea of Private Law* (Cambridge, Mass, Harvard University Press, 1995) 151–2; RW Wright, 'Right, Justice and Tort Law' in D Owen (ed), *The Philosophical Foundations of Tort Law* (Oxford, Clarendon Press, 1995) 159 ff.

[5] P Cane, *Atiyah's Accidents, Compensation and the Law*, 6th edn (London, Butterworths, 1999) 331 ff.

[6] See JG Fleming, *The Law of Torts*, 8th edn (Sydney, The Law Book Co Ltd, 1992) 6 ff.

much enthusiasm for the principle, reflecting the Kantian ideal of the 'equal freedom' of persons, as well as the historical research of the Pandectist school, which saw in it a moral advance over earlier forms of strict liability. In this context the jurist Rudolf von Jhering famously compared the emergence of fault with the 'discovery by chemists that it is not light itself that burns, but oxygen in the air'.[7] These ideas were influential in the drafting of the German Civil Code (*Bürgerliches Gesetzbuch* (BGB)) towards the end of the nineteenth century, and assured the principle a dominant role within the Code.[8]

Even though in both countries, with the development of the modern welfare state and the prevalence of third party insurance, there has been some dilution of this position—with an increase in areas governed by strict (or causal) liability—the principle still retains much of its persuasive force: at any rate, some extra justification is usually regarded as necessary to depart from it. Typically, this justification is that the defendant's activity, while socially legitimate and beneficial in advancing their interests, imposes on others a higher than normal risk of harm. Here it appears right to require the defendant to make good such damage (from the risk in question) as may from time to time occur, as with the common law rule in *Rylands v Fletcher*[9] or the liability in Germany of operators of technical apparatus and machinery.[10] However, it is also generally accepted that such a justification is absent in the case of therapeutic and consensual medical treatment: risky it may be, but it is carried out primarily for the patient's benefit, not that of the doctor.[11]

(a) England: Negligence Liability

As we saw in chapter one, most patients in England (viz, those receiving treatment under the NHS) will be required to bring a claim for medical injury in negligence. Here the need for faulty conduct by the doctor may be regarded as axiomatic: it is woven into the very fabric of the tort, with its requirement—to be discussed shortly—that, in order to be liable, the defendant must fail to take the care expected of a reasonable person in the circumstances. In this context the courts have been mindful of the inherent uncertainty of medicine—the inability of the doctor to control all variables. As Lord Diplock remarked in *Sidaway v Bethlem Royal Hospital*,

[7] Cited in E von Caemmerer, 'Das Verschuldensprinzip in rechtsvergleichender Sicht' (1978) 42 *Rabels Zeitschrift* 5 at 6.

[8] Von Caemmerer, *ibid.* C Katzenmeier, *Arzthaftung* (Tübingen, Mohr Siebeck, 2002) 150 ff. As further discussed below, under the BGB not only tortious, but also contractual liability is subject to the operation of the fault principle.

[9] *Rylands v Fletcher* (1868) LR 3 HL 330. The case establishes the strict liability of a landowner for the escape of dangerous substances accumulated on its land.

[10] See generally, K Zweigert and H Kötz, *An Introduction to Comparative Law* (trans T Weir) (Oxford, Clarendon Press, 1998) 646 ff. In Germany, more activities have been subjected to strict liability than in England. These are regulated in special statutes outside the BGB and include the liability of car-drivers (under the *Straßenverkehrsgesetz*). More recently strict liability for defective consumer products has been introduced in both countries as a result of initiatives at EC level: see further ch 5 pt III.

[11] Admittedly, there have been reform proposals in both countries that have suggested dispensing with fault-based liability in medical malpractice cases. There are examined in ch 5 below.

[i]nevitably all treatment, medical or surgical, involves some degree of risk that the patient's condition will be worse rather than better for undergoing it. Statistically, the chances of any risk of the proposed treatment going awry at all may be small—but . . . it is never totally absent and the degree of possible worsening involved may cover a whole spectrum of disabilities from mild occasional discomfort to what might justify the epithet catastrophic.[12]

The same fault-based approach applies to medical malpractice claims brought in contract law by patients in private care. In particular, in such cases, the treatment contract will not be construed as warranting a successful outcome.[13] In *Thake v Maurice*, where a private patient sued following the failure of his vasectomy, Neill LJ in the Court of Appeal commented:

I do not consider that a reasonable person would have expected a responsible medical man to be intending to give a guarantee. Medicine, though a highly skilled profession, is not, and is not generally regarded as being, an exact science. The reasonable man would have expected the defendant to exercise all the special care and skill of a surgeon in that speciality; he would not in my view have expected the defendant to give a guarantee of 100% success.[14]

In short, absent an express term to the contrary, the private doctor will be held merely to have promised to apply due skill and care in performing the treatment.[15] In implying the level of skill warranted, the courts have held this to be identical to the standard of 'reasonable' care required to avoid a claim in negligence.[16] This is also the position under statute. Thus section 13 of the Supply of Goods and Services Act 1982, which applies to contracts for services generally, provides that a person who supplies (contractual) services in the course of a business must carry them out with reasonable care and skill.

(b) Germany: Negligent Breach of Contract

As noted, in Germany too, the fault principle remains of central importance in determining the liability of actors in private law and permeates the *Bürgerliches Gesetzbuch.* Indeed one aspect of the dominance of the fault principle within the BGB is that (more explicitly than under the common law) fault has been made a condition for liability not only in tort, but in contract as well: a party's objective contractual breach leads initially to a presumption of culpability, which they may rebut (pursuant to § 280 I 2 BGB) by showing that they were 'not answerable' for

[12] *Sidaway v Board of Governors of the Bethlem Royal Hospital* [1985] AC 871 (HL) 890.

[13] This may be contrasted with the tendency under the common law for contractual obligations often to be construed strictly—eg in contracts for sale or for the supply of goods: see generally G Treitel, *The Law of Contract*, 11th edn (London, Sweet & Maxwell, 2003) 838 ff.

[14] *Thake v Maurice* [1986] QB 644 (CA) 685.

[15] See A Grubb (ed), *Principles of Medical Law*, 2nd edn (Oxford, Oxford University Press, 2004) paras 5.17 ff, who notes that it will be rare for such a warranty to be found. For an exceptional Canadian case on point (involving unsuccessful cosmetic surgery) see *LaFleur v Cornelis* (1979) 28 NBR (2d) 569.

[16] *Eyre v Measday* [1986] 1 All ER 488 (CA).

the breach in question.[17] In this context, § 276 I BGB provides that a party will (only) be answerable for willful or negligent breaches.

Given that, as discussed in chapter one, the doctor's obligations to the patient in Germany arise primarily in contract, this possibility for him to exculpate himself by showing lack of fault may seem of considerable significance. In fact, this is only true up to a point. The reason is that, before the stage is reached at which the doctor is required to raise the argument, a breach of contract must first have been made out. And here, as in England, a breach does not arise merely from the failure to achieve a given outcome (nor, usually, from the fact the patient suffers iatrogenic injury). In this regard, the courts have classified the contract for medical treatment as a *Dienstvertrag* (contract for services) under the BGB, obliging the doctor to exercise due skill and care, not as a *Werkvertrag* (contract for work) warranting a particular result.[18]

This classification admittedly has the conceptually unattractive result that, as the doctor's breach of contract (where established) will in effect already involve fault, § 280 I 2—offering him the chance to redeem himself by showing its absence—becomes redundant. In an attempt to escape from this, some commentators have here mooted a distinction between 'outer and inner care' (*äußere und innere Sorgfalt*): the idea is that while the (objectively faulty) breach of contract represents a failure to satisfy 'outer care', the doctor may yet exceptionally escape liability by showing that, subjectively, he held to the required 'inner care'.[19] This approach, though, is not easy to reconcile with the objective nature of fault generally sufficient for private law liability.[20] An alternative suggested by other commentators is for the doctor's contractual obligations to be construed generally from the outset, as part of a *Werkvertrag*. Accordingly, whenever treatment failed to produce the hoped for result, the doctor—to escape liability—would be required to demonstrate that he performed it with due skill and care.[21]

Nevertheless, the dominant view (and that endorsed by the courts) is that the latter model, shifting the burden of proof to the doctor, would be unjust in the light of the number of factors conducing to the treatment's success or failure that lie beyond his control.[22] As the BGH has noted,

[17] § 280 I BGB was introduced in 2002 and broadly consolidates the rules relating to breach of contract (*positive Vertragsverletzung*), previously developed by the courts.

[18] The model of the *Dienstvertrag* is set out at §§ 611 ff BGB; that of the *Werkvertrag* at §§ 631 ff BGB. Occasionally, a treatment contract may include elements of a *Werkvertrag*, eg where an orthopaedic surgeon agrees to prepare and fit a prosthetic limb: see Geiß and Greiner, *Arzthaftpflichtrecht* (n 2 above) para A4.

[19] E Deutsch and A Spickhoff, *Medizinrecht*, 5th edn (Berlin, Springer, 2003) para 136; see also Katzenmeier, *Arzthaftung* (n 8 above) 186 ff.

[20] S Heidelk, *Gesundheitsverletzung und Gesundheitsschaden: Ärztliche Verantwortung im Kontext des § 280 Abs. 1 BGB* (Berlin, Duncker & Humblot, 2005) 118 ff. The objective approach to the breach of duty question is discussed in pt II 2 (b) below.

[21] Giesen supported such an approach on the basis that the doctor is generally in the best position to know why treatment fails: see Giesen, *Arzthaftung* (n 1 above) paras 372 ff.

[22] Katzenmeier, *Arzthaftung* (n 8 above) 99 ff.

> the doctor can as a rule vouch only for a skilled attempt, not for a cure—and often not even for a correct diagnosis.[23]

At any rate this consideration holds good for the doctor's primary, positive duties (directed at trying to cure or ameliorate the patient's condition). By contrast, as we shall see later, a different approach has been taken to certain subsidiary obligations owed by the treating side—in particular the provision of a safe background environment for the treatment.[24]

Turning to the German doctor's concurrent tortious duties under § 823 I BGB, liability there—as with the tort of negligence in England—is based squarely on the defendant's faulty conduct. Thus the provision requires that, for a duty to compensate to arise, the defendant's unjustified invasion of another's protected interests must be either willful (*vorsätzlich*) or negligent (*fahrlässig*): in this regard, the same definition of 'negligence' (under § 276 II BGB) applies as for a breach of contract. As previously suggested, since the 2002 reforms to the BGB, tort law in this area may be regarded largely as duplicating contractual liability, rather than contributing distinct rules of its own.

2. The Standard of Care Expected of the Doctor

As we have just seen, the fault principle that underpins much of English and German private law involves a rejection of straightforward liability for the adverse outcomes of an individual's conduct. Applied to a doctor, this means that in cases of injurious medical treatment (including where it fails to bring the expected benefit) this alone does not make him liable. Instead he must have failed to exercise proper skill and care in carrying out the treatment. This raises the question of what is meant by 'proper skill and care': ie to what abstract standard of conduct will a doctor be held, in order not to be at fault? As we shall see below, in answering this, English and German law show a high degree of similarity.

(a) England: The Reasonably Skilled Practitioner

In general terms, to avoid being negligent (or 'in breach of duty'[25]), an individual must perform activities involving a risk of harm to others with the care expected of a 'reasonable person'. In the classic formulation of Alderson B in *Blyth v Birmingham Waterworks Co*,

> [n]egligence is the omission to do something which a reasonable man, guided upon those considerations which ordinarily regulate the conduct of human affairs, would do, or doing something which a prudent and reasonable man would not do.[26]

[23] BGH, 11 October 1977, NJW 1978, 584 (584).

[24] Here, in line with the doctrine of 'fully-masterable risks' (*voll beherrschbare Risiken*), the duties in question will be construed strictly: see the discussion in pt II 3 (b) below.

[25] The courts use these two expressions synonymously.

[26] *Blyth v Birmingham Waterworks Co* (1856) 11 Exch 781, 784.

Though the notion of a 'reasonable' person at first sight suggests the care of 'average' or 'ordinary' citizens, in reality it embodies a prescriptive element, reflecting the court's sense of how a person *ought* to behave. In the words of Lord MacMillan in *Glasgow Corporation v Muir*,

> [s]ome persons are by nature unduly timorous and imagine every path beset with lions. Others, of a more robust temperament fail to foresee or nonchalantly disregard even the most obvious dangers. The reasonable man is presumed to be free both from over-apprehension and from over-confidence.[27]

It is clear that what is required of a person will vary according to the nature of the activity in question. As Lord MacMillan, again, stated in *Glasgow Corporation v Muir*,

> [t]hose who engage in operations inherently dangerous must take precautions that are not required of persons engaged in the ordinary routine of daily life.[28]

This is of direct relevance to doctors and other professionals, who hold themselves out as possessing special skill to deal with the risks that arise in the course of their work. It means that a given doctor is required to display the degree of aptitude that would be possessed by a reasonable doctor. This point is reflected in McNair J's famous jury-direction in the case of *Bolam v Friern Hospital Management Committee*:

> In an ordinary case it is generally said you judge [negligence] by the action of the man in the street. He is the ordinary man. In one case it has been said you judge it by the conduct of the man on the top of a Clapham omnibus. He is the ordinary man. But where you get a situation which involves the use of some special skill or competence, then the test as to whether there has been negligence or not is not the test of the man on the top of a Clapham omnibus, because he has not got this special skill. The test is the standard of the ordinary skilled man exercising and professing to have that special skill.[29]

In fact, the courts will differentiate further according to the defendant's particular speciality. As Lord Bridge remarked in *Sidaway v Board of Governors of Bethlem Royal Hospital*,

> [t]he language of the *Bolam* test clearly requires a different degree of skill from a specialist in his own special field than from a general practitioner. In the field of neuro-surgery it would be necessary to substitute for [the] phrase 'no doctor of ordinary skill', the phrase 'no neuro-surgeon of ordinary skill'.[30]

In this context, it is apparent that 'skill' is being used in a broad sense to encompass not only technical ability in executing treatment, but the knowledge and experience necessary to form judgements in relation to diagnosis and treatment. With regard to a field of activity such as medicine, an important aspect of this will

[27] *Glasgow Corporation v Muir* [1943] AC 448 (HL) 457.
[28] *Ibid*, 456
[29] *Bolam v Friern Hospital Management Committee* [1957] 1 WLR 582 (QBD) 586.
[30] *Sidaway v Board of Governors of Bethlem Royal Hospital* [1985] AC 871 (HL) 897.

relate to the awareness of the risks attaching to a given intervention. Here doctors will be expected to keep reasonably up to date with medical literature and familiarise themselves with new research findings and techniques (either showing that an existing technique involves dangers not previously known, or that there is a newer method involving lower risks).[31] However, the courts will be careful to judge the defendant's conduct by reference to those risks knowable at the time. A famous case in point is *Roe v Minister of Health*, where two patients were paralysed following the administration of contaminated anaesthetic. The contamination had occurred through antiseptic solution seeping through invisible fissures in the storage ampoules—a previously unknown risk. In the Court of Appeal, Denning LJ, in finding against the hospital's liability, commented as follows:

> It is so easy to be wise after the event and to condemn as negligence that which was only a misadventure. We ought always to be on our guard against it, especially in cases against hospitals and doctors. Medical science has conferred great benefits on mankind, but these benefits are attended by considerable risks . . . Doctors, like the rest of us, have to learn by experience; and experience often teaches in a hard way.[32]

A central feature of the reasonable skill and care approach is its objectivity: as Lord MacMillan put it in *Glasgow Corporation v Muir*,

> [i]t eliminates the personal equation and is independent of the idiosyncrasies of the particular person whose conduct is in question.[33]

Thus the defendant is measured not by how well they personally could have acted, but against how a reasonable person (placed in those circumstances) would have acted. In this regard, a doctor who is particularly skilled will not be negligent if he fails to meet his own exceptional standard on a given occasion (provided he still performs as well as a reasonable doctor). As McNair J observed in the *Bolam* case,

> [a] man need not possess the highest expert skill at the risk of being found negligent. It is well established law that it is sufficient if he exercises the ordinary skill of an ordinary competent man exercising that particular art.[34]

Conversely, though, for conduct to qualify as negligent it is enough that there was a one-off failure of ordinary skill; the average level of care offered by the defendant over a range of cases is irrelevant.[35] Another effect of the objective standard is that liability may be found against a defendant who was never in a position to exercise the level of care required: a well-known example, outside the medical malpractice context, is *Nettleship v Weston*, in which a learner-driver, who caused

[31] *Crawford v Charing Cross Hospital* (CA), *The Times*, 8 December 1953; Grubb, *Principles of Medical Law* (n 15 above) 6.28 ff.

[32] *Roe v Minister of Health* [1954] 2 QB 66 (CA) 83.

[33] *Glasgow Corporation v Muir* [1943] AC 448 (HL) 457.

[34] *Bolam* [1957] 1 WLR 582 (QBD) 586; see also Jones, *Medical Negligence* (n 1 above) paras 3-084 ff. It may, though, be negligent for a doctor not to make use of extra knowledge that he (subjectively) possesses: for a suggestion to this effect, see *Stokes v Guest, Keen and Nettlefold (Bolts and Nuts) Ltd* [1968] 1 WLR 1776, 1783 (Swanwick J).

[35] *Wilsher v Essex Area Health Authority* [1987] QB 730 (CA) 746 (Mustill LJ).

an accident on her second driving lesson, was held liable despite her argument that she was doing her incompetent best.[36]

The same approach has been taken in medical injury cases with respect to mistakes made by inexperienced doctors. The leading case is *Wilsher v Essex Area Health Authority*, in which a junior doctor in a specialist baby unit took faulty blood-oxygen measurements for a premature baby; this led to the baby being over-saturated with oxygen, which allegedly caused his subsequent blindness. In his judgment Glidewell LJ stated:

> In my view, the law requires the trainee or learner to be judged by the same standard as his more experienced colleagues. If it did not, inexperience would frequently be urged as a defence to an action for professional negligence.[37]

As he further noted,

> [i]f this test appears unduly harsh in relation to the inexperienced, I should add that, in my view, the inexperienced doctor called upon to exercise a specialist skill will, as part of that skill, seek the advice and help of his superiors when he does or may need it. If he does seek such help, he will often have satisfied the test, even though he may himself have made a mistake.[38]

Another situation where the courts have insisted on a threshold standard of medical care is in the face of arguments based on shortages of health care resources. In practice, such a claim is likely to be brought not against an individual doctor, but directly against a health trust or hospital, in respect of institutional negligence—ie arguing that the overall system of care it operated was flawed. Here, given that the provision of health care is a public benefit, there might be felt to be an argument for relaxing the standard on occasion: after all, the effect of a court finding that a given hospital department is unable to operate safely due to inadequate resources may be that the hospital simply closes it down. On a strict utilitarian calculus, this may represent a loss to the overall community—many patients who would have used (and could have been successfully treated by) the department will henceforth have to travel a greater distance to another hospital.

However, the courts have refused to be swayed by such considerations. A case in point is that of *Bull v Devon Area Health Authority*, in which one of the claimant's twins was born brain damaged due to the delay in getting the registrar to attend her. The defendants maintained maternity services on different sites, but only employed a single registrar, and the system for calling him over to assist in the

36 *Nettleship v Weston* [1971] 2 QB 691 (CA).

37 *Wilsher v Essex Area Health Authority* [1987] QB 730 (CA) 774.

38 *Ibid.* But see the dissenting view of Sir Nicolas Browne-Wilkinson VC, at 777, who would have made allowance for the doctor's inexperience: 'so long as the English law rests liability on personal fault, a doctor who has properly accepted a post in a hospital in order to gain necessary experience should only be held liable for acts or omissions which a careful doctor with his qualifications and experience would not have done or omitted'. His solution would have been to impose liability on the hospital/Health Authority alone for institutional negligence in failing to supervise the junior doctor.

delivery had broken down.[39] The Court of Appeal unanimously held the health authority liable. In his judgment, Mustill LJ commented:

> The . . . suggested answer [to the claim of negligence] was on these lines: that hospitals such as the Devon and Exeter were in the dilemma of having to supply a maternity service, and yet not disposing of sufficient manpower to provide immediate cover, the more so since the small number of consultants and registrars had to deal with three different sites. They could not be expected to do more than their best, allocating their limited resources as favourably as possible . . . I have some reservations about this contention, which are not allayed by the submission that hospital medicine is a public service. So it is, but there are other public services in respect of which it is not necessarily an answer to allegations of unsafety that there were insufficient resources to enable the administrators to do everything which they would like to do.[40]

The upshot, as Jones argues, is that policy-makers must choose between the provision of no service and of a reasonably safe service (otherwise they could choose between no service and an unreasonably risky service). As he further notes, the courts here proceed on the background assumption that sufficient funding/resources are available from other areas of the public purse, which can be made available without undue damage to the overall polity.[41] At the same time, what is at issue here is the provision of a minimum level of care. Over and above this, a degree of disparity in treatment services will be tolerated between different geographical regions and types of hospital. Thus the fact that a district hospital fails to provide the patient with the level of specialist care he would have received in a university hospital is not itself negligent; the issue will instead be whether, in the light of the patient's condition, it was negligent not to refer him for such specialist care.[42] On the other hand it will be negligent for a hospital that possesses more advanced technical equipment than average not to employ it in an appropriate case: unlike the subjective (and evidentially problematic) issue of the more than averagely skilled individual doctor, the potential availability of such equipment will form one of the external circumstances against which its conduct is judged.[43]

A related set of questions concerns the standard of care expected in emergency situations: an 'emergency' might indeed be defined as a sudden disjunction between an unusual event and the resources available to deal with it. This sometimes, again, raises the issue of institutional liability, namely whether the hospital or health authority, in its second-order planning for eventualities, allowed for an adequate provision of care over a range of cases. Here the courts will hold to a

[39] *Bull v Devon Area Health Authority* (1993) 4 Med LR 117 (CA).

[40] *Ibid*, 141.

[41] Jones, *Medical Negligence* (n 1 above) paras 4-099 ff. For an argument that the courts should be mindful of the public good dimension in medical care and forgive 'systemic' negligence due to insufficient resources, see C Witting, 'National Health Service Rationing: Implications for the Standard of Care in Negligence' (2001) 21 *Oxford Journal of Legal Studies* 443.

[42] *Ball v Wirral Health Authority* [2003] Lloyd's Rep Med 165 (QBD); Jones, *Medical Negligence* (n 1 above) para 4-101.

[43] Jones, *Medical Negligence* (n 1 above) para 4-107.

threshold standard, based upon the range of events deemed to have been reasonably foreseeable as possibilities during the relevant period. Thus a hospital will not be required to have extra (specialist) staff in constant attendance in case, by unlucky coincidence, two patients suddenly require their attention at the same time.[44]

As regards the potential liability of an individual doctor who acts in an emergency, the courts, while retaining an objective starting point, will take account of the unusual circumstances. As Mustill LJ observed in the *Wilsher* case,

> [a]n emergency may overburden the available resources, and, if an individual is forced by circumstances to do too many things at once, the fact that he does one of them incorrectly should not lightly be taken as negligence.[45]

The courts will be mindful that the defendant may have been required to take swift decisions on the basis of incomplete knowledge. Similarly, if the existence of the emergency justified intervention by someone without the specialist skills ideally required, the latter will only be held to the standard of someone with their actual skills.[46]

(b) Germany: Required Care Under § 276 II BGB

The starting point in defining the relevant standard of care in German law is § 276 II BGB, which provides that, to avoid negligence (*Fahrlässigkeit*), a person must bring to a task 'the socially required level of care' (*die im Verkehr erforderliche Sorgfalt*). This provision immediately makes apparent—indeed more clearly than the common law's reference to 'reasonable care'—that the standard at issue is prescriptive, not descriptive. In particular, the ordinary or customary standard of care (*übliche Sorgfalt*) prevailing in society does not provide the benchmark; rather it is the court that defines the standard.[47]

In terms of their general reference point, the German courts, like their English counterparts, have regard to the notional conduct of a careful person engaging in the same sphere of activity as the defendant. As van Gerven, Lever and Larouche note, various descriptions have been used over the years:

> 'Typical formulations include the bonus pater familias, the average, orderly, intelligent person, and the circumspect and conscientious member of the relevant social group.'[48]

[44] *Smithers v Taunton and Somerset NHS Trust* [2004] EWHC 1179. There the trust was found not liable for the brain damage of a baby, caused by the delay in delivering him while the doctors dealt with another emergency.

[45] *Wilsher v Essex Area Health Authority* [1987] QB 730 (CA) 749. See also *Kent v Griffiths* [2001] QB 36 (CA) 53 (Lord Woolf MR).

[46] Grubb, *Principles of Medical Law* (n 15 above) para 6.48.

[47] See eg BGH, 27 November 1952, NJW 1953, 257, discussed further at n 92 below.

[48] W van Gerven, J Lever and P Larouche, *Tort Law: Common Law of Europe Casebooks* (Oxford, Hart Publishing, 2000) 314; see also H Kötz and G Wagner, *Deliktsrecht*, 10th edn (Neuwied, Luchterhand, 2006) para 113.

As in England, the degree of care will vary according to the difficulty and risk inherent in the defendant's undertaking. In this regard, the German Federal Court (*Bundesgerichtshof* (BGH)) has held that doctors must demonstrate the standard of care of 'a respectable and conscientious medical professional of average expertise in the relevant field'.[49]

In this context, doctors should remain up to date with medical literature and familiarise themselves with new techniques and may be negligent if they fail to apply a new method involving fewer risks than an older method. For example, in one case a doctor was found negligent for treating an infection with a medicine which had arsenical poisoning as a side effect instead of using penicillin.[50] At the same time, the courts will remain mindful of the state of knowledge and technical possibilities available to the defendant at the time. Thus in another case the BGH was required to decide, in 1960, if it had been negligent for a doctor in 1948 to miss signs of the claimant's tuberculosis on an X-ray slide. It endorsed the view of the Appellate Court that the issue needed to be judged relative to conditions prevailing in 1948.[51]

As in England, the courts will distinguish according to the specialism in which the doctor operates: thus, a specialist doctor is required to show the knowledge and skill of a reasonable specialist.[52] It will, accordingly, be negligent if a particularly difficult operation, such as thyroid gland surgery, is performed by other than specialist surgeons.[53] Here, a key concern of the law is to safeguard the justified expectations of patients when submitting themselves to medical care. In this context less may sometimes be demanded of practitioners who *to the patient's knowledge* possess a lower degree of expertise. In one case, the BGH considered the liability of an alternative health therapist (*Heilpraktiker*) for the unexpected death of a patient following ozone-injection therapy.[54] In its decision the Court held that such a therapist was

> under an obligation to acquire sufficient competence with regard to the treatment methods used by him (including their risks) and especially the correct techniques for using those techniques without danger. Accordingly, in the same way as a physician, he fails to exercise the required care if he chooses a therapy without being familiar in advance to the necessary extent, with its use, specific characteristics and risks.[55]

On the facts, though, the BGH was prepared to exonerate the therapist: the risk—while it might have been known to a specialist in the field—was so rare that the defendant could not be expected to be aware of it.

As with the standard of care in negligence in England, the care required by § 276 II BGB is objective; by setting out to practise in a given field, a doctor automatically falls to be judged by the standard of a reasonable peer. In Dieter Giesen's words,

[49] BGH, 13 June 1960, NJW 1961, 600 (600).
[50] BGH, 16 May 1972, VersR 1972, 887.
[51] BGH, 13 June 1960, NJW 1961, 600.
[52] BGH, 13 February 2001, NJW 2001, 1786.
[53] Giesen, *Arzthaftung* (n 1 above) para 134.
[54] BGH, 29 January 1991, VersR 1991, 469.
[55] *Ibid*, 470 (as translated in van Gerven, Lever and Larouche, *Tort Law* (n 48 above) 317).

a physician, through accepting a patient for treatment, impliedly warrants that he possesses the competence to perform his art and specialty carefully and competently inclusive of his proper and skilful judgment whether and when his patient needs a referral to a specialist . . . for a second opinion or further treatment.[56]

In fact, it appears a subjective approach may be applied upwards (above the threshold of reasonable care), so that a particular doctor with more than the average knowledge and experience must offer a commensurately higher standard of care; thus it would be negligent, for example, if a general practitioner with previous training as an orthopaedic surgeon failed to draw upon his specialist knowledge in an appropriate case.[57] In this regard, the legal position in Germany is arguably stricter than that in England.[58]

Nonetheless, what is beyond doubt is that the objective standard of care operates downwards, identifying a threshold level of care that must be met by all. In this context, the doctor's personal deficiencies, eg due to overwork or advanced years, are irrelevant to the issue of liability.[59] It follows too that a junior doctor (*Assistenzarzt*) cannot rely on inexperience to excuse a mistake. Insofar as he falls short of the required standard, the reproach that can be levelled against him is that he undertook a task for which he lacked the qualifications, so-called *Übernahmeverschulden* (ie the faulty assumption of a task). In a leading decision in this area the BGH held that

[a junior doctor] owes the same duty of skill and care to the patient as any other doctor . . . If he recognises, or ought to recognise, that the patient will be exposed to a heightened risk of injury as a result of his inexperience, he should not proceed to treat against the dictates of his medical conscience and own better judgment[60]

In such a case the Court emphasised the need for self-critical appraisal and suggested the junior doctor should, if necessary, inform the patient of his inexperience, so that the latter might reconsider his consent. This was so even if the doctor's training and advancement might thereby suffer. At the same time, though, it recognised that this may be hard on a defendant whose very inexperience prevents them from recognising their limitations. In this regard, there has been a tendency in practice to shift liability away from junior doctors. Thus in the case at hand, the BGH set aside the defendant's liability where he was instructed by his supervising doctor to carry out an operation for which he (unknown to himself) lacked the requisite skill. Instead liability was imposed on the hospital authority for an organisational failure to see that each of its employees was working within the scope and limits of their competence.

[56] D Giesen, *International Medical Malpractice Law* (Tübingen, Mohr, 1988) para 137.

[57] M Gehrlein, *Umriss der Arzthaftpflicht* (n 2 above) para B9. See also BGH, 24 June 1997, NJW 1997, 3090; BGH, 10 February 1987, NJW 1987, 1479.

[58] See the discussion in n 34 above. In Germany too, though, an objective approach would arguably apply where 'skill' in the narrow sense of physical dexterity is at issue: evidentially it is unclear how a subjective fault finding would here be reached.

[59] BGH, 10 February 1987, NJW 1987, 1479; Giesen, *Arzthaftung* (n 1 above) para 72.

[60] BGH, 27 September 1983, NJW 1984, 655 (657).

As regards the potential effect of shortages in resources on the relevant level of care, the emphasis in Germany, as in England, is on maintaining a threshold minimum standard. As Geiß and Greiner suggest, the case law here is characterised by an attempt to steer a middle course between the pressure to use the most modern and costly equipment on the one hand, and guaranteeing the quality of patient care on the other.[61] In this context, the courts accept a degree of local discrepancy in the care offered to patients, depending on the type of hospital and level of expertise of its doctors.[62] A municipal hospital is thus not required to achieve the optimal possible standard of the treatment-leaders: on the other hand it may be obliged to advise a particularly needy patient of the possibility of securing more advanced treatment elsewhere.[63] As in England, where a given hospital has at its disposal more advanced equipment than average, it will be negligent to fail to make use of it in an appropriate case.[64]

Turning to the related issue of the applicable standard in emergencies, one may distinguish, as in our discussion of the English law, between cases where the hospital as a whole does not have adequate physical resources to cope, and where the conduct of a particular doctor is impugned. In relation to the former situation, eg where there are insufficient staff on duty to provide medical cover to two patients who simultaneously require attention,[65] German law in fact appears more claimant-friendly than the common law: the risks stemming from the lack of available staff would be regarded as within the hospital's sphere, ie a matter it could have addressed by appropriate planning. As is discussed more fully below, in such cases (of so-called 'fully-masterable risks') the onus will rest on the hospital to persuade the court that, in making the relevant staffing arrangements, it exercised all due care.[66]

By contrast, a mistake by an overburdened individual doctor is, as in England, more likely to be forgiven: here the difficulty of the circumstances facing him will be taken into account.[67] Indeed, in principle the German doctor may avail himself of a special statutory provision to defend his conduct, namely §680 BGB. The latter restricts the liability of a 'rescuer' to cases where his conduct was willful or grossly negligent. Even so, as Katzenmeier notes, the provision is aimed principally at 'Good Samaritan' interventions on the part of ordinary citizens; it is not clear that it would be extended to a doctor with professional medical training. The latter is arguably sufficiently protected by the fact that he would only be expected to achieve the standard of a reasonable doctor of his actual speciality.[68]

[61] Geiß and Greiner, *Arzthaftpflichtrecht* (n 2 above) para B6. See also Katzenmeier, *Arzthaftung* (n 8 above) 283 ff.

[62] BGH 22 September 1987, NJW 1988, 763.

[63] Katzenmeier, *Arzthaftung* (n 8 above) 284.

[64] BGH, 30 May 1989, NJW 1989, 2321.

[65] Eg, as occurred in the *Smithers v Taunton* case in England: see n 44 above.

[66] See by analogy BGH, 11 December 1990, NJW 1991, 1543. As to fully-masterable risks, see further the discussion in pt II 3 (b) below.

[67] Geiß and Greiner, *Arzthaftpflichtrecht* (n 2 above) para B27.

[68] Katzenmeier, *Arzthaftung* (n 8 above) 110–11; A Laufs and W Uhlenbruck, *Handbuch des Arztrechts*, 3rd edn (Munich, Beck, 2002) § 45, para 19. Admittedly, in one case the BGH suggested that the non-specialist doctor who assists in an emergency will be objectively liable for not attaining the

3. Establishing Lack of Care: the Role of Accepted Practice

In general terms, to decide if a given defendant has satisfied the relevant standard of care, the courts focus on the risk of injury, as against the hoped-for benefits attaching to their conduct. Assuming that some degree of risk was inherent and unavoidable, the question is whether in all the circumstances this was justified. In England the issue is often characterised as one of 'fact', meaning that a court's decision will be specific to the case at hand and of limited precedential value. However, this should not detract from its normative nature, viz did the defendant behave in the circumstances as the law deems they *ought* to have?

In cases of 'everyday' negligence, the courts are able to decide this question directly: the judge is aware of the risks of ordinary activities and the norms that have developed in response to the same, eg what counts as careful driving, etc. However, the position is different in complex matters of medical (or other professional) expertise, where the defendant's conduct is assessed by reference to that of other specialists. There, the courts will be reliant to a significant degree on the opinion evidence of the latter as to how far the defendant's actions were acceptable.[69] In this regard, a central issue is how far the defendant should be exonerated by a finding—on the basis of such evidence—that his conduct was in line with normal medical practice. Here, at least in the past, there has been a perceptible divergence between the relevant English and German law.

(a) *England: The* Bolam *Test*

In England, the courts have traditionally attached great weight to the doctor's compliance with 'accepted practice': a defendant whose conduct is approved by other doctors (testifying as expert witnesses) is most unlikely to be found in breach of duty. This approach informed McNair J's well-known jury direction in the 1957 case of *Bolam v Friern Hospital Management Committee*:

> Counsel for the plaintiff put it in this way, that in the case of a medical man, negligence means failure to act in accordance with the standards of reasonably competent medical men at the time. That is a perfectly accurate statement, as long as it is remembered that there may be one or more perfectly proper standards; and if a medical man conforms with one of those standards then he is not negligent . . . a doctor is not negligent if he is acting in accordance with such a practice merely because there is a body of opinion that takes a contrary view.[70]

standard of the specialist: see BGH, 13 February 2001, NJW 2001, 1786. However, that decision concerned a doctor who, though not yet himself a qualified specialist, was working in the relevant specialist unit.

[69] See eg the remarks of Sir Christopher Staughton in *Adams v Rhymney Borough Council* (2000) 150 NLJ 1231 (CA) para 38.

[70] *Bolam v Friern Hospital Management Committee* [1957] 1 WLR 582 (QBD) 587.

The courts have endorsed the use of this '*Bolam* test' in numerous subsequent decisions, including at the highest level. In the House of Lords case of *Maynard v West Midlands Regional Health Authority*, Lord Scarman remarked as follows:

> Differences of opinion and practice exist, and will always exist, in the medical as other professions. There is seldom any one answer exclusive of all others to problems of medical judgment. A court may prefer one body of opinion to the other, but that is no basis for a conclusion for negligence . . . [I]n the realm of diagnosis and treatment negligence is not established by preferring one respectable body of opinion to another. Failure to exercise the ordinary skill of a doctor (in the appropriate speciality if he be a specialist) is necessary.[71]

As this makes clear, 'accepted practice' is not a unitary concept: the courts recognise that medicine is an imprecise and developing science where, at a given time, a plurality of accepted practices may co-exist. However, a significant ambiguity in the operation of the *Bolam* test over the years concerned the role of the court itself: did a finding that a doctor had complied with a currently accepted practice *automatically* absolve him of a breach of duty, or was the judge still entitled in an appropriate case to find him liable (in effect, by condemning the practice as a whole)?

In dealing with other (non-medical) professional activity, the English courts were certainly prepared on occasion to find accepted practice wanting.[72] However, for a time, it seemed as though doctors had been accorded a special dispensation: as Lord Scarman put it in *Sidaway v Board of Governors of Bethlem Royal Hospital*, 'the law imposes the duty of care, but the standard of care is a matter of medical judgment'.[73] This approach was often fatal to the patient's claim: however many experts he mustered who were of the view that the defendant had been negligent, this could be nullified by the defence leading the opinion evidence of perhaps a small minority of other experts that it had not been. A good illustration is provided by the case of *De Freitas v O'Brien*, where the patient suffered serious injury in the course of risky spinal surgery carried out by the defendant.[74] Though 'normal medical opinion' (of some 1,000 orthopaedic surgeons countrywide) would not have countenanced such surgery, the defendant's decision to operate was supported by a handful of 'spinal surgeons'. The Court of Appeal deemed this to constitute a 'responsible body of opinion' and dismissed the claim. In his judgment, Otton LJ remarked that the question of negligence 'could not be determined by counting heads'.[75]

This state of affairs attracted criticism over the years from both academic commentators and patient support groups, concerned at the degree to which doctors

[71] *Maynard v West Midlands Regional Health Authority* [1984] 1 WLR 634 (HL) 638.

[72] See eg *Edward Wong Finance Co Ltd v Johnston Stokes and Masters* [1984] AC 296 (PC), where a solicitor was found negligent despite following the conveyancing practice universally adopted in Hong Kong.

[73] *Sidaway v Board of Governors of the Bethlem Royal Hospital* [1985] AC 871 (HL) 881.

[74] *De Freitas v O'Brien* [1995] PIQR P281 (CA).

[75] *Ibid*, P291.

were able to immunise themselves from findings of negligence.[76] As Kennedy and Grubb suggest, one explanation for the judges' reticence in challenging medical testimony may have been that the technical complexity of many cases—requiring expert input to clarify the factual issues—carried over into an uncritical approach to the experts' views as to whether the doctor was justified in acting as he did.[77] Nonetheless, a further policy-based reason is likely to have been the fear of encouraging an explosion of malpractice litigation (on the lines of the US medical malpractice crisis) against the National Health Service. This concern was alluded to explicitly by Lord Denning MR in the Court of Appeal in *Whitehouse v Jordan*, where his Lordship commented:

> Take heed of what has happened in the United States. 'Medical malpractice' cases there are very worrying, especially as they are tried by juries who have sympathy for the patient and none for the doctor, who is insured. The damages are colossal . . . Experienced practitioners are known to have refused to treat patients for fear of being accused of negligence. Young men are even deterred from entering the profession because of the risks involved. In the interests of all, we must avoid such consequences in England.[78]

Be that as it may, more recently, in *Bolitho v City and Hackney Health Authority*, the House of Lords has reaffirmed the court's ultimate role in evaluating the reasonableness of accepted medical practice, however distinguished its proponents. In that decision, Lord Browne-Wilkinson commented as follows:

> [I]n my view, the court is not bound to hold that a defendant doctor escapes liability for negligent treatment or diagnosis just because he leads evidence from a number of medical experts who are genuinely of the opinion that the defendant's treatment or diagnosis accorded with sound medical practice . . . the court has to be satisfied that the exponents of the body of opinion relied upon can demonstrate that such opinion has a logical basis. In particular in cases involving, as they so often do, the weighing of risks against benefits, the judge before accepting a body of opinion as being responsible, reasonable or respectable, will need to be satisfied that, in forming their views, the experts have directed their minds to the question of comparative risks and benefits and have reached a defensible conclusion on the matter.[79]

At the same time, his Lordship urged trial judges to remain cautious in such cases in finding a breach of duty: after all it is the experts, not the judge, who have the relevant expertise (and will presumably try to avoid practices containing unreasonable risks[80]):

[76] See generally M Brazier and J Miola, 'Bye-bye *Bolam*: a medical litigation revolution?' (2000) 8 *Medical Law Review* 85.

[77] IM Kennedy and A Grubb, *Medical Law: Text, Cases and Materials*, 3rd edn (London, Butterworths, 2000) 429.

[78] *Whitehouse v Jordan* [1980] 1 All ER 650 (CA) 658.

[79] *Bolitho v City and Hackney Health Authority* [1998] AC 232 (HL) 241–2. See also *Joyce v Merton, Sutton and Wandsworth Health Authority* (1996) 7 Med LR 1 (CA) 13–14 (Roch LJ).

[80] As Sopinka J commented in the Canadian Supreme Court in *ter Neuzen v Korn* (1995) 127 DLR (4th) 577, 590, the professional 'is assumed to have adopted procedures which . . . are not inherently negligent'.

> It is only where a judge can be satisfied that the body of expert opinion cannot be logically supported at all that such opinion will not provide the bench mark by reference to which the defendant's conduct falls to be assessed.[81]

Applying this approach, there have so far only been a handful of cases where trial judges have found conduct negligent in the face of supportive testimony from other doctors, and here more where the doctor was offering a personal assessment (as opposed to asserting that the conduct in question conformed with 'accepted practice').[82]

In fact, there has in recent years been a trend in the National Health Service towards a more monolithic approach to medical practice, deriving from the findings of 'evidence-based medicine'. In this regard, there has been a proliferation of 'best practice' guidelines from quality assurance agencies, which aim to set out in some detail the procedures to be followed in relation to given forms of treatment.[83] Here, it is evident that compliance with such guidance will be a persuasive indicator of non-negligence[84]; certainly, it will be very difficult here for a patient to demonstrate that the relevant practice is illogical and hence not truly responsible. Instead, perhaps the more interesting question is how far *deviation* from such (near universal) accepted practice will be regarded automatically as negligent?

The latter issue was addressed in general terms in the case of *Clark v MacLennan*, where a gynaecologist performed an operation on his patient to relieve stress incontinence one month after she had given birth, rather than waiting the normal three months. In finding a breach of duty, Peter Pain J suggested that the 'burden of proof', in such a case, moved to the doctor to show he was not in breach.[85] Though, subsequently in the *Wilsher* case, Mustill LJ rejected the idea that the proof burden would shift in formal terms, he agreed that, at a practical level, the onus would pass to the defendant to justify his conduct. This was in accord with

> the forensic commonplace that, where one party has, in the course of the trial, hit the ball into the other's court, it is for that other to return it.[86]

Such a justification will clearly be hard to bring if the accepted practice was universal and specifically directed against the risk that materialised. A case in point is *Chin Keow v Government of Malaysia* in which a doctor was found liable for the death of a patient to whom he gave penicillin without taking the normal step of

[81] *Bolitho v City and Hackney Health Authority* [1998] AC 232 (HL) 243.

[82] See eg *Marriott v West Midlands Health Authority* [1999] Lloyds Rep Med 23 (CA); *Burne v A* [2006] EWCA Civ 24.

[83] See Grubb, *Principles of Medical Law* (n 15 above) para 6.23. The key agency is the National Institute for Health and Clinical Excellence (NICE), which was set up in 1999 with the task of assessing treatments available for various conditions in terms of clinical and cost effectiveness.

[84] See *Penney v East Kent Health Authority* [2000] Lloyd's Rep Med 41 (CA); Kennedy and Grubb, *Medical Law: Text, Cases and Materials* (n 77 above) 455.

[85] *Clark v MacLennan* [1983] 1 All ER 416 (QBD) 427. In fact the term 'burden of justification' arguably better captures the normative status of what is at stake.

[86] *Wilsher v Essex Area Health Authority* [1987] QB 730 (CA) 754. The proof rules operative in medical negligence cases are discussed in ch 3 below.

checking for an allergy: he was aware of the danger, but continued with his own approach as he had never suffered a mishap before.[87]

However, sometimes the doctor may be able to provide cogent reasons for his deviation. Indeed, the importance of giving doctors latitude to try out innovative forms of treatment was noted by Lord Diplock in *Sidaway v Board of Governors of Bethlem Royal Hospital*:

> Those members of the public who seek medical or surgical aid would be badly served by the adoption of any legal principle that would confine the doctor to some long-established, well tried method of treatment only, although its past record of success might be small, if he wanted to be confident that he would not run the risk of being held liable in negligence simply because he tried some more modern treatment, and by some unavoidable mischance it failed to heal but did some harm to the patient.[88]

(b) Germany: A Stricter Approach

As in England, a doctor in Germany is liable for taking risks that a reasonably skilled doctor would not have taken in like circumstances. As the BGH noted in a 1987 decision,

> [t]he question of the doctor's liability for an error in treatment, causative of injury to the patient, can only be answered by reference to whether, in the concrete case, he manifested the required medical skill and experience in reaching defensible decisions as to diagnostic and therapeutic measures, and in carrying out the latter carefully.[89]

It is evident (again as in England) that the opinions of the medical experts will have an important bearing upon this question. They supply the starting point for the court's deliberations by giving the medical view of the defendant's conduct in terms of risks and benefits, and the extent to which it constituted normal, accepted practice; indeed the BGH has held that a judge may not find negligence on the basis of ideas of his own, without support from the experts.[90]

Nevertheless, against this background, the German courts have traditionally evinced a more critical attitude towards expert opinion evidence than their English counterparts. Insofar as the existence of a given practice is established, the fact that the defendant is found to have conformed to it does not preclude negligence. This critical approach has its germ in the definition of 'negligence' in §276 II BGB, which—as noted earlier—is a more overtly prescriptive test than the 'reasonable care' approach favoured in England.[91] Thus, in a case from 1952 the BGH was engaged with a claim brought against a dentist by a patient who swallowed a needle that the dentist momentarily dropped in the course of the dental work. The

[87] *Chin Keow v Government of Malaysia* [1967] 1 WLR 813 (PC).

[88] *Sidaway v Board of Governors of the Bethlem Royal Hospital* [1985] AC 871 (HL) 893. See also *Hunter v Hanley* (1955) SC 200.

[89] BGH, 10 March 1987, NJW 1987, 2291 (2292).

[90] BGH, 17 September 1985, VersR 1985, 1187; BGH, 2 March 1993, NJW 1993, 2378.

[91] See the discussion in pt II 2 (b) above.

evidence was that it was then commonplace for dentists to use such unsecured needles, as attaching them—eg by cotton thread—was uncomfortable for the patient and time-consuming. In finding the dentist liable, the Court commented:

> It may admittedly be concluded, from the fact that experienced dental practitioners habitually tend to work with unattached needles, that the defendant was exercising the care customary among his profession. However, that is not ultimately determinative. The decisive question is instead whether he observed the socially required care. Particularly in cases involving medical professionals, the dominant concern must be the protection of the patient from avoidable risks arising from treatment mishaps.[92]

Again, as the BGH held in a case from 1964,

> [t]he fact a given practice is customary will not be sufficient to negative negligence if at the same time there is a failure to do all that is necessary, according to the rules and experience of medical science, to safeguard the patient from bodily harm.[93]

In this context the German courts sometimes make reference to a generic 'standard' of practice in relation to treating a given medical condition, such as that embodied in best practice guidelines from professional organisations. As Katzenmeier notes, the 'standard' in question will derive from a combination of scientific knowledge, medical experience and professional acceptance. In so doing it serves to particularise 'required care' in relation to a given set of circumstances. In such cases a medical expert who refers to it in the course of their testimony in a malpractice trial is able to give an institutional, rather than merely a personal view.[94]

Nonetheless, in practice much discretion will remain with the doctor in terms of deciding which specific treatment method to adopt in a given case. Not only is the field of medical practice characterised by individual variation among patients and their illnesses but medical science itself is in a constant process of flux and development, where often a single universally accepted practice does not exist. Here, the law will need to leave room for rival schools of thought, with the courts functioning 'as a form of border control' ('*in einer Art Grenzkontrolle*') in checking if a particular method involved undue risks, or was carelessly executed.[95]

It follows too that, where a failure to abide by standard practice is made out, this is not automatically to be equated with negligence: rather, as under English law, a doctor will be entitled to deviate from a usual treatment method in view of his patient's particular circumstances. Here though, again as in England, he will be required to show that his divergent approach was a considered one, which could

[92] BGH, 27 November 1952, NJW 1953, 257 (257–58).

[93] BGH, 13 October 1964, NJW 1965, 345 (346).

[94] Katzenmeier, *Arzthaftung* (n 8 above) at 277ff; see also D Hart, 'Ärztliche Leitlinien—Definitionen, Funktionen, rechtliche Beziehung. Gleichzeitig ein Beitrag zum medizinrechtlichen und rechtlichen Standardbegriff' (1998) *Medizinrecht* 8. Even so, as noted, the relevant 'standard' must ultimately also be approved by the court.

[95] Katzenmeier, *Arzthaftung* (n 8 above) 282; Hart, 'Ärztliche Leitlinien' (n 94 above) 13.

be plausibly justified by reference to the risks and benefits to the individual patient.[96] In this context, the BGH remarked in a decision of 7 July 1987 that

> [i]t is true that the doctor need not always choose the safest therapeutic approach; however, the taking of a higher risk will require to be objectively justified by reference to the exigencies of the particular case or by a more favourable prospect of a cure.[97]

So far the applicable German approach resembles that now prevailing in England following the *Bolitho* decision. The main difference appears to be one of degree—namely that the presumption *against* fault, in cases where the doctor is found to have conformed to accepted practice, remains rather stronger in England than in Germany. However, there is lastly a significant category of cases recognised by the German law, where at a conceptual level, a different approach operates, which has no parallel under the common law. This is in relation to situations of so-called 'fully-masterable risks' (*voll beherrschbare Risiken*), in which harm to the patient stems from a risk that, rather than emanating from the patient's medical condition, arises out of the treatment environment. One example is of injury caused by defective medical apparatus; another is of injury that occurs through an organisational mix-up of some kind, eg a break down in communication between the medical staff.[98]

Analytically, in such a case the materialisation of the risk ranks as a breach of one of the doctor/hospital's ancillary obligations under the treatment contract, which (unlike the main, positive duties under it) are construed strictly. As the BGH observed in a leading case from 1977, where a patient suffered brain damage during anaesthesia due to problems with the oxygen supply,

> [t]he hospital authority owed a contractual duty of care with respect to the provision of a properly functioning oxygen machine. The objective breach of this led to the damage in question . . . The principle [that the doctor will not be held contractually to the achievement of a given outcome] does not apply to the fulfilment of fully-masterable subsidiary obligations, in particular the guaranteeing of safe technical equipment during treatment.[99]

Here, in accordance with the scheme of contractual liability contained in §280 I (together with §276 I) BGB, it will be for the doctor to show that he is not answerable for the breach.[100] Nonetheless, the burden of justification will be a heavy one: the court is always liable (with the benefit of hindsight) to identify some additional precaution that could and should have been taken against the risk. The upshot, as

[96] BGH, 19 June 1979, VersR 1979, 826; Giesen, *Arzthaftung* (n 1 above) para 95.

[97] BGH, 7 July 1987, NJW 1987, 2927 (2927).

[98] Eg in one case, the claimant suffered injury after the keys to the operating theatre went missing at the critical time: OLG Stuttgart, 13 April 1999, VersR 2000, 1108.

[99] BGH, 11 October 1977, NJW 1978, 584 (584–5).

[100] See pt II 1 (b) above. This is also consistent with a more general approach in the German law of obligations, based on the concept of '*Verkehrspflichten*' (duties on those controlling a given situation or activity to ensure a safe environment): see Kötz and Wagner, *Deliktsrecht* (n 48 above) paras 123 ff and 168 ff; BS Markesinis and H Unberath, *The German Law of Torts*, 3rd edn (Oxford, Hart Publishing, 2002) 86; Stauch, 'Approaches to Fault in German Tort Law' (n 2 above) 252 ff.

Katzenmeier has argued, is that the doctor's liability in this type of case approaches strict liability.[101] In recent years the German courts have subjected an increasing number of the doctor's duties to this form of analysis, developing in the process extensive case law.[102] As we shall see further in chapter three, the approach is also of considerable significance in cases of evidential uncertainty, ie where the underlying facts of the accident in which injury occurred remain unclear.[103]

III. Causation of Damage

In both English and German law, to obtain compensation, it is not enough for the patient to establish that the doctor behaved faultily. Rather, like any other private law litigant, he must show the effect that such conduct had on him, in bringing about his injury. This element of the claimant's action—causation (*Kausalzusammenhang*)—can be regarded as an essential adjunct to the fault principle, which, as we saw, distinguishes between harm that is natural or 'fateful', and that attributable to faulty human conduct. If, notwithstanding that an agent behaved faultily (in creating an unjustified risk of harm), the risk did not materialise, the claimant's injury is after all to be ascribed to fate; the claimant will here have no claim to reparation as a matter of corrective justice from the defendant.[104] In both England and Germany the causation element is generally recognised as falling into two parts, namely factual causation (*äquivalenter Kausalzusammenhang*) and legal causation (often also termed remoteness of damage) (*adäquater Kausalzusammenhang*).[105]

1. Factual Causation

In the ordinary case, for factual causation to be present under either English or German law, it is enough that the defendant's conduct was a necessary condition (*condicio sine qua non*) for the injury suffered by the claimant. It is certainly not required to be a sufficient condition: it is accepted that many conditions are present in producing any given outcome in the world. In this regard, the conduct will be just one member of a larger 'causal set' of conditions that were necessary and together sufficient for the injury. The German label of *äquivalenter Kausalzusammenhang* captures this in its allusion to the scientifically 'equivalent' status enjoyed by the

[101] Katzenmeier, *Arzthaftung* (n 8 above) 167; see also A Laufs, 'Delikt und Gefährdung—Von der Schadenszurechnung zur Schadensverteilung?' in A Laufs (ed), *Die Entwicklung der Artzhaftung* (Berlin, Springer, 1995) 1 ff.

[102] For detailed references to the various authorities, see Geiß and Greiner, *Arzthaftpflichtrecht* (n 2 above) paras B 241 ff.

[103] See ch 3 pt III 2 (b) (ii).

[104] On the need for a causal nexus, establishing the bilateral relation between parties in private law, see Weinrib, *The Idea of Private Law* (n 4 above) 153 ff.

[105] The American term is 'proximate causation'.

defendant's conduct and those other conditions.[106] Generally the (critical) question of whether the conduct was indeed *one* of the necessary conditions at work is perceived in both countries as a neutral issue of fact—it admits of a straightforward yes or no answer (in contrast to the more evaluative issues that arise at the legal causation/remoteness stage).

(a) England: The 'But For' Test

Under the common law, the courts approach the issue of causal necessity by using the 'but for' test. As Denning LJ put it in the case of *Cork v Kirby Maclean Ltd*,

> [i]f you can say that the damage would not have happened but for a particular fault then that fault is in fact a cause of the damage; but if you can say that the damage would have happened just the same, fault or no fault, then the fault is not a cause of the damage.[107]

In the medical malpractice context, a well-known decision that illustrates the workings of the test is *Barnett v Chelsea and Kensington Hospital Management Committee*.[108] There a doctor failed to examine a night watchman who attended the hospital's casualty department with symptoms of sickness and nausea after drinking some tea. The man later died from what it transpired were the effects of arsenical poisoning. However, the court accepted the expert evidence that, even if the doctor had properly examined the man, his condition would have been diagnosed too late to apply an antidote. Accordingly, it dismissed the claim brought by the man's widow against the hospital.

Barnett was a case where treatment was straightforwardly omitted, and the patient's injury took the form of the progression of his underlying medical condition. However, the same basic approach applies where actual medical treatment gave rise to iatrogenic injury: here the issue is whether, absent the careless feature of treatment, such injury would have been avoided. For example, in *Robinson v Post Office* a man attended hospital following a work accident and was given an anti-tetanus vaccination. However, the doctor negligently failed to check first (by means of a small test dose) whether he was allergic to it.[109] In the event the man suffered a severe allergic reaction leading to brain damage. Given, though, that this did not manifest itself until three days later, the court was satisfied that a test dose would not have revealed the allergy in time to prevent him from receiving the full vaccine. Thus, as in *Barnett*, the claim (against the hospital) failed.[110]

[106] See van Gerven, Lever and Larouche, *Tort Law* (n 48 above) 397. For an illuminating analysis of factual causation problems in terms of 'causal sets', see RW Wright, 'Causation in Tort Law' (1985) 73 *California Law Review* 1735.

[107] *Cork v Kirby Maclean Ltd* [1952] 2 All ER 402 (CA) 407.

[108] *Barnett v Chelsea and Kensington Hospital Management Committee* [1969] 1 QB 428.

[109] *Robinson v Post Office* [1974] 2 All ER 737 (CA).

[110] Instead, the claimant recovered full damages (including for brain damage) from his employer, responsible for the earlier injury requiring his attendance at hospital.

As these decisions point up, the inquiry into factual causation is invariably hypothetical in form, requiring the court to compare events as they turned out (following the defendant's breach of duty) with how they would have turned out had there been no breach. In practice, the greatest problem in such cases is usually an evidential one. Since the patient's underlying medical condition (and/or treatment for it given without fault) often has the potential to cause injury of the kind allegedly stemming from the treatment error, the court must select between competing explanations for the harm—typically against a backdrop of scientific uncertainty. In chapter three we shall look in detail at how the courts in England and Germany have attempted to address this problem.[111]

Nonetheless, an added complication is that, occasionally, the 'but for' test may fail to provide a result in principle. This occurs in relation to 'causal overdetermination' cases (viz, where the claimant's injury stems from two or more concurrent tortious occurrences, each by itself sufficient for the harm).[112] An example, involving medical malpractice, is where two doctors, acting independently, give the patient an overdose of a drug, and each alone would have killed him. Admittedly such cases are in practice rare, at least as a basis for disputing causation at all (more commonly, the point may figure in the court's deliberations when assessing damages—the doctor may argue that, if they had not caused injury, the patient would later have suffered the same harm through his illness progressing).[113] However, a recent English case which did raise the problem is *Bolitho v City and Hackney Health Authority*.[114]

In *Bolitho* a doctor failed to attend the infant claimant who had a breathing problem; the infant subsequently suffered a complete respiratory collapse, leaving him with severe brain damage. The non-attendance was conceded to be negligent, but the doctor argued that even had she attended she would not have instigated the one procedure, intubation, which—as known at trial—would have saved him. In the House of Lords, this argument denying factual causation on the basis of the doctor's hypothetical non-intubation was accepted. However this was subject to the important caveat (satisfied on the facts) that the hypothetical conduct in question must not itself amount to negligence.[115] As Lord Browne-Wilkinson commented in his speech,

[111] See ch 3 pt III 3.

[112] An old US authority in point is *Corey v Havener* (1902) 182 Mass 250, 65 NE 69, where the claimant was injured when his horse was overtaken on both sides by the defendants racing their motorbikes.

[113] If made out, the latter argument will lead to a reduction in damages (see eg *Jobling v Associated Dairies* [1982] AC 794 (HL)); but it does not cast doubt on the defendant's responsibility for the injury as such. See also the discussion of the German law: text at n 120 ff below.

[114] *Bolitho v City and Hackney Health Authority* [1998] AC 232 (HL).

[115] *Bolitho* was the decision in which the House of Lords clarified that the practice adopted by the doctor must not only be accepted within the medical profession, but the court must be satisfied that it stands up to logical analysis: see the text at n 79 ff above. Here there were found to be defensible grounds ex ante, which supported the (hypothetical) decision not to intubate the claimant.

> in the present case the answer to the question 'what would have happened?' is not determinative of the issue of causation . . . A defendant cannot escape liability by saying that the damage would have occurred in any event because he would have committed some other breach of duty thereafter.[116]

In other words, where two tortious items of conduct are (or would have been) independently sufficient for the harm in issue, then—notwithstanding its corresponding lack of causal necessity—the law will treat each as a cause. In the *Bolitho* case a single defendant would have been responsible for both items—the initial non-attendance as well as the decision not to intubate; but it seems certain that the same result would apply where separate defendants contribute independent sufficient causes of the damage (as in the example of the two doctors who each gave the patient an overdose).

(b) *Germany:* The Condicio Sine Qua Non *Formula*

In Germany, the factual causation issue is addressed by means of the so-called 'condicio sine qua non formula'. This approach is not set out in the BGB, but has been developed by commentators and the courts. According to it, an event (conduct by the defendant) will be a cause of some given outcome (injury to the claimant) if it cannot be 'eliminated in thought' (*hinweggedacht*) without the outcome too ceasing to occur.[117] In this regard, it is apparent that the German approach is identical to the 'but for' test employed by the common law. Under both systems the crucial question is simply whether the defendant's behaviour affected the way things turned out, leading to harm where there would otherwise have been none. In the context of treatment malpractice claims, this means that if the patient's injury would have occurred anyway the claim will fail. For example in one decision, discussed by Deutsch and Spickhoff, a dermatologist, whom the patient engaged to remove a discoloured patch of skin, negligently failed to advise her to be tested for a possible melanoma. However, though she in fact had a melanoma, it was later identified and successfully treated by another doctor. The *Oberlandesgericht Frankfurt* rejected the patient's claim against the dermatologist, as she was unable to show the delay in diagnosis had made any difference to her condition, or to the subsequent treatment she was required to undergo.[118]

As in England, the fact that the patient was typically at independent risk of the harm that befell him means that proving that faulty treatment was a necessary condition for the same will often be very difficult: the doctor may argue that the injury was wholly attributable to the patient's underlying ailment. Indeed, as we shall see

[116] *Bolitho v City and Hackney Health Authority* [1998] AC 232 (HL) 240.

[117] Markesinis and Unberath, *The German Law of Torts* (n 100 above) 104; U Magnus, 'Causation in German Tort Law' in J Spier (ed), *Common Law of Europe: Causation* (The Hague, Kluwer Law International, 2000) 63, 64.

[118] OLG Frankfurt, 26 January 1978, VersR 1979, 39; Deutsch and Spickhoff, *Medizinrecht* (n 19 above) para 174. See also Giesen, *Arzthaftung* (n 1 above) para 183.

in chapter three, German law is even more vulnerable to such evidential uncertainty, due to the higher civil standard of proof that operates there. Certainly, it is the issue of proof—and the development of mechanisms to address the patient's difficulties here—that has tended to dominate academic and judicial discussion of the factual causation issue.[119]

However, remaining for now at the level of substantive law, German commentators are, like those in England, familiar with the occasional limitations of the sine qua non approach that arise in causal over-determination cases. In this regard, one situation which has received particular attention concerns the problem of alternative causation (*überholende Kausalität*; *Reserveursachen*)—ie cases where, if the claimant had not suffered injury due to the defendant's negligence, he would have suffered some other injury soon afterwards of a similar or greater form. An example in the treatment malpractice context is where a patient goes blind after a doctor gives him the wrong drug, but the patient would have gone blind anyway within a few months (due to the progress of his illness). This is an issue the common law would usually deal with under quantum: damage has undoubtedly been caused by the defendant, but is limited to the period in which the claimant would otherwise have remained free of it, and is hence of less 'value'.[120] Be that as it may, the solution adopted appears to be identical under both systems. Where—as with the blinded patient—the hypothetical superseding event would have been of a natural character, damages will be limited to the intervening period.[121] Similarly (in a case of simultaneous independent causes), if it were established that the act of each defendant was by itself sufficient for the claimant's injury, the solution would be the same as under the common law: the defendants will be jointly and severally liable.[122]

Finally, though, a complication in the German approach to factual causation must be addressed, which has no counterpart in the common law. This consists in the distinction, often drawn by courts and commentators, between *haftungsbegründende Kausalität* and *haftungsausfüllende Kausalität*. The first of these, 'liability-grounding causation', denotes the link from the defendant's faulty conduct and *initial* harm to the claimant (in the form of an invasion of one of his abstract protected interests). By contrast, the latter, 'liability-completing causation', refers to the subsequent link between that invasion and the further, tangible injuries suffered by the claimant (which form the subject of his claim for substantial damages).[123] In terms of German tort, this approach—with its double test of (factual)

[119] See ch 3 pt III 3 (b).

[120] Though under the common law too, the distinction between causation and quantum is often blurred: see generally J King, 'Causation, Valuation, and Chance in Personal Injury Torts Involving Pre-existing Conditions and Future Consequences' (1981) 90 *Yale Law Journal* 1353.

[121] E Steffen 'Haftung des Arztes für Fehler bei der Risikoaufklärung—Zurechnungsbeschränkungen oder *versari in re illicita*?' in V Beuthien (ed), *Festschrift für Medicus* (Cologne, Heymann, 1999) 643; Markesinis and Unberath, *The German Law of Torts* (n 100 above) 109 ff.

[122] Kötz and Wagner, *Deliktsrecht* (n 48 above) para 187.

[123] See van Gerven, Lever and Larouche, *Tort Law* (n 48 above) 396–7; Magnus, 'Causation in German Tort Law' (n 117 above) 63–4.

causation—derives from the wording of § 823 I BGB, which requires 'a person who intentionally or negligently injures another's life, body, health' to compensate them 'for the injury arising therefrom'. However, the courts have held that the same approach will apply in relation to breaches of contract that lead to the infringement of an interest of the kind protected in tort (under § 823 I).[124]

Admittedly, as Magnus has noted, the distinction is not always necessary or workable in practice: the claimant's injury may be an instant and indivisible event.[125] Moreover, the character of the initial harmful event (*Erfolg*), which lies between the primary and subsequent causal links, arguably remains ambiguous.[126] Thus, as noted, this has been equated in theory with the invasion of one of the claimant's abstract protected interests, with the residual issue—the secondary causal link—going to the need to show a substantial loss deriving from that invasion. However, in practice as applied by the courts, the initial event often appears to constitute a concrete injury (already involving substantial loss). For example, in one case involving medical malpractice the defendant prescribed the patient a skin cream; this caused the latter to suffer an allergic reaction, which allegedly later led to his death from bone marrow depression. Here the BGH treated the allergic reaction as the primary injury, with death the further and secondary consequence.[127] In this guise, the distinction has an affinity to the issue of 'ulterior harm' in the common law, which we will look at below as an aspect of remoteness of damage.[128]

In the light of these uncertainties, some commentators have doubted the continued utility of distinguishing in this way between two stages of causation.[129] Nevertheless, in the treatment malpractice context the distinction's importance is that the courts have used it to support a relaxation of proof in some cases. In particular, once the patient establishes the initial link between the doctor's wrong and the invasion of his interests, he need only prove the secondary link to further harm (ie *haftungsausfüllende Kausalität*) to a lower standard.[130] This aspect of matters is looked at further in chapter three below.[131]

2. Legal Causation/Remoteness of Damage

Even after factual causation is established, there remains, both in English and German law, the question whether the damage should be legally attributed to the defendant. In particular, despite the latter's fault and its factual causal link to the

[124] BGH, 24 June 1986, NJW 1987, 705.

[125] Magnus, 'Causation in German Tort Law' (n 117 above) 63–4.

[126] See H Lange and G Schiemann, *Schadensersatz*, 3rd edn (Tübingen, Mohr Siebeck, 2003) 78.

[127] BGH, 13 November 1962, VersR 1963, 67.

[128] See the text at n 142 ff, below. There the issue is how far a defendant who causes a given harm should remain liable for discrete harm later in time for which that initial harm was a necessary condition.

[129] C Wendehorst, *Anspruch und Ausgleich: Theorie einer Vorteils- und Nachteils-Ausgleichung im Schuldrecht* (Tübingen, Mohr Siebeck, 1999), 82 ff; Lange and Schiemann, *Schadensersatz* (n 126 above) 78; P Gottwald, *Schadenszurechnung und Schadensschätzung* (Munich, Beck, 1979) 74 ff.

[130] Under § 287 (rather than § 286) of the Code of Civil Procedure (*Zivilprozessordnung*—ZPO).

[131] See ch 3 pt III 3 (b) (i).

claimant's injury, it may sometimes be felt impolitic or unjust to hold them liable. Typically, this hesitation arises where the injury appears unexpected or freakish—not at all the type of consequence usually associated with the risky behaviour in question.

Analytically, this is connected to the fact that, at the factual causation stage, the focus of the enquiry is upon causal necessity. Thus, as we saw, the sine qua non approach asks simply if the defendant's conduct was *a* necessary condition for the harm (out of a causal set of conditions that were necessary and together sufficient for it). This is unexceptional where the further conditions making up the set are ordinary features of the environment (of which the defendant must be taken to be aware); there the risk posed by their conduct was precisely that, in conjunction with those other conditions, the harm in suit would ensue. The problem occurs in cases where the further conditions contributing to the harm are themselves of an unusual character, which the defendant could not have anticipated, or which otherwise render their responsibility slight by comparison.[132]

(a) England: The 'Reasonable Foreseeability' Test

The courts approach legal causation (or remoteness of damage) in negligence by asking if, at the time of the defendant's faulty act, the risk of it causing the harm in suit was 'reasonably foreseeable'.[133] This is also the approach taken in cases of breaches of contract resulting in physical damage. 'Reasonable foreseeability' is in practice a relatively elastic test: the courts retain significant room for manoeuvre in deciding which risks the defendant should have foreseen in a given case. Moreover, two 'glosses' on the approach have been recognised: first, so long as the broad nature of the harm was foreseeable, the precise manner of its upshot need not be[134]; and secondly, in the context of a personal injury claim, provided actionable injury to the claimant could have been foreseen, the defendant will be liable for its full extent, including where this was exacerbated by an unforeseeable weakness in the claimant's metabolism. The latter is known as the 'eggshell skull principle'.[135]

In medical negligence cases it is, in line with the above, unusual for legal causation to create difficulty for the patient. Generally, the courts will refuse to draw fine distinctions between the type of harm the doctor ought to have foreseen and that which actually materialised. For example, in *Hepworth v Kerr* the defendant anaesthetist was held liable for using an experimental anaesthetic technique on a patient that resulted in a spinal stroke. The risk of inducing a spinal stroke was in fact not known about, but the risk of a cerebral stroke (thus, making the procedure's use

[132] See further M Stauch, 'Risk and Remoteness of Damage in Negligence' (2001) 64 *MLR* 191.

[133] Following the decision of the Privy Council in *The Wagon Mound (No 1)* [1961] AC 388; see also *Carslogie Steamship Co Ltd v Royal Norwegian Government* [1952] AC 292 (HL).

[134] *Hughes v Lord Advocate* [1963] AC 837 (HL).

[135] See *Smith v Leech Brain and Co Ltd* [1962] 2 QB 405 (QBD).

negligent) was.[136] Similarly, in *Wisniewski v Central Manchester Health Authority* the defendant health authority attempted to deny liability for the claimant's hypoxia, suffered during birth. The defendant had negligently failed to manage the birth, but argued that, while the injury had been foreseeable, the mechanics of it in the particular case (involving a rare instance of a knot in the umbilical cord) had not been. In the Court of Appeal, Brooke LJ commented that to allow such an argument would be 'an affront to common sense, and the law would look an ass'.[137]

Nonetheless, where the risks are appreciably different in kind, the courts have indicated that the patient's action may sometimes fail on remoteness grounds. An example is *Brown v Lewisham and North Southwark Health Authority*, where the claimant was negligently discharged from hospital following heart surgery, despite having a chest infection. He subsequently suffered a thrombosis, which ultimately led to the loss of one of his legs. In the Court of Appeal, Beldam LJ stated:

> The public policy of limiting the liability of tortfeasors by the control mechanism of foreseeability seems to me as necessary in cases of medical as in any other type of negligence. I do not see on what policy ground it would be fair or just to hold a doctor [liable] who failed to diagnose an asymptomatic and undetectable illness merely because he was at fault in the management of a correctly diagnosed but unrelated condition.[138]

This dictum was obiter, as on the facts the Court rejected the existence of a factual causal link (ie it was not persuaded that, had the claimant remained in hospital, his thrombosis and loss of leg would have been avoided). However, it was approved in *Thompson v Bradford*, in which the Court of Appeal denied the liability of a doctor for vaccine injuries to a child following immunisation for polio.[139] The doctor had failed to advise the parents that a boil the child had was a contra-indication for the vaccination—advice which would have led to the procedure being postponed. In the event, the boil played a factually causative role in the vaccine damage. Nonetheless, the reason the advice should have been given was not the added risk of such damage (which had been unforeseeable), but the discomfort to the child of vaccinating him in those circumstances.

Occasionally, the English courts have also adverted to the limited scope of the defendant's duty to the claimant so as to restrict negligence liability. In particular, this is relevant where the injury stemmed from a risk that, while foreseeable in itself, can be said from the outset not to be one that the defendant undertook to protect the claimant against. Interestingly, in *South Australia Asset Management Corp (SAAMCo) v York Montague Ltd*, the leading English case on the general applicability of this approach, Lord Hoffmann used a medical negligence scenario by way of illustration:

136 *Hepworth v Kerr* (1995) 6 Med LR 139 (QBD).
137 *Wisniewski v Central Manchester Health Authority* [1998] PIQR P324 (CA) P344.
138 *Brown v Lewisham and North Southwark Health Authority* [1999] Lloyd's Rep Med 110 (CA) 117.
139 *Thompson v Bradford* [2005] EWCA 1439.

A mountaineer about to undertake a difficult climb is concerned about the fitness of his knee. He goes to a doctor who negligently makes a superficial examination and pronounces the knee fit. The climber goes on the expedition, which he would not have undertaken if the doctor had told him the true state of his knee. He suffers an injury which is an entirely foreseeable consequence of mountaineering but has nothing to do with his knee . . . On what I have suggested is the . . . usual principle, the doctor is not liable.[140]

The *SAAMCo* decision itself concerned the liability of a surveyor for a negligent property valuation. However, a medical malpractice case in which the approach was applied is *R v Croydon Health Authority*, where a radiographer failed to spot the claimant's pulmonary aorta in the course of a pre-employment health check. This was a contra-indication for pregnancy and it was accepted that, had she known of her condition, the claimant would not have had a child. Nonetheless, the court held that any duty of care owed by the radiologist was directed at guarding the claimant from risks in the course of her employment, not those arising in the course of her domestic life (including pregnancy and childbirth).[141]

Finally, under the heading of legal causation/remoteness, there is a category of case involving so-called 'ulterior harm', in which initial injury caused by the defendant is a necessary condition for a discrete further injury suffered by the claimant later in time.[142] This raises the issue of how far an agent should be liable for harm as a knock-on effect of earlier harm, notwithstanding that other agents (a third party or the claimant) could in principle have acted so as to avert it. In some instances the second injury will be a consequence of the claimant's inability to cope with his compromised physical state due to the first injury, and here the tendency (at least if the second injury occurs within a short time span) is to extend the defendant's liability to the latter as well.[143] Similarly, where a doctor negligently injures a patient, who then suffers further injury due to the fault of a second doctor in treating the initial injury, the first doctor will generally be jointly and severally liable for the later injury.[144] This is subject, though, to an exception if the second doctor's intervention was so disproportionately faulty or unrelated to the earlier negligence as to qualify as a 'novus actus interveniens', which 'breaks the chain of causation' between the first doctor's fault and the second injury.[145]

(b) Germany: Adäquater Kausalzusammenhang *and* Schutzzweck

In Germany, the courts approach the legal causation/remoteness issue (*adäquater Kausalzusammenhang*) by asking if the defendant's conduct was 'generally apt'

[140] *South Australia Asset Management Corp v York Montague Ltd* [1997] AC 191 (HL) 213

[141] *R v Croydon Health Authority* (1997) 40 BMLR 40 (CA). This case was decided prior to the House of Lords' decision in *McFarlane v Tayside Health Board* [2000] 2 AC 59, rejecting maintenance claims for healthy children as a matter of legal policy (by denying 'a duty of care'). See ch 1 above, fn 65 ff.

[142] See HLA Hart and AM Honoré, *Causation in the Law*, 2nd edn (Oxford, Clarendon Press, 1985) 109.

[143] See eg *Wieland v Cyril Lord Carpets* [1969] 3 All ER 1006 (QBD).

[144] See by analogy *Rahman v Arearose Ltd* [2000] 3 WLR 1184 (CA).

[145] *Hogan v Bentinck Collieries* [1949] 1 All ER 588 (HL).

(*generell geeignet*) to bring about the type of harm that in fact occurred; as a rule they will find an adequate causal connection made out where the conduct,

> in general and not only under abnormal, completely improbable and in the ordinary course of things neglectable circumstances would have led to the occurrence of the result that happened.[146]

In assessing this question, the courts will adopt the perspective of an optimal observer who is deemed to be familiar with all possible causal processes. There has in fact been some dispute as to whether the optimal observer is also equipped with hindsight, so that liability extends to damage resulting from a previously unknown causal process; certainly this is implicit in one view, according to which the decisive question is simply if the defendant's conduct 'objectively increased' the probability of the damage occurring in an appreciable way.[147] In addition, like the common law, German law recognises the eggshell skull principle, so that personal injury arising out of some freakish susceptibility of the claimant's physical metabolism will never count as unforeseeable.[148]

Compared to the common law approach of reasonable foreseeability, the above approach is arguably stricter (leading to liability in a wider set of circumstances); indeed the only sort of case for which the adequacy test will unambiguously exclude liability is that of 'coincidence' (where the ex ante probability of the injury remains unaffected by the defendant's faulty act).[149] Nonetheless, conscious of the expansive liability to which this may lead, the German courts have supplemented the test with a second limiting device: this takes the form of asking whether the claimant's injury fell within the protective purpose of the rule prohibiting the defendant's conduct (*Schutzzweck der Norm*).[150] As noted, in discussing the emergence of a similar approach in the English law of negligence, this will rule out liability for injuries that, while in themselves the 'foreseeable' or 'adequate' consequence of the defendant's conduct, were not part of the justification for the rule requiring them to take care.[151]

In fact, in the context of treatment malpractice, neither of the above approaches will often lead to the exclusion of liability for injury factually arising from a doctor's default.[152] For its part, the adequacy test will virtually always be satisfied—it is difficult to conceive of a case where the treatment error will not objectively have

[146] BGH, 4 July 1994, NJW 1995, 126 (127), cited by Magnus, 'Causation in German Tort Law' (n 117 above).

[147] Markesinis and Unberath, *The German Law of Torts* (n 100 above) 107–8; Hart and Honoré, *Causation in the Law* (n 142 above) 478 ff.

[148] Deutsch and Spickhoff, *Medizinrecht* (n 19 above) para 336.

[149] Ie over a range of similar cases there is no link between acts and harms of the relevant kinds. An example (provided by the 19th century German physiologist, Johannes von Kries) is of a coach that deviates from its path after the driver falls asleep and the passenger is then injured by a lightning strike: see Hart and Honoré, *Causation in the Law* (n 142 above) 470–71.

[150] Markesinis and Unberath, *The German Law of Torts* (n 100 above) 108; Kötz and Wagner, *Deliktsrecht* (n 48 above) paras 229 ff.

[151] See the text at n 140 ff above.

[152] See the illustrative cases in Giesen, *Arzthaftung* (n 1 above) para 188.

increased the risk of the harm to the patient to some degree.[153] As regards the *Schutzzweck* limitation, much will depend on the way the courts interpret the purpose of the treatment contract: if this is seen broadly as 'the protection of the patient's health', then liability will be correspondingly wide. Similarly, the prohibition on tortious conduct in § 823 I BGB is widely drawn, allowing significant room for interpretation by the court as to whether a given injury fell within its ambit.[154] On the other hand, it may sometimes be apparent from the surrounding context that the patient engaged the doctor for a specific reason only, and here it is easier to exclude liability for the consequences of his faulty conduct beyond this. As discussed in chapter one, one context where such considerations have applied in German medical malpractice law is in respect of claims for maintenance costs following a child's wrongful conception or birth.[155]

Lastly, there remains the question of how far a doctor who faultily injures his patient may also be liable for secondary (or 'ulterior') harm suffered by the patient as a further consequence of this, eg through faulty remedial treatment by a second doctor. Here, as in England, the default position is that the first doctor will be (jointly and severally) liable for the further injury. However, there is an exception where the second doctor's conduct was grossly and disproportionately negligent, or if the latter simply uses the occasion to treat the patient (faultily) for a separate ailment.[156] The BGH commented in a decision in point from 1988:

> Where the ultimate injury stands in a physical relation to the original actor's conduct, but was decisively triggered by the wholly exceptional and unreasonable conduct of a third party, the boundary may be crossed at which it is still appropriate to attribute these further consequences to the first actor . . . In this regard . . . an evaluative assessment will be required. If, from this standpoint, the injury bound up with the second intervention is no longer to be seen as the materialisation of a risk of the original conduct; if the connection between the two was rather only of an 'external' or 'incidental' kind, then it will no longer be just to demand reparation for it from the original actor.[157]

In such a case, notwithstanding that objectively the first doctor's mistake increased the risk of the ultimate injury,[158] he will be relieved of liability. Here the German approach appears to be identical to that adopted in England; interestingly, the exception is also presented in similar metaphorical terms—viz 'interruption of the chain of liability' (*Unterbrechung des Haftungszusammenhangs*).[159]

[153] Eg in a case like *Thompson v Bradford* (n 139 above) the doctor would remain liable: clearly the vaccination increased the objective risk of the injury, albeit this could not have been foreseen at the time.

[154] Markesinis and Unberath, *The German Law of Torts* (n 100 above) 109.

[155] See ch 1 pt III 2 (b). Two other contexts in which *Schutzzweck* considerations are relevant in German medical malpractice law are in the deployment of proof reversals—see ch 3 pt III 3 (b) (iii); and in cases of disclosure malpractice—see ch 4 pt IV 2 (a).

[156] BGH, 20 September 1988, NJW 1989, 767; BGH, 2 July 1957, NJW 1958, 627.

[157] BGH, 20 September 1988, NJW 1989, 767 (768).

[158] If he had not caused the first injury, the second doctor would not have had the opportunity to cause further injury.

[159] See E Deutsch, 'Anmerkung zu BGH, 20 September 1988' *NJW* 1989, 769.

IV. Comparative Assessment

As will be apparent, there is in terms of overall framework, and indeed also as regards many of the detailed rules, much similarity between the English and German approaches to identifying and holding doctors to account for treatment errors. In both cases, the rules are embedded in the broader system of private law. Thus, whether the patient brings his claim in contract or tort, both systems require that the patient demonstrate faulty treatment by the doctor (ie treatment that fell below the legally required standard of skill and care). Here, the alternative of a 'strict liability' approach—making the doctor liable for an unfavourable outcome per se—has been rejected, and in both countries for the same reason: namely that in this field of activity where, by common agreement, many of the variables that conduce to success or failure lie beyond the doctor's control, such an approach is recognised as unfair.

At the same time, both systems agree that in this context subjective culpability on the doctor's part is not required; it is enough that he failed to exhibit the care of a skilful doctor in the relevant speciality. Here, while both systems have acknowledged tensions that may arise with regard to inexperienced junior doctors (and the need for them to 'learn on the job'), the protection of the patient is regarded as paramount. In practice the tendency has been to shift liability in such a case to the doctor's employing institution (for using them for a task beyond their skill). The same objective approach applies with regard to resource issues: the law in both countries, while not certain in every detail, appears to be directed towards ensuring the maintenance of a threshold level of care. Attempts by defendant hospitals to bring in the 'public good' dimension of health care, and to argue that an imperfect service is better than none at all, will not be entertained. On the other hand, above the requisite threshold, a certain variation in the quality of care provided across different hospitals or regions has been accepted.

Nonetheless, where the two jurisdictions diverge—and liability is stricter in Germany—is in relation to the normative determination by the courts of when, in the circumstances, there was fault. In particular, while in both countries, the opinion of medical experts provides the starting point, the German courts—applying § 276 II BGB with its reference to 'required care'—have been more prepared than their English counterparts to look critically at practices supported by experts and, at times, find them wanting. By contrast in England, the *Bolam* test as traditionally applied left the setting of standards within the discretion of the doctors. Though, following *Bolitho*, the position has changed in formal terms, the threshold conditions before a judge will go against exculpatory expert medical opinion remain high. As suggested, a factor that may have influenced the English courts is their fear of otherwise encouraging an explosion of malpractice litigation. In this regard the scarcity of health resources within the centralised NHS system has arguably played a role—a concern that has less resonance in the devolved, insurance-based German scheme.[160]

[160] See further the discussion in ch 6 below.

As we saw, another way in which German law is notably stricter than that in England has been in identifying injury in certain cases as being within the doctor's sphere of controllable risk, and putting the onus on them of persuading the court that they took all practicable precautions. This has no counterpart in English law: there is, it is true, something close to a presumption of fault in cases of divergence from normal practice (as there is in German law too), but in the latter situation the doctor's deviation from established rules has already been established. Instead the German approach illustrates the tendency, in contexts where the patient's illness was not the primary source of risk, for the courts to ratchet up the standard of care, so that it becomes in practice close to one of strict liability.[161]

Moving on to issues of causation, we again find that the conceptual approach is similar in both countries: for liability to arise, faulty treatment by the doctor must usually be a necessary condition for non-remote injury to the patient.[162] As regards the first, factual causation aspect, this serves to distinguish patients whose injury could and should have been avoided with reasonable care from those where the injury must be ascribed simply to 'fate' or bad luck. Arguably, factual causation will be a necessary element in any workable private law system of compensation—in particular, it serves to connect the injury to the defendant's faulty agency, thus marking them out as the person owing redress. Insofar as we accept the need for such a link, the remaining question for each legal system is a practical one of its efficient application. That is to say, how well in practice do the courts succeed in distinguishing cases where fault was necessary for injury, from those where the latter would have occurred anyway? This question in fact raises acute difficulties in treatment malpractice cases, but not so much at the level of substantive law; rather in relation to proof. We shall have occasion to consider this problem in chapter three.

Finally, as to legal causation, both legal systems have recognised that sometimes there may be a mismatch between the faultiness of the defendant's conduct (in terms of the unjustified risk they ran) and the nature of the claimant's injury as it actually materialised. Here the German system is on the whole stricter in holding the defendant to account also for unforeseeable factual consequences, provided these do not occur through coincidence. However, as we saw, this issue is in any case of peripheral importance in treatment malpractice cases: the injury suffered by a patient through the doctor's default will nearly always be foreseeable. Thus, in England too it is extremely rare for a doctor's liability to be excluded on this basis. Similarly, the use—particularly by the German courts—of *Schutzzweck* considerations to limit liability (by seeking a link between the harm and the infringed norm) adds little in this context. Normally the patient's injury will fall foursquare within the risk against which the doctor was supposed to protect him.

[161] As noted, this applies to iatrogenic risks in the treatment environment; it does not impinge on the principle (where treatment fails to yield a positive benefit) that the doctor does not guarantee a cure.

[162] As we saw, both systems make an exception for rare instances of causal over-determination.

As already hinted, there is an important sense in which the conclusions just summarised are incomplete: this is because we have in this chapter restricted ourselves to the *substantive* legal rules that apply in England and Germany, respectively. However, in practice procedural law—in particular the rules of proof—plays a central part in determining the success or failure of treatment malpractice claims: it is only after considering proof issues that one obtains a complete picture of the way the law in each country operates in this field. The examination of these rules is the subject of the next chapter.

3

Treatment Malpractice—Proof Issues

I. Introduction

IN CHAPTER TWO, we looked at the substantive elements that must be satisfied in order for a patient's claim against a doctor for treatment malpractice to succeed. Implicit in the discussion was that the court could be satisfied on the evidence that the elements in question were present. However, in practice, the main dispute between the parties to a medical malpractice case often centres on contested issues of fact. Thus they may offer differing accounts of the background circumstances in which the doctor was called upon to treat the patient, as well as how he acted in response. (By way of contrast, it may be accepted by both sides that, *if* the circumstance were 'x' and the doctor did 'y', this would be a breach of duty.)

As with the substantive law, neither England nor Germany has any formally distinct rules relating to the proof of medical malpractice claims. Rather, the ordinary rules of private litigation apply. Such rules, which are often treated as an aspect of civil procedure, are ancillary to the substantive law: whereas the substantive law prescribes the elements required in the abstract, the rules of proof determine when those elements will be found to be historically present. In this regard a method of testing whether a given rule belongs to substantive law or goes to proof, is to invoke a hypothetical state of omniscience: 'if every fact about the case were known, would there still be scope for applying this rule?' If the answer is no, the rule concerns problems of proof. Nevertheless, since in practice virtually every case contains some degree of factual uncertainty, such rules will play a direct role in combination with the substantive law in determining the result of a given action.

This is nowhere truer than in the treatment malpractice context where, compared to other private law claims for personal injury, there are special factors that conduce to evidential uncertainty and dispute. The first is the pronounced informational inequality between the two sides: it is the doctor who has professional knowledge of the patient's condition; he alone will have detailed awareness of the treatment method he adopted, what he hoped it to achieve and how—if it went wrong—this seemed to occur. By contrast, the patient as a medical layman will know only fragments of the above. He may have been under anaesthetic and unable to observe what was done to him; even when conscious, his perceptive faculties will often be compromised by stress and anxiety. Subsequently, he may not be aware that he has suffered an actionable injury at all; he may believe for example that the (in reality) negligently caused injury was the treatment's normal consequence.[1]

In the second place the court, in reconstructing events, is heavily reliant upon the testimony provided by expert medical witnesses.[2] In chapter two we considered the role of the experts in assisting the judge on the normative question of fault: the issue there was how far the judge might go against expert opinion that the doctor was justified in acting as he did.[3] However, also of great significance is the experts' contribution to the judge's understanding of the factual background of the case: typically this includes the range of diagnoses that came into question in relation to the claimant; the actual nature of the latter's condition (and prognosis), and the various treatment options available together with their respective risks and benefits.

Thirdly, though, there are not infrequently cases of medical injury where the experts themselves will remain baffled. Sometimes, in the light of gaps in the evidence, they may be able to do little more than speculate as to what happened (including what some missing piece of evidence might have shown). In this regard, the most common occasion for perplexity is in relation to the inherently hypothetical issue of factual causation. As noted in chapter two, the substantive enquiry here concerns whether, absent faulty treatment, the patient would have avoided injury.[4] However, the fact that the patient was typically ill at the time—ie exposed to other risks of injury besides those stemming from the treatment—makes its resolution particularly problematic.

As we shall see later, a central issue for both the English and German legal systems has been how far, in treatment malpractice cases, the courts may have recourse to special proof modifications to address some of the above difficulties. First, though, to put that discussion into context, we shall briefly consider the underlying approach taken to civil proof in the two jurisdictions, as this bears upon medical injury claims.

II. The General Approach to Proof

In both English and German private law, the general proof rules cast the burden of proof upon the claimant to establish the substantive elements necessary to

[1] Conversely, patients are more likely than other litigants to bring unfounded claims (seeing negligent injury in what was—in actual fact—an inevitable outcome).

[2] Admittedly this point is not unique to medical negligence cases; it will also apply to other types of professional negligence cases involving defendants with special knowledge and skill.

[3] See ch 2 pt II 3.

[4] See ch 2 pt III 1.

ground his claim. In an action for treatment malpractice it is thus the patient who must normally prove both that the doctor was in breach of duty to him, and that this caused his injury.[5] This reflects the fact that in bringing the action it is he, not the doctor, who is inviting the court to disturb the status quo (by ordering the transfer of monetary damages). However, beyond this starting point, there are important differences between the English and German systems of civil procedure. This is so both as regards the general approach to judicial fact-finding, and with respect to the relevant standard of proof.

1. England: An Adversarial System

In accordance with the adversarial system of litigation under the common law, the gathering and presentation of the proof in respect of a given claim has been seen as part of the wider contest between the parties.[6] It is for them to decide what evidence to adduce to support their respective contentions, ie in the form of witnesses, documents and other real evidence. In the past it was then for the jury, having heard such evidence at the trial, to decide whose account of events it preferred on the issues in dispute, and to make findings of fact accordingly. Though nowadays the judge (besides determining legal questions) has taken over the jury's function as fact-finder in negligence,[7] the underlying approach to litigation persists. Thus, the judge remains a relatively passive figure, who is expected to leave the presentation of the evidence and legal argumentation to Counsel.

A significant feature, connected to the adversarial approach, is the relatively low standard of proof that operates in private law, namely that of the 'balance of probabilities'.[8] In accordance with this, the judge need only be satisfied, at the close of the evidence, that a party's contentions (on an issue on which that party bears the burden of proof) are *more likely than not* to be true. In effect, a form of relative truth prevails: the court must decide whether it prefers A's account that a given fact was 'x', to the opposing version offered by B (that the fact was 'not-x'); it matters not that, in A's version too, various unclarified circumstances or gaps remain. Admittedly, in relation to allegations of professional negligence, the courts on occasion have suggested they will need persuading to a greater level than a simple preponderance of probabilities.[9] Even so, such a higher putative standard (which

[5] For England, see generally JA Jolowicz, *On Civil Procedure* (Cambridge, Cambridge University Press, 2000); for Germany, see A Laufs and W Uhlenbruck (eds), *Handbuch des Arztrechts*, 3rd edn (Munich, Beck, 2002) § 107; U Graf, *Die Beweislast bei Behandlungsfehlern im Arzthaftungsprozess* (Munich, VVF, 2001) 7 ff.

[6] Jolowicz, *ibid*, 375.

[7] One of the last medical negligence cases to be tried before a jury was *Bolam v Friern Hospital Management Committee* [1957] 1 WLR 582 (QBD).

[8] Contrast the criminal law standard according to which proof is required 'beyond reasonable doubt'.

[9] See eg *Whitehouse v Jordan* [1980] 1 All ER 650 (CA) 659 (Lawton LJ). This accords with the idea that the supporting evidence should increase with the gravity of a given allegation: see further A Grubb (ed), *Principles of Medical Law*, 2nd edn (Oxford, Oxford University Press, 2004) para 6.107.

applies only to breach of duty, not causation) would still allow a liability finding in the face of reasonable doubt.

As noted above, it is an inescapable feature of medical malpractice cases that the court, in making its findings, will rely on the assistance of expert medical witnesses. In England, in accordance with the adversarial approach, the court itself does not appoint such experts (ie as neutral advisors). Rather, they are called by the respective parties and present their evidence on behalf of them. Here the main safeguard against tendentious testimony is that the judge will also hear the experts appearing for the other side. Indeed, it is a key principle of the adversarial system that witnesses (including experts) should normally attend the trial in person, where their demeanour under questioning can be observed. In this regard, the process of cross-examination of the witnesses by Counsel plays an important role.[10]

Insofar as the expert evidence on a given fact is in conflict, the judge must decide which of the parties' experts he prefers. Here, in contrast to the experts' opinions on the normative issue of fault (see chapter two), the court may not simply exonerate the defendant on the basis that responsible medical experts disagree on the matter.[11] At the same time, as in the case of expert opinion evidence, a criticism—made especially by patient support groups—has been that the courts have deferred too readily to the defence experts on issues of fact. The neutrality of such experts on both types of question may be queried, given that they are from the same profession (and, in the case of attesting to what occurred, the same hospital) as the defendant doctor.[12] These tensions were recognised by Lord Woolf in his 1996 Report into reforming the civil justice system, where he noted concerns as to the relative shortage of experts willing to appear for the patient, and the way these witnesses had been drawn into the adversarial culture of litigation.[13] Following the recommendations of his Report, there is now a greater use made where possible of jointly instructed experts. A further suggestion (not yet taken up) was for specialist training in medical issues for judges hearing such cases.[14]

2. Germany: An Inquisitorial System[15]

In Germany, where juries—in the common law tradition—have featured less in the legal process, the approach to matters of civil procedure and proof has devel-

[10] Ie the process by which counsel attempts—through probing questioning—to expose weak points and inconsistencies in the testimony of witnesses for the other side

[11] See *Penney v East Kent Health Authority* [2000] Lloyd's Rep Med 41 (CA).

[12] J Healy, *Medical Negligence: Common Law Perspectives* (London, Sweet & Maxwell, 1999) 73 ff. But see A Merry and A McCall Smith, *Errors, Medicine and the Law* (Cambridge, Cambridge University Press 2001) 181 ff, who argue that, if anything, expert evidence tends to operate in favour of the patient.

[13] Woolf, *Access to Justice: Final Report to the Lord Chancellor on the Civil Justice System in England and Wales* (London, HMSO, 1996) ch 15, paras 63 ff.

[14] See the Chief Medical Officer (Sir Liam Donaldson), *Making Amends: A consultation paper setting out proposals for reforming the approach to clinical negligence in the NHS* (London, Department of Health, 2003) 90–91.

[15] The terminology of 'adversarial' and 'inquisitorial' procedure, while capturing the style of the common and civil law systems respectively, should not be treated as a rigid dichotomy. In practice each

oped as an inquisitorial system. Here, while the parties initiate the proceedings, and to that extent determine the subject-matter of their dispute (including the facts necessary to resolve it), the judge from the outset assumes a more proactive role than in England. Thus, the court will normally inform the parties where it requires further evidence on a given point. It will also be expected to give them the opportunity to refine their contentions if the initial statement of claim contains irrelevancies or contradictions. This is a corollary to the lower degree of legal specialisation in Germany, including the absence of a distinct class of barristers experienced in trial work. The investigation proceeds in a gradual and dialectical fashion with less distinction, compared to the common law, between pre-trial and trial stages.[16] Moreover, the preference is often for written rather than oral testimony. In one treatment malpractice case the BGH indeed stressed the desirability of written evidence on the key points, so as to give the other side a chance to respond.[17]

For a common lawyer, undoubtedly the most striking difference thrown up by the German approach to civil litigation concerns the high standard of proof that applies. In particular, under § 286 of the Code of Civil Procedure (*Zivilprozessordnung*—ZPO), the court in reaching its findings must be overwhelmingly convinced of the facts (*Überzeugung des Richters*). The BGH has interpreted this as entailing,

> full judicial conviction in the form of a degree of certainty that silences doubts for practical purposes, even if it does not eliminate them entirely.[18]

This approach ties in with the more inquisitorial culture of civil law litigation, emphasising the court's role in seeking the independent truth (rather than simply adjudicating as to whose case is stronger on the day).[19] At the same time, though, it means cases of *non liquet* (not proven) will be more prevalent than under the common law. The judge may think A's version of the facts more likely to be true than B's, but neither meets the threshold standard.

Given their inherent potential for evidential uncertainty, this is likely to occur especially frequently in cases of treatment malpractice.[20] On the face of things, it is the patient, having the burden of proof, who will then lose. In fact, however, the German courts have reacted by making special allowance for such cases. As we shall see in part III, this has in part involved fashioning a number of proof modifications that will apply. However, at a more general level too, the BGH has stressed the importance in such cases of judges adopting a flexible approach to

system contains some elements from the other approach: see Jolowicz, *On Civil Procedure* (n 5 above) 175.

[16] See generally M Bohlander, 'The German Advantage Revisited: An Inside View of German Civil Procedure in the Nineties' (1998) 13 *Tulane European and Civil Law Forum* 25.

[17] BGH, 17 April 1984, NJW 1984, 1823.

[18] BGH, 17 February 1970, BGHZ 53, 245 (256).

[19] For a comparative discussion of the standard of proof used for private law cases in common and civil law jurisdictions, see K Clermont and E Sherwin, 'A Comparative View of Standards of Proof' (2002) 50 *American Journal of Comparative Law* 243.

[20] See generally Graf, *Die Beweislast bei Behandlungsfehlern im Arzthaftungsprozess* (n 5 above) 14 ff.

procedure and evidence. They should remain mindful of the patient's difficulties and—while not renouncing their neutrality—be ready to intervene and ask questions or suggest lines of questioning to the patient's legal representative.[21] Less, correspondingly, is expected of the patient's side than in other types of action. Often the patient, in formulating the statement of claim, will be able to do little more than point to the fact of his injury and its temporal proximity to the medical treatment.[22]

In an important case from 1979 the Federal Constitutional Court (*Bundesverfassungsgericht*) affirmed the need for the courts to ensure 'equality of arms' (*Waffengleichheit*) between the parties in medical malpractice litigation. This derived from the patient's constitutional right to due process under Article 103 I of the *Grundgesetz*.[23] Indeed the court there queried whether, in order to guarantee this right, the patient should receive the benefit of a general reversal of the burden of proof against the treating side. Ultimately, the view prevailed that it would be sufficient for trial judges to apply proof modifications as the circumstances of the case demanded. This had also been the conclusion of the BGH in its slightly earlier '*Dammschnitt-Urteil*', where, in upholding the default rule as to the burden of proof, it noted that

> the doctor [too] has the difficulty that in many areas of medical treatment, harm whose occurrence points in general to negligence, may in fact sometimes occur naturally due to the vagaries of the human organism.[24]

As discussed earlier, one of the most important factors in determining the outcome of a treatment malpractice action will be the evidence of the medical experts. Unlike England, where the latter are commissioned by each side, in Germany the court will typically appoint one or more experts to act as its impartial helper(s). These then ordinarily submit a written report, detailing their findings on the facts of the case, including their opinion as to whether negligence was involved.[25] Although it is then for the judge to pronounce definitively on the issue, as discussed in chapter two, he may not do so on the basis of unsupported theories of his own.[26] In this regard, as in England, an important issue concerns the experts' objectivity: indeed, this is even more relevant in the context of the German inquisitorial system, where one expert's view is less likely to be challenged by another.

In fact in a number of critical utterances from the 1970s the BGH queried the impartiality of experts in treatment malpractice cases. In one decision it commented that,

[21] BGH, 15 May 1979, NJW 1979, 1933; BGH, 24 June 1980, NJW 1980, 2751; BGH, 17 April 1984, NJW 1984, 1823; C Katzenmeier, *Arzthaftung* (Tübingen, Mohr Siebeck, 2002) 390 ff.

[22] Katzenmeier, *ibid*, 392.

[23] BVerfG, 25 July 1979, NJW 1979, 1925.

[24] BGH, 14 March 1978, NJW 1978, 1681 (1682).

[25] See Bohlander, 'The German Advantage Revisited' (n 16 above) 41 ff.

[26] BGH, 2 March 1993, NJW 1993, 2378; BGH, 10 May 1994, NJW 1994, 2419.

> even today there are not a few medical experts, who in carrying out their functions find it difficult to free themselves from outdated (and in this context legally unacceptable) mores of professional solidarity.[27]

Accordingly, trial judges needed to critically examine such evidence for fullness and freedom from inconsistency.[28] Since then, it appears the problem of bias in medical witnesses has eased. Indeed some commentators have argued that the courts remain unduly distrusting of exculpatory testimony.[29] Be that as it may, it is now normal practice, where doubts as to neutrality arise, to obtain a second expert opinion. In addition, the patient retains the right to commission his own partisan expert. In such a case, the court should take the latter's contentions seriously and, if need be, invite him to clarify points in his report.[30]

III. Modifying the Normal Proof Rules to Assist the Patient?

As noted, the factual uncertainties inherent in treatment malpractice litigation—plus the fact that it is the patient who ordinarily carries the burden of proof—will often pose a serious obstacle to a successful claim. In this regard, a question of primary importance is how far the courts may on occasion invoke special rules modifying the general rules in respect of civil proof, so as to assist the patient. This has received a different response in England and Germany. The courts in the first country (albeit from the lower starting point of the 'balance of probabilities' standard) have been reluctant to countenance modifications. By contrast, in Germany an elaborate case law has developed, providing for them in a variety of circumstances.[31] This divergence of approach can be observed in three main contexts: first, in relation to disputed primary facts; secondly, in deciding in what circumstances negligence may be inferred from the occurrence of injury; and thirdly, in resolving issues of causal uncertainty.

1. Establishing the Primary Facts

At the outset, and as a precondition for its normative judgement of whether the defendant doctor acted with the required skill and care, the court must establish the primary facts of the case. In this regard, it will need to make findings as to the concrete circumstances facing the doctor and what he did in response.

[27] BGH, 22 April 1975, NJW 1975, 1463 (1464).
[28] BGH, 17 September 1985, VersR 1985, 1187; BGH, 10 May 1994, NJW 1994, 2419.
[29] Katzenmeier, *Arzthaftung* (n 21 above) 409.
[30] BGH, 19 May 1981, VersR 1981, 752.
[31] Katzenmeier, *Arzthaftung* (n 21 above) 424, notes that such rules have been characterised as 'the most important source of judicial law making . . . the dynamic motor for liability-shifting'.

(a) England: Inferences from the Information Available

Usually, in arriving at its findings of fact in a treatment malpractice case, the court will have in front of it a body of more or less direct evidence, including the testimony of those present, contemporary or near-contemporary medical notes and records, mechanically-generated test results, and so forth. In this regard an important procedure—serving to address the informational inequality between the parties—is that of disclosure (formerly known as 'discovery'), requiring the defendant hospital to make relevant documents available to the claimant, including those that inculpate the doctor.[32] Witness statements (including from the experts) will also be exchanged prior to trial. As noted earlier, the witnesses are then normally required to attend the trial in person. The most prized form of evidence is oral evidence, particularly as it emerges through the process of cross-examination.

In the event that key items of evidence are lost at the time of trial, the court will do its best to reconstruct the contents of the missing evidence in the light of such evidence as is available. This includes situations where the evidence was lost through the treating side's default. For example in *Kay v Ayrshire and Arran Health Board* the question was whether a missing blood-sugar test more likely than not showed that the claimant's meningitis had reached its peak prior to the defendant's faulty intervention. Having heard the rival arguments of the expert witnesses (offering reasoned speculation on the basis of the pattern from surviving records), the court answered this in the affirmative.[33] Similarly, where the doctor's notes are incomplete and he cannot remember the details of the particular case, he may when on the witness stand tender evidence of his normal careful practice in support of the proposition that he took care on the occasion in question.[34] It is the circumstances overall that are decisive. Thus, even where a doctor is found to have falsified his operation notes after the event, this will not automatically lead to a finding that he performed the treatment negligently.[35] However, sometimes an inference may lie close at hand that a witness has avoided taking the stand, or evidence has been withheld or concealed, to avoid exposing information adverse to the defendant's case; and this will tilt matters in favour of the claimant.[36]

(b) Germany: Presumptions in Cases of Missing Records

As noted earlier, in German civil litigation it is more common than in England for evidence to be presented to the court in written form. In this context, the patient's

[32] See Jolowicz, *On Civil Procedure* (n 5 above) 56–7. The patient enjoys in addition a general statutory right of access to his medical records under the Data Protection Act 1998.

[33] *Kay v Ayrshire and Arran Health Board* [1987] 2 All ER 417 (HL).

[34] *Ratcliffe v Plymouth and Torbay Health Authority* [1998] PIQR P170 (CA); see also *Maynard v West Midlands Regional Health Authority* [1984] 1 WLR 634 (HL).

[35] *De Freitas v O'Brien* [1995] PIQR P281 (CA).

[36] See *Wisniewski v Central Manchester Health Authority* [1998] PIQR P324 (CA), where an adverse inference was drawn from a doctor's failure to attend the trial in person.

medical records and notes play a central role in helping to substantiate any claim; not least, they will form the starting point for the medical expert's report.[37] Although for a long time such records were regarded simply as an aide memoir for the doctor, in two important cases from 1978 the BGH reclassified their retention as an essential, albeit subsidiary, component of the doctor's principal duty to provide treatment and care.[38] In so far as this duty is breached (*Verletzung der Dokumentationspflicht*), the doctor is subject to a procedural sanction. This takes the form of a presumption that a treatment measure, for which the record is now missing, was omitted.[39]

Admittedly, in such cases the normative question of whether the (presumed) omission amounts to a faulty treatment error must already be in issue: merely to point to the absence of a record that a given procedure was performed will be pointless if there was no reason to expect it to be performed.[40] The BGH noted in one decision:

> The doctor's failure to record does not give rise to an independent cause of action. It can lead to relief only where the patient's ability to prove a given allegation has been specifically impaired by the absence of the record. Accordingly it is for the patient to show, at the outset, that prima facie there is the indication of a faulty treatment error causative of his injury, albeit the demands imposed on him in this regard should not be too high.[41]

In determining whether the records are sufficient (or if there is a gap warranting an adverse inference) the courts will ask if they contain the essential information regarding the patient's treatment in terms comprehensible to another doctor.[42] However, the BGH has held that heightened recording duties—extending to routine information—may apply in relation to patients known to be at an especially high risk of harm, as well as to treatment carried out by junior doctors.[43]

An important sub-category of cases—which, while related to the above, is recognised as raising special difficulties—concerns a doctor's failure to record or preserve the results of diagnostic tests. As with the non-documentation of actual treatment, the non-preservation of such findings will be adjudged a breach of a subsidiary duty of care (*Verletzung der Befundsicherungspflicht*),[44] with similar procedural consequences—viz a presumption that the doctor omitted to carry out the test. Insofar as the doctor is unable to rebut this, then—assuming the test was medically indicated—the case will turn into one of faulty misdiagnosis. A breach of duty will have been established and the remaining proof issues will concern factual causation—ie what would the test have revealed, and would subsequent therapy have cured (or ameliorated) the patient's condition?[45]

[37] As in England, the patient has a general right of access to his records: BGH, 23 November 1982, NJW 1983, 328; Laufs and Uhlenbruck, *Handbuch des Arztrechts* (n 5 above) § 111 paras 1–2.

[38] BGH, 14 March 1978, NJW 1978, 1681; BGH, 26 June 1978, NJW 1978, 2337.

[39] BGH, 14 February 1995, NJW 1995, 1611; Katzenmeier, *Arzthaftung* (n 21 above) 470 ff.

[40] G Müller, 'Beweislast und Beweisführung im Arzthaftungsprozeß' NJW 1997, 3049 (3054).

[41] BGH, 9 November 1982, NJW 1983, 332 (332); see also BGH, 28 June 1988, NJW 1988, 2949.

[42] BGH, 24 January 1984, NJW 1984, 1403; BGH, 24 January 1989, NJW, 1989, 2330.

[43] BGH, 7 May 1985, NJW 1985, 2193.

[44] BGH, 21 November 1985, NJW 1996, 779.

[45] See Graf, *Die Beweislast bei Behandlungsfehlern im Arzthaftungsprozess* (n 5above) 87.

We shall consider the (still considerable) problem of showing causation in such cases below.[46] However, relevant at this stage of the discussion are those cases where the doctor *succeeds* in rebutting the presumption through compelling independent evidence that he performed the test in question. Here, where no or inadequate treatment was provided for the patient's condition (as now known at trial), the German courts have been exercised with how to accommodate the patient's difficulty in showing that such (non-) treatment was a breach of duty. After all, with the test result no longer to hand it will be hard to impugn either the diagnosis reached or the doctor's decision regarding therapy. The courts' solution has been to presume a breach, if in the light of other evidence it seems 'sufficiently likely' that the missing test showed something relevant that the doctor ought to have reacted to.[47]

2. Inferring Malpractice from the Occurrence of Injury

Sometimes, despite the best efforts of the witnesses, and even where reasonably complete records were kept, the full facts surrounding a given medical injury will remain obscure. Clearly, though, *something* must have happened to cause it. In this context, both English and German law have developed rules that may allow the patient to present the fact of injury itself as prima facie evidence of causative negligence on the doctor's part.

(a) England: Res Ipsa Loquitur

In England the relevant evidential doctrine bears the Latin tag of *res ipsa loquitur* (literally, 'the thing speaks for itself') and is of general and longstanding application in the law of negligence. It enables a court to infer a breach of duty where: (i) it is unclear on the evidence what actually happened; but (ii) the situation was under the defendant's control; and (iii) the damage that occurred does not normally do so without negligence.[48] Though the precise effect of this doctrine has been disputed over the years, it is now generally accepted that the overall burden of proof remains with the claimant: the defendant is not required positively to show that the accident did not result from negligence.[49] At the same time, though, he cannot remain silent. Rather, to disarm the claimant's prima facie case, he must adduce evidence—either showing that he took reasonable care in the circumstances, or that the same injury could plausibly have resulted from the operation of independent factors (over which he had no control).[50]

[46] See the discussion in pt III 3 (b) (ii) below.

[47] BGH, 3 February 1987, NJW 1987, 1482; BGH, 13 February 1996, NJW 1996, 1589; BGH, 6 October 1998, NJW 1999, 860.

[48] See *Scott v London and St Katherine's Docks Co* (1865) 3 H & C 596, where some bags of flour fell in unexplained circumstances from the defendant's warehouse, injuring the claimant.

[49] See the decision of the Privy Council in *Ng Chun Pui v Lee Chuen Tat* [1988] RTR 298.

[50] *Delaney v Southmead Health Authority* (1995) 6 Med LR 355 (CA); see Grubb, *Principles of Medical Law* (n 9 above) paras 6.101 ff.

In the context of treatment malpractice, *res ipsa loquitur* has been pleaded in a number of cases over the years, typically where there has been some untoward consequence of surgery or anaesthesia.[51] For example, in the well-known case of *Roe v Minister of Health*, the claimants were left paralysed following routine surgery, which had been carried out under general anaesthetic. In the Court of Appeal, Denning LJ stated:

> The [trial] judge has said that those facts do not speak for themselves, but I think that they do. They certainly call for an explanation. Each of these men is entitled to say to the hospital: 'While I was in your hands something has been done to me which has wrecked my life. Please explain how this has come to pass'.[52]

Similarly, in *Cassidy v Ministry of Health* the doctrine was applied in favour of a patient whose hand was left useless following treatment to correct two stiff fingers.[53] He had been in the care of a number of different doctors and nurses, and it was unclear which of these might have been negligent. However, they were all employees of the relevant hospital, and the hospital offered no evidence at all as to how such an injury could occur without negligence.

Nonetheless, in more recent years the courts have equivocated with regard to the usefulness of *res ipsa loquitur* in such cases. In *Glass v Cambridge Health Authority*, the doctrine was invoked in relation to a claim of negligent anaesthetic management. The court commented that 'the heart of a healthy child does not stop for no reason under anaesthetic', and rejected the explanation offered by the defendant as to how this could have occurred (consistently with non-negligence) as far-fetched.[54] By contrast, in *Delaney v Southmead Health Authority*—where the patient alleged injury from faulty positioning during an operation—the court, having heard positive evidence that the defendant had taken due care, was prepared to accept this even though the upshot was that the claimant's injury remained unexplained.[55]

In fact, as the Court of Appeal has recognised in the leading modern case of *Ratcliffe v Plymouth and Torbay Health Authority*, the general availability of at least some evidence in treatment malpractice cases prevents *res ipsa loquitur* from applying in a pure form. Rather, the judge will decide the case on the whole of the available evidence (including that of the medical experts). As Hobhouse LJ noted in his judgment,

> in practical terms, few, if any, medical negligence cases are brought to trial without full discovery having been given, particulars having been obtained where necessary of the

[51] See Brooke LJ's discussion of the relevant authorities in *Ratcliffe v Plymouth and Torbay Health Authority* [1998] PIQR P170 (CA) P180ff; see also M Jones, *Medical Negligence*, 3rd edn (London, Sweet & Maxwell, 2003) paras 3-121 ff.

[52] *Roe v Minister of Health* [1954] 2 QB 66 (CA) 81; in the event (as noted in ch 2 above, fn 32), the hospital succeeded in rebutting liability by pointing to the (unforeseeable) contamination of anaesthetic as the cause.

[53] *Cassidy v Ministry of Health* [1951] 2 KB 343 (CA).

[54] *Glass v Cambridge Health Authority* (1995) 6 Med LR 91 (CA).

[55] *Delaney v Southmead Health Authority* (1995) 6 Med LR 355 (CA).

> defendant's pleading, witness statements having been exchanged and experts' reports lodged. Therefore, the trial opens not in the vacuum of available evidence and explanation as sometimes occurs in road traffic accident cases, but with expert evidence on both sides and defined battle-lines drawn . . . The viable allegations or inferences of negligence will have been identified, and the parties and the trial judge will have a reasonable idea of the specific factual issues which are going to have to be investigated and determined at the trial.[56]

Importantly, the application of *res ipsa loquitur* is also limited fundamentally by the requirement that the claimant's injury not be such as could plausibly have arisen in the absence of negligence. This is rarely the case in medical treatment situations, where the existence of a given background risk of injury (through the operation of causal factors over which the doctor has no control), is a characteristic feature. As a Canadian judge remarked in this context,

> the human body is not a container filled with a material whose performance can be predictably charted and analysed . . . medical science has not yet reached the stage where the law ought to presume that a patient must come out of an operation as well or better than he went into it.[57]

This point will be relevant in those iatrogenic harm cases, where it is accepted that the treatment carried a non-eliminable, residual risk of harm of the form that occurred.[58] On the face of things, it is even more telling in cases where the patient simply fails to benefit from a procedure, eg following misdiagnosis. There, given the inherent possibility that the illness might not have been cured or ameliorated with proper treatment, the *res ipsa loquitur* doctrine appears to have no purchase.

Nonetheless, an exceptional category of misdiagnosis claim, where an approach with some affinity to the doctrine has been recognised, concerns the failure to detect foetal abnormalities. Here, where a foetal scan is interpreted as normal, but the child is born with significant disabilities, the doctor involved will come under an onus to justify the error. Thus in *Lillywhite v University College University Hospitals NHS Trust*, the Court of Appeal inferred negligence by a consultant who identified a child in utero as having a normal brain structure, who was subsequently born with a severe brain malformation.[59] Direct photographic evidence as to what the scan had shown was no longer available, but the majority of the Court rejected the consultant's explanation (itself only put forward late in the proceedings) as to how, consistently with due care, he could have recorded structures to be present that were not there.

[56] *Ratcliffe v Plymouth and Torbay Health Authority* [1998] PIQR P170 (CA) P187.

[57] *Girard v Royal Columbian Hospital* (1976) 66 DLR (3d) 676 (Andrews J).

[58] See Grubb, *Principles of Medical Law* (n 9 above) para 6.106.

[59] *Lillywhite v University College University Hospitals NHS Trust* [2005] EWCA Civ 1466. It was accepted (as to causation) that, if she had known of the true state of affairs the claimant (the child's mother) would have had her pregnancy terminated. See also *Pithers v Leeds Teaching Hospitals NHS Trust* [2004] EWHC 1392.

(b) The Position in Germany

(i) *Anscheinsbeweis*

German law has recognised an evidential doctrine very similar to *res ipsa loquitur*, which it terms *Anscheinsbeweis* or *Prima Facie Beweis* (prima facie proof). As with its common law cousin, the doctrine's application extends well beyond the confines of treatment malpractice to cases of unexplained injury generally; namely, in circumstances where the injury does not 'in the typical course of events' occur absent negligence. Again, as in the case of *res ipsa loquitur*, there has been some debate in the academic literature as to whether the doctrine shifts the burden of proof to the defendant, with the modern consensus being that it does not. Rather, it is a matter the court will consider in deciding (under § 286 ZPO) whether the claimant has made out a sufficiently strong case as to the defendant's fault.[60]

Over the years the courts have invoked *Anscheinsbeweis* in quite a number of treatment malpractice cases. As with *res ipsa loquitur*, the doctrine's primary application will lie in circumstances of unexpected iatrogenic injury, for example where objects have been left inside patients during surgery or unusual injury occurs immediately following an injection.[61] In one case, the doctrine was used to assist a patient who suffered burns in the course of treatment with high frequency surgical equipment (in conjunction with expert evidence that this did not usually occur).[62] More recently, it was applied in favour of a patient—not otherwise in a high-risk category—who was found to have contracted the HIV virus following a blood transfusion from an infected source.[63] However, in other situations the use of *Anscheinsbeweis* has been rejected from the outset, eg in the context of unsuccessful sterilisations.[64] This is in keeping with the courts' unwillingness to assume fault where treatment fails to achieve a positive desired outcome. A striking illustration is provided by a decision of the *Oberlandesgericht* Hamm, refusing to apply the doctrine in circumstances where, after numerous unsuccessful fistula operations on the patient by the defendant, another doctor performed the surgery with immediate success.[65]

Even in unexpected iatrogenic injury cases, it will (as with *res ipsa loquitur* under the common law) remain open to the defendant to rebut the inference of negligence as the cause by pointing to other possible explanations.[66] As Müller has noted, the unpredictability of human organisms means that it is nearly always

[60] Katzenmeier, *Arzthaftung* (n 21 above) 431; Graf, *Die Beweislast bei Behandlungsfehlern im Arzthaftungsprozess* (n 5 above) 45–7.

[61] BGH, 27 February 1952, VersR 1952, 180; Laufs and Uhlenbruck, *Handbuch des Arztrechts* (n 5 above) § 108, Rn 5.

[62] BGH, 22 June 1955, VersR 1955, 573.

[63] BGH, 30 April 1991, NJW 1991, 1948.

[64] Graf, *Die Beweislast bei Behandlungsfehlern im Arzthaftungsprozess* (n 5 above) 53.

[65] OLG Hamm, 30 April 1986, VersR 1987, 1119.

[66] OLG Zweibruecken, 13 May 1997, MedR 1997, 358; Graf, *Die Beweislast bei Behandlungsfehlern im Arzthaftungsprozess* (n 5 above) 58 ff.

possible for some poorly understood variable to materialise and injure.[67] In this regard, the BGH has stressed the need for restraint by trial judges in drawing causal inferences based on the 'typical course of events'.[68] In more recent years, the reliance by the patient upon *Anscheinsbeweis* appears in any case to have declined. The reason is that the courts have developed other, more advantageous mechanisms (from the patient's viewpoint), allowing negligence to be presumed in certain fact situations.[69] Most significant in this regard are approaches deriving from the notion of 'fully-masterable risks', which are looked at next.

(ii) Fully-Masterable Risks

We previously touched upon the concept of fully masterable risks (*voll beherrschbare Risiken*) in chapter two.[70] As discussed there, the German courts have—in the context of damage arising within the doctor's 'sphere of risk' (as opposed to risks connected to the vagaries of the patient's illness)—been prepared to presume fault, and cast the onus on the doctor to show otherwise. An example would be where the patient suffers injury as a result of receiving a contaminated medical substance.[71] Implicit in our earlier discussion was that the court's knowledge of the primary facts was complete. There was no mystery as to what happened—the issue was instead a normative one (in practice approaching a strict liability standard), in which the defendant was required to justify the failure to take a given precaution. Nevertheless, the same approach is also highly pertinent when there are gaps in the primary facts: indeed, here the defendant's inability to explain fully how the injury occurred will make a finding of negligence inevitable. The slim chance he might otherwise have had of exonerating himself (by showing the injury stemmed from a risk he could not possibly be expected to guard against) will be foreclosed.

An illustration of the latter 'evidential' application of the 'fully masterable risks' approach is provided by a well-known case in which a patient suffered brain damage under anesthetic, and a tube in the oxygen machine was subsequently found to have been disconnected. It remained unclear how and when the disconnection occurred, but it was known the machine had stood unattended for a time in a hospital corridor. On these facts the BGH held the hospital straightforwardly liable.[72] Other cases have involved patients who suffer unexplained accidents in the course of their general care, eg where they have fallen off a trolley, or stumbled while being walked by a nurse.[73] As will be apparent, the factual scenarios here are ones where *Anscheinsbeweis* could also be applied. Indeed, certain scenarios—for exam-

[67] Müller, 'Beweislast und Beweisführung im Arzthaftungsprozeß' (n 40 above) 3052.
[68] BGH, 11 June 1965, VersR 1965, 792.
[69] Katzenmeier, *Arzthaftung* (n 21 above) 437.
[70] See ch 2 pt II 3 (b).
[71] BGH, 9 May 1978, NJW 1978, 1683.
[72] BGH, 11 October 1977, NJW 1978, 584.
[73] BGH, 18 December 1990, NJW 1991, 1540; see the discussion of the cases in Graf, *Die Beweislast bei Behandlungsfehlern im Arzthaftungsprozess* (n 5 above) 145 ff.

ple where objects are left inside patients—where the courts formerly applied that doctrine will nowadays be dealt with as 'fully-masterable risks'.[74] Nonetheless, a significant advantage of the latter approach, for the patient, is that a formal reversal of the burden of proof operates.

Usually, the risk that the defendants failed to master will stand in a close and undisputed causal relation to the patient's injury: there is no alternative explanation (in the form of a competing background risk) as to how the injury may have occurred. In this regard again, there is much similarity with the doctrine of *Anscheinsbeweis.* However, on occasion the 'fully-masterable risks' approach has been extended beyond such situations to ones where independent risks of injury were also in play. At the same time, its application will here be subject to further caveats. An example is of cases of post-operative infection in which the BGH has recognised only limited scope for the approach. In particular, the court will first need to be satisfied that the source of infection was 'hygienically controllable'.[75] Only then does the onus shift to the defendant to show he had indeed taken all relevant precautions. The court noted in a case from 1991:

> The absolute freedom from bacteria of the doctors and other members of the surgical team is unattainable . . . Infection occasioned by them that occurs unavoidably and despite all requisite hygienic measures having been taken by the hospital must be regarded as a matter within the patient's sphere of risk and not compensable.[76]

A second situation in which the fully-masterable risk approach will apply in a qualified form is when the patient alleges injury from being wrongly positioned on the operating table. Here the starting point is that the treating side has the onus of showing that the positioning corresponded to the required medical standard, albeit the evidential demands on it here will not be especially high (eg detailed documentary evidence is not usually required).[77] The question remains though—where the hospital fails to discharge this burden—whether the injury should without more be attributed to the faulty positioning? Here the BGH has held that as a rule the burden is also on the treating side to show absence of causation (ie that the same injury would have occurred with correct positioning).[78] However, this does not apply where the patient had a rare physical anomaly, increasing his susceptibility to the injury in question:

> The reversal of proof in respect of positioning injuries is based on the consideration that the risk-factors—including from the patient's physical constitution—conducing to such injuries can be planned for and eliminated by the doctors; thus it is for them to explain why an injury of this type nonetheless occurred . . . But, in the case of a rare and unforeseeable anomaly on the patient's part, the risks are no longer wholly controllable, and there is thus no room for such a reversal.[79]

[74] OLG Köln, 18 December 1986, VersR 1988, 140.
[75] BGH, 8 January 1991, NJW 1991, 1541.
[76] *Ibid*, 1542.
[77] BGH, 24 January 1984, NJW 1984, 1403.
[78] BGH, 24 January 1995, NJW 1995, 1618.
[79] *Ibid*, 1618.

In such a case, to escape liability the hospital must thus establish the presence of the additional background risk (due to the patient's anomaly), but need not show that this actually materialised and caused the injury.[80]

A final group of cases relevant in this context concerns treatment carried out by junior doctors. Here, while it is accepted that such doctors must train on the job, the onus will be on the hospital to take special steps to mitigate the extra dangers their inexperience poses to the patient.[81] Thus, full supervision is required, which includes the presence of an experienced doctor ready to take over if the need arises. Moreover, the junior doctor's actions should be fully documented, to show that he brought to bear the standard of care of an experienced doctor. Failing such steps, there will be a primary breach of duty—at an organisation level—on the part of the hospital.[82] In addition, where the patient suffers injury of a kind which is generally avoidable and *often attributable* to lack of experience, the burden of clarifying events will be upon the hospital. In other words, as regards causation, it is for the latter to show that it was not the extra risk presented by the junior doctor's inexperience that materialised in the case at hand.[83]

3. Dealing with Problems of Causal Uncertainty

The situations considered above (in part II 2) were for the most part ones where, apart from a breach of duty by the doctor, there was no other plausible account as to why the patient suffered the injury he did.[84] The only risk factor normally associated with that kind of injury was presented by the treatment, a risk moreover that could be avoided by due care. It was these features that made permissible the inference back from the patient's injury to the doctor's breach of duty. Nonetheless, the issues need only be presented in this way for it to become clear that such cases form the exception in the treatment malpractice context. In most cases, there *will* be other possible explanations besides negligence for the harm, namely that it stemmed from an inherent treatment risk (beyond the doctor's control), or from a risk connected to the patient's underlying condition.

As noted earlier, a feature of treatment malpractice cases is that even the experts may not fully understand the causal processes at work. This is due to the complexity and idiosyncrasies of individual human organisms, and the illnesses that afflict them, combined with uncertainty as to a treatment's potential to injure rather than cure. Cases of injury following misdiagnosis often present particular difficulty: there the question whether the patient's illness would have responded to

[80] See also the decision of the OLG Hamm, 18 June 1997, VersR 1998, 1243, which is discussed (as case no 4) in M Faure and H Koziol (eds), *Cases on Medical Malpractice in a Comparative Perspective* (Vienna, Springer, 2001).

[81] BGH, 27 September 1983, NJW 1984, 655; Katzenmeier, *Arzthaftung* (n 21 above) 486 ff.

[82] Graf, *Die Beweislast bei Behandlungsfehlern im Arzthaftungsprozess* (n 5 above) 157–8.

[83] BGH, 27 September 1983, NJW 1984, 655; BGH, 7 May 1985, NJW 1985, 2193. The reversal in question appears to be limited to cases where iatrogenic injury occurs, not ones where there is (simply) a failure to make the patient better.

[84] As just discussed, some of the German 'fully-masterable risk' cases offer a partial exception.

treatment, is inherently speculative—turning on various imponderables as to its stage of progress (at the time the diagnosis ought to have been made) and the form that the omitted treatment might have taken.

Clearly the response of the courts to such endemic uncertainty will often be determinative as to whether the patient receives any compensation. In this regard, the English and German courts have in line with their general approach to questions of proof adopted divergent approaches—the jurisprudence of the latter country revealing a notably more 'patient-friendly' stance than that of the former.

(a) The Position in England

As with the breach of duty issue, the general starting point is that it is for the patient to prove the existence of causation on the balance of probabilities. The courts, while acknowledging that this may give rise to difficulties for him in the medical malpractice context, have refused to modify this approach by allowing for reversals of proof. They have also so far rejected claims for proportionate recovery in misdiagnosis cases based on statistical evidence as to the patient's lost chance of a cure.

(i) Keeping the Burden on the Patient

To start with the patient must show the doctor's or hospital's faulty conduct was capable of causing injury of the type he suffered—ie that it presented a risk at all. This may occasionally pose problems in cases relating to unusual treatment reactions: for example in *Kay v Ayrshire and Arran Health Board* it was held that the claimant had failed to establish even a putative link between an overdose of penicillin (that he had mistakenly received during treatment for meningitis) and his subsequent deafness.[85] Nonetheless far more problematic as a general rule is the further requirement—once a risk is established—that the patient show it was *that* risk (as opposed to an independent background risk) that materialised and injured him in the case at hand.

In *Barnett v Kensington and Chelsea Hospital Management Committee* whose facts were referred to in chapter two,[86] counsel for the claimant argued that, since the doctor by failing to attend and treat the patient had added to his risk of death, the burden of disproving causation (by showing he could not have been saved) should shift to the hospital.[87] However the judge, Nield J, rejected this suggestion in robust terms:

[85] *Kay v Ayrshire and Arran Health Board* [1987] 2 All ER 417 (HL). See also *Loveday v Renton* (1990) 1 Med LR 117 (QBD).

[86] *Barnett v Chelsea and Kensington Hospital Management Committee* [1969] 1 QB 428 (QBD); see ch 2 above, fn 108.

[87] In faulty non-treatment cases the risk posed by the doctor's conduct is that it denies the patient the chance he would otherwise have of benefiting from the omitted treatment.

> Mr Pain submitted that the casualty officer should have examined the deceased and had he done so he would have caused tests to be made which would have indicated the treatment required and that, since the defendants were at fault in these respects, therefore the onus of proof passed to the defendants to show that the appropriate treatment would have failed, and authorities were cited to me. I find myself unable to accept that argument, and I am of the view that the onus of proof remains upon the plaintiff.[88]

In reaching this conclusion Nield J referred in particular to *Bonnington Castings Ltd v Wardlaw*, where the House of Lords had reiterated that the general burden of proving causation remains on the claimant.[89]

In fact, in the years since *Barnett* the House of Lords has relaxed the law in this regard in certain cases outside the medical negligence field. A well-known decision is that of *McGhee v National Coal Board*, where the claimant sued his employer for the dermatitis he contracted following exposure to brick dust at his workplace. Such exposure was not itself negligent, but the defendant had negligently added to it (and hence to the risk of injury) by failing to provide adequate washing facilities. On these facts—and given the impossibility of telling if the washing facilities would have prevented the dermatitis—the House of Lords put the onus on the employer to show that the additional exposure had *not* played a causative role.[90] More recently, in *Fairchild v Glenhaven Funeral Services*, the House of Lords permitted a similar reversal of the burden of proof in respect of a multiple-tortfeasor problem (where it was unclear which of several, equally negligent defendants had caused the claimant's injury).[91]

Nevertheless, in *Wilsher v Essex Area Health Authority*,[92] the House of Lords emphatically denied the applicability of this approach to a medical negligence claim. In that case the claimant was a baby, who suffered retrolental fibroplasia (RLF) and became virtually blind, following treatment in the defendant's post-natal unit. It was established that, due to a breach of duty by hospital staff, he had been over-saturated with oxygen during the first weeks of his life.[93] However, whilst this might, according to some of the evidence, have caused the RLF, there were four other natural conditions (stemming from the claimant's prematurity), which could equally have been responsible. On these facts, a majority of the Court of Appeal had decided (following the *McGhee* decision) that a reversal of the burden of proof should operate to assist the claimant. The House of Lords disagreed. In his speech (with which the rest of the House concurred), Lord Bridge instead approved the dissenting judgment of Browne-Wilkinson V-C in the Court of Appeal that the instant case was distinguishable:

[88] *Barnett v Chelsea and Kensington Hospital Management Committee* [1969] 1 QB 428 (QBD) 438.

[89] *Bonnington Castings Ltd v Wardlaw* [1956] AC 613 (HL).

[90] *McGhee v National Coal Board* [1972] 3 All ER 1008 (HL).

[91] *Fairchild v Glenhaven Funeral Services* [2002] 3 WLR 89 (HL). There the claimant, who suffered from asbestos-related mesothelimia, had worked for several firms, each which had exposed him to asbestos; it was unclear when he had inhaled the 'fatal fibre'.

[92] *Wilsher v Essex Area Health Authority* [1988] AC 1074 (HL).

[93] This aspect of the case is discussed in ch 2 above, fn 37 ff.

> The position, to my mind, is wholly different from that in *McGhee*, where there was only one candidate (brick dust) which could have caused the dermatitis, and the failure to take a precaution against brick dust causing dermatitis was followed by dermatitis caused by brick dust. [By contrast, the] failure to take preventive measures against one out of five possible causes is no evidence as to which of those five caused the injury.[94]

In its subsequent decision in the *Fairchild v Glenhaven* case, the House of Lords—while doubtful of certain aspects of the reasoning in *Wilsher*—took the opportunity to affirm the correctness of the outcome in relation to a medical negligence action. In his speech, Lord Hoffmann adverted to policy considerations as a powerful factor militating against a reversal of the burden of proof in such cases:

> It is true that actions for clinical negligence notoriously give rise to difficult questions of causation. But . . . the political and economic arguments involved in the massive increase in the liability of the National Health Service which would have been a consequence of the broad rule favoured by the Court of Appeal in *Wilsher's* case are far more complicated than the reasons given [in *McGhee*] for imposing liability upon an employer who has failed to take simple precautions.[95]

(ii) The Rejection of Claims for 'Loss of Chance'

As we have just seen, the effect of the *Wilsher* decision is to deny recovery in treatment malpractice cases, even when it is clear that the doctor's mistake created a significant additional risk to the patient. At the same time, a feature of cases like *Wilsher* (where faulty treatment adds to the risks in play) is that it is not normally possible to quantify the risks with any precision. This is because such accidents are usually the exception to the norm of proper treatment.[96] Rather the most that can be said—and what the balance of probabilities standard invites the court to say—is that the risk from the doctor's error remains a less (or sometimes more) likely explanation for the patient's injury than some alternative source of risk for which he was not responsible.

Nonetheless, in other cases evidence will be available measuring fairly precisely the risk that the breach of duty presented to the patient's prospects. In particular, this is true in misdiagnosis cases, where the breach consists of an omission (the failure to provide appropriate and/or timely treatment). The evidence takes the form of class statistics compiled in relation to other patients with a similar medical condition to the claimant, who *were* given the proper treatment. The statistics

[94] *Wilsher v Essex Area Health Authority* [1988] AC 1074 (HL) 1090–91.

[95] *Fairchild v Glenhaven Funeral Services* [2002] 3 WLR 89 (HL) para 69. See also the recent mesothelimia case of *Barker v Corus Ltd* [2006] UKHL 20. There Lord Walker remarked (para 114) that: 'it would be a very long step indeed, which I would not contemplate, to extend an analysis based on 'increase in risk' . . . to a case like *Wilsher* . . . Such an extension would lead to great uncertainty in a large number of clinical negligence cases'. See also Lord Hoffmann (para 5); and Lord Scott (para 64).

[96] Thus in *Wilsher* there were no statistics showing the relative risk of a premature baby (with the claimant's natural ailments) suffering from RLF with and without the administration of excess oxygen.

record the percentage of patients who responded to the treatment (and hence avoided injury), as opposed to those who went on to suffer the injury anyway. In such situations the question arises whether the misdiagnosed patient may make use of such evidence and sue for proportionate damages based on the statistical chance he lost, including where this was below 50 per cent.[97]

The courts first had occasion to consider a treatment malpractice claim framed in these terms, ie as a so-called action for 'loss of chance', in *Hotson v East Berkshire Health Authority*.[98] In that case a schoolboy attended the defendant's casualty department after falling from a tree and injuring his hip. The defendant failed, in breach of duty, to carry out an X-ray and by the time the extent of the injury was discovered necrosis had set in, making permanent disability unavoidable. The medical evidence as to causation was to the effect that, with immediate diagnosis, 25 per cent of patients with that injury could be successfully treated while the remaining 75 per cent would suffer the disability anyway.

On these facts the High Court accepted the claimant's claim in respect of the lost 25 per cent chance that proper treatment would have prevented his disability, and awarded him proportionate recovery.[99] This approach was subsequently upheld by the Court of Appeal, Sir John Donaldson MR commenting:

> As a matter of common sense, it is unjust that there should be no liability for failure to treat a patient, simply because the chances of a successful cure by that treatment were less than 50 per cent. Nor, by the same token, can it be just that if the chances of a successful cure only marginally exceed 50 per cent, the doctor or his employer should be liable to the same extent as if the treatment could be guaranteed to cure.[100]

However, the House of Lords unanimously allowed the health authority's appeal and reiterated the need for medical negligence claimants to prove causation of the injury itself on an all-or-nothing basis, in accordance with the balance of probabilities. In his speech Lord Bridge stated:

> This was a conflict, like any other about some relevant past event, which the judge could not avoid resolving on a balance of probabilities . . . But the judge's findings of fact . . . are unmistakably to the effect that on a balance of probabilities the injury caused by the plaintiff's fall left insufficient blood vessels intact to keep the epiphysis alive. This amounts to a finding of fact that the fall was the sole cause of the avascular necrosis.[101]

More recently, in *Gregg v Scott*,[102] the second such case to reach the House of Lords, the claimant sued for his reduced chance of a cure for cancer following a negligent misdiagnosis. He had consulted the defendant doctor about a lump under his arm, but the doctor failed to refer him to hospital for tests and it was not

[97] Ie such that he cannot show, on the balance of probabilities, that he would have achieved a cure.
[98] *Hotson v East Berkshire Health Authority* [1987] 1 AC 750 (HL).
[99] The full injury to the hip was valued at £46,000. Accordingly the High Court awarded the claimant damages of £11,500 for the lost chance.
[100] *Hotson v East Berkshire Health Authority* [1987] AC 750 (CA) 759–60.
[101] *Ibid*, (HL) 782.
[102] *Gregg v Scott* [2005] UKHL 2.

until a year later that non-Hodgkin's lymphoma was diagnosed. The effect of this delay was that the cancer had spread and, statistically, the claimant's chance of a 'cure' (defined medically as 10-year disease-free survival) had fallen from 42 to 25 per cent. The claimant subsequently underwent a number of painful and distressing treatments, though at the time of the final hearing—nearly 10 years after the original misdiagnosis—was still alive.[103]

For his part, Lord Nicholls would have allowed the claim. His Lordship commented in his speech as follows:

> What the patient loses depends, of course, on the circumstances of the individual case. No doubt in some cases medical opinion will be that, given his pre-existing condition, the patient lost nothing by the delay in treatment because he never had any realistic prospect of recovery... In other cases medical opinion may be that the patient lost everything . . . But there are also many cases . . . where medical opinion will be that, given prompt and appropriate treatment, the outcome was uncertain but the patient's prospects of recovery were appreciable, sometimes exceeding 50 per cent, sometimes not ... Given this uncertainty of outcome, the appropriate characterisation of a patient's loss in this type of case must surely be that it comprises the loss of the chance of a favourable outcome, rather than the loss of the outcome itself. Justice so requires, because this matches medical reality.[104]

However, a majority of their Lordships disagreed. In his speech, Lord Hoffmann, adverted (as he had in *Fairchild v Glenhaven Funeral Services*) to the possible negative resource implications of permitting such claims:

> [A] wholesale adoption of possible rather than probable causation as the criterion of liability would be so radical a change in our law as to amount to a legislative act. It would have enormous consequences for insurance companies and the National Health Service.[105]

By contrast the other members of majority, Lord Phillips and Baroness Hale, appear to have been swayed principally by the particular complexities of the case at hand. Above all, this arose from the fact that the damage for which the patient was claiming the lost (or more precisely, *reduced*) chance, namely the lack of a 'cure', had not accrued at the time of the action, and quite possibly would not do so. As Lord Phillips noted,

> The likelihood seems to be that Dr Scott's negligence has not prevented Mr Gregg's cure, but has made that cure more painful.[106]

His Lordship concluded:

> The complications of this case have persuaded me that it is not a suitable vehicle for introducing into the law of clinical negligence the right to recover damages for the loss

[103] As to the significance of this point, see the text at n 114 ff below.

[104] *Gregg v Scott* [2005] UKHL 2, paras 21 ff.

[105] *Ibid*, para 90.

[106] *Gregg v Scott* (n 104 above) para 190. As Baroness Hale noted (at paras 206 ff), if the claimant had claimed damages for the more distressing and painful treatment required, that part of his claim would have succeeded.

> of a chance of a cure . . . Where medical treatment has resulted in an adverse outcome and negligence has increased the chance of that outcome, there may be a case for permitting a recovery of damages that is proportionate to the increase in the chance of the adverse outcome. That is not a case that has been made out on the present appeal.[107]

The decision in *Hotson*, and now in *Gregg*, has given rise to a vast academic literature.[108] Unsurprisingly given the complexity of the issues, commentators have been divided as to the merits of recognising loss of chance actions. Particular concerns, which feature also in the judgments of the House of Lords, relate to the proper meaning to be attached to the statistics used, and how far—if proportionate recovery were allowed—this is reconcilable with the traditional need for a 'but for' causal link between fault and injury. There is also the fear that allowing recovery for loss of chance in medical negligence cases could lead to a tide of speculative litigation against the NHS, with adverse resource implications.

Within the space available here it must suffice to repeat the author's view that such concerns have been exaggerated, and that loss of chance claims following medical misdiagnoses should be allowed.[109] As noted earlier, the statistics at issue are derived empirically by reference to how patients with the claimant's condition generally fare (ie with the proper treatment). It is true that this does not offer certainty in a particular case. As Lord Nicholls noted in his dissenting speech in *Gregg v Scott*,

> [s]tatistics record retrospectively what happened to other patients in more or less comparable situations . . . They are general in nature. The different way other patients responded in a similar position says nothing about how the claimant would have responded.[110]

Nonetheless, the crucial point is that the traditional balance of probabilities test is no different. In finding that a given patient's condition was *probably* untreatable, the court also draws upon past experience as to how other patients with a similar condition responded to treatment (ie that the majority did not benefit). It does not tell us that the *claimant* individually could not have been helped: he might have been one of the (perhaps substantial) minority whose condition would have responded. In this context, the use of statistics providing an accurate measure of the opportunity lost as a precursor to an award of proportionate damages appears significantly fairer than the present 'all or nothing' approach.[111]

[107] *Gregg v Scott* (n 104 above) para 190.

[108] For an overview see H Luntz, 'Loss of Chance' in I Freckleton and D Mendelson (eds), *Causation in Law and Medicine* (Aldershot, Ashgate, 2002) 152; for a comparative treatment by a German author, see M Kasche, *Verlust von Heilungschancen—eine rechtsvergleichende Untersuchung* (Frankfurt am Main, Peter Lang, 1999).

[109] See further M Stauch, 'Causation, Risk and Loss of Chance in Medical Negligence' (1997) 17 *Oxford Journal of Legal Studies* 205.

[110] *Gregg v Scott* [2005] UKHL 2, para 28.

[111] It is true that the statistical evidence may be complex or disputed. Nonetheless, this does not raise any special difficulty: indeed in calculating damages at the quantum stage, the courts habitually resolve disputes of this kind (eg in assessing the likelihood that a claimant will later develop arthritis in his injured leg).

Similarly, the fear that allowing claims for proportionate recovery would undermine general principles of causation in personal injury cases is not justified. In the first place, such claims, which depend on the availability of empirical statistical evidence, would normally be confined to medical misdiagnosis cases. As discussed above, it is much less likely that such evidence will be at hand where the doctor's mistake actively added to the risks to the patient.[112] Secondly, it is important to reiterate that—in common with other proof modifications considered in this chapter—loss of chance claims arise as a response to factual uncertainty (ie in default of individuating evidence as to what would have happened in the particular case). In this regard, the relevant rules operate on a different plane to the substantive law elements, including 'but for' causation.[113]

Thus, following on from the above, it would remain necessary for the (substantive law) requirement of *actual* injury to the claimant to be satisfied—these cases are not about treating exposure to risk per se as a recoverable form of injury.[114] This, it is submitted, was the key difficulty with *Gregg v Scott*, where the claimant's injury (the lost benefit of a cure) had not yet occurred, and it was uncertain whether it would do so in the future. In this regard, Lord Phillips was, with respect, correct to assert that the case was not a suitable one for recognising loss of chance in medical negligence law. By contrast, in the most scenarios of this type—such as in *Hotson*—this problem does not arise.

Finally, as to the concern that permitting loss of chance claims could lead to a flood of additional litigation against the NHS, we should be clear that, in terms of overall compensation, no more would be paid out in faulty diagnosis claims than before. This is because, logically, the use of statistics as a basis for proportionate recovery 'must cut both ways'.[115] Thus a patient who had, say, a 60 per cent chance of benefiting from wrongfully omitted treatment should only receive 60 per cent of damages in respect of his injury, not 100 per cent as at present.[116] It remains true that the total number of claims may increase, as patients will no longer be deterred, as at present, from litigating in cases where their prospects of successful treatment

[112] See n 96 above.

[113] Eg consider a patient who goes deaf following the faulty treatment of an ear infection, where the evidence is that 30 % of patients avoid deafness if properly treated. Here, if recovery for 'loss of chance' were permitted, the patient would recover 30 % of the damages payable for deafness. However, suppose next that the fog of scientific uncertainty lifts: new evidence shows conclusively that, had he been treated, *this* patient would have escaped deafness. No one would now be inclined to award damages by percentages; we should pay out full damages.

[114] It has occasionally been mooted that recovery should be based on risk exposure alone: see GO Robinson, 'Probabilistic Causation and Compensation for Tortious Risk' (1985) 14 *Journal of Legal Studies* 779; however, this would be a radical departure from normal principles of private law based upon corrective justice: see EJ Weinrib, *The Idea of Private Law* (Cambridge MA, Harvard University Press, 1995) 155 ff.

[115] *Gregg v Scott* [2005] UKHL 2, para 225 (Baroness Hale); her Ladyship remained sceptical as to the propriety of such discounting, but the reason for this is, with respect, not entirely clear.

[116] In a few first instance cases, courts have engaged in this type of discounting: see *Clark v MacLennan* [1983] 1 All ER 416 (QBD); *Bagley v North Hertfordshire Health Authority* (1986) 136 NLJ 1014 (QBD); *Judge v Huntingdon Health Authority* (1995) 6 Med LR 223 (QBD).

were low. Arguably, to guard against a proliferation of low-value actions, the law (in a pragmatic vein) should demand that the chance lost was a substantial one.[117]

(b) The Position in Germany

As discussed previously, in Germany the underlying effect of the law of civil evidence is that the claimant must satisfy the burden of proof as to factual causation to the strict standard of 'judicial conviction'.[118] It scarcely needs to be said—given the difficulties already noted in relation to the 'balance of probabilities' standard in England—that if this approach were adhered to rigidly the patient would fail in the large majority of cases. This will include situations where the probability that the patient would have escaped injury but for the doctor's fault was quite high. Indeed in one decision the BGH upheld the view of the lower courts that causation had not been sufficiently established in a non-diagnosis case, notwithstanding expert testimony that there had been a 70 per cent chance that prompt treatment would have prevented the injury.[119]

Importantly, though, as with the breach of duty issue, the German courts have developed special proof concessions to help patients over the causation hurdle.[120] Of greatest significance in this regard is the full reversal of proof that operates where the doctor committed a 'gross' breach of duty. To start with, though, we consider two other modifications deployed sometimes, namely the relaxations of proof with regard to 'secondary harm' and where there was a failure to carry out appropriate diagnostic tests.

(i) Proof Relaxations in Cases of 'Secondary Harm'

As we have seen, the general strict standard of proof in German private law is contained in § 286 ZPO. However, the ZPO also provides on occasion for a lower standard of so-called 'free-' as opposed to 'strict-' proof to apply. In particular, under § 287 ZPO, the court may sometimes treat a fact (which attains a certain threshold of plausibility) as proven, without strictly being convinced of it—ie a standard more akin to the 'balance of probabilities'. One area where this standard operates is in relation to quantum, ie in valuing what a given injury has cost the claimant in financial terns (eg by having to travel to hospital for treatment, miss

[117] In *Hotson*, the lower courts would have restricted loss of chance claims in this way. See also the US case of *Herskovits v Group Health Cooperative of Puget Sound* (1983) 664 P 2d 474.

[118] Under § 286 ZPO.

[119] BGH, 6 October 1998, NJW 1999, 860. In the event, the BGH applied a proof modification to assist the patient on the basis of the doctor's failure to conduct a proper diagnostic test: see n 135 below.

[120] In one type of case a modification of the proof rules has been specifically allowed for in the Civil Code, namely where it is unclear in multiple-defendant cases, who caused the claimant's injury—ie the type of situation that arose in the English *Fairchild* case (see n 91 above). Here § 830 I BGB provides that each defendant will be jointly and severally liable unless they can prove the non-causality of their conduct. Nonetheless, this rule is of limited relevance in the medical malpractice context.

days off work, etc).[121] However, the courts have also extended it to an aspect of the causation inquiry. In particular, as we saw in chapter two, they have evolved a distinction between 'primary' (*haftungsbegründende*) and 'secondary' (*haftungsausfüllende*) causation of harm.[122] Whereas the first relates to initial injury to the claimant (ie the infringement of one of his protected interests under § 823 I BGB), the second concerns the link between such injury and further injury that occurs as its consequence. In their case law, the courts have held that the latter link is subject merely to proof in accordance with § 287 ZPO.

An example, in the treatment malpractice context, is provided by a BGH judgment from 1962 in respect of a patient who suffered an allergic reaction to skin-cream negligently prescribed by the defendant. She subsequently developed a bone marrow disorder, which led to her death. The court held that the alleged link between the allergic reaction and the bone marrow disorder concerned secondary harm, and thus fell to be decided according to the lower standard of proof.[123] In another case a patient developed a skin reaction due to the contamination of disinfectant used in her caesarian section. She later suffered toxic shock syndrome, and kidney failure, necessitating treatment with powerful antibiotic drugs, and was left with serious sensory impairments. For its part, the hospital argued that the cause of the toxic shock was a different, naturally occurring infection. Here the court held that the (uncontested) link between the disinfectant and the skin reaction was the primary harm, and accordingly the connection between this and the later complications required proof only to the standard under §287 ZPO.[124] In other cases, where patients have been injected with the wrong drug, the courts have located the primary harm in the penetration of the patient's skin by the needle.[125]

As discussed in chapter two, the distinction between 'primary' and 'secondary' causation of harm is not free from conceptual difficulty. Moreover, its effect may be regarded as fortuitous. The standard of proof will depend on whether the patient can point to some earlier invasion of his interests by the doctor, which the court is prepared to classify as primary. Sometimes there may be significant ambiguity as to this, eg where the claim relates to a negligent omission by the doctor.[126] However that may be, it has been argued by Katzenmeier that the primary-secondary harm distinction (and concomitant use of § 287 ZPO) is now of declining significance in treatment malpractice cases.[127] Generally, where the

[121] Graf, *Die Beweislast bei Behandlungsfehlern im Arzthaftungsprozess* (n 5 above) 38; D Giesen, *Arzthaftung*, 4th edn (Tübingen, Mohr, 1995) para 401.

[122] See ch 2 pt III 1 (b).

[123] BGH, 13 November 1962, VersR 1963, 67.

[124] BGH, 9 May 1978, NJW 1978, 1683.

[125] H Helbron, *Entwicklungen und Fehlentwicklungen im Arzthaftungsrecht* (Munich, Utz, 2001) 27.

[126] For a case where the BGH held that the progress of the patient's tuberculosis following initial misdiagnosis was primary harm, and the side-effects allegedly flowing from the drug treatment later given for it secondary, see BGH, 26 June 1988, NJW 1988, 2948.

[127] Katzenmeier, *Arzthaftung* (n 21 above) 429.

circumstances are apt, the patient is likely to prefer to use other, more attractive proof concessions that have increased in importance in the meantime.[128]

(ii) Proof Relaxations in Misdiagnosis Cases

As suggested previously, in cases where a doctor's faulty conduct takes a passive form—eg he fails, following a misdiagnosis, to provide the treatment he ought to have—causation often poses particular difficulties of proof. The doctor may argue that the patient's illness could not have been treated in any event. In some such cases, the patient's difficulties may also be exacerbated by uncertainty as to the primary facts. One situation is where the doctor fails to preserve the test results that served as the basis of the course of treatment he provided (*Verletzung der Befundsicherungspflicht*). On other occasions he may have failed to carry out appropriate diagnostic tests in the first place (*Verletzung der Befunderhebungspflicht*).

As we saw earlier,[129] in the former type of case the German courts have applied a relaxation of proof requirements in relation to the breach of duty question, by presuming, in cases where this appears 'sufficiently likely', that the lost test revealed a condition to which the doctor ought to have reacted. Similarly, in cases where no test was carried out (or at any rate cannot be shown to have been[130]) the doctor's breach will consist precisely in that omission. Nevertheless, in both situations, further facts vital to showing causation may remain impossible to establish. The court is faced with a series of speculative and/or hypothetical questions: what did the test show (or what would it have shown) about the patient's illness, what would a careful doctor have done in response, and how far would the treatment have helped?

In cases of this type, the BGH was for a time prepared to relax the standard of proof in relation to causation as well as breach. Thus in a 1987 case, the doctor was found to have negligently failed to perform a follow-up lung X-ray on a patient, whom he diagnosed with bronchial-pneumonia (but who in fact had tuberculosis).[131] The Court held that at this point, the further questions were: first, would the omitted X-ray *probably* have shown up something requiring a reaction by the doctor? And, secondly, would such reaction *probably* have availed the patient? These were matters within the discretion of the trial judge to be decided on a case-by-case basis.[132] However, in its case law since 1996, the BGH has repudiated this approach. The reason is that a claimant in respect of whom the original test was never carried out (or was, but the result lost) should not stand better than one for whom the result of the test is to hand, and where the doctor subsequently failed to

[128] In particular the full reversal of proof of causation allowed in cases of gross treatment errors: see pt III 3 (b) (iii) below.

[129] See the discussion in pt III 1 (b) above.

[130] As noted above, absent independent evidence that the test took place, the presumption will be that it was omitted.

[131] BGH, 3 February 1987, NJW, 1987, 1482.

[132] *Ibid*, 1484; see also BGH, 14 December 1993, NJW 1994, 1596.

offer the appropriate treatment. Instead, the courts will now only presume that the test would have shown something that the doctor ought to have reacted to, not that their response would have been effective.[133]

At this point the burden of proof (in accordance with the strict standard under §286 ZPO) will ordinarily be on the claimant. However, there is an exception to the extent that the doctor's failure to react to the missing or omitted diagnostic test amounted (or would have amounted) to gross negligence. Here, in accordance with the general reversal of proof of causation allowed in cases of gross error—to be discussed shortly—it will be for the doctor to prove that the appropriate response would not have helped the patient.[134] Thus in one case the doctor negligently failed to carry out a blood test on a patient with pains in the kidney region following a road accident, and who subsequently suffered kidney failure. The BGH, in putting the burden of proof on the doctor to show that treatment (following such a test) would not have prevented this outcome, stated:

> As this [court] has held in its more recent case law, the doctor's breach of his duty to conduct and preserve diagnostic tests gives rise, in the first instance, only to a presumption—in cases where this appears sufficiently likely—that the test result would have required a reaction on his part. In addition, though, the patient may sometimes also obtain a proof dispensation in relation to the causation issue, namely if in the particular circumstances it is possible at the same time to discern a gross treatment error. This will be the case where it is sufficiently likely that the test result in question would have revealed such a clear and grave state of affairs, that the doctor's failure to recognise this would amount to a fundamental error.[135]

As will be apparent, in such cases the gross negligence by the doctor remains in the realms of the hypothetical—a point whose artificiality has drawn criticism. In particular, it appears somewhat paradoxical to classify the hypothetical failure to react to a test as gross negligence where the prior failure to perform it was only ordinarily negligent.[136]

(iii) Reversals of Proof in Cases of 'Gross' Treatment Errors

As has already been hinted, the most significant development in the proof of treatment malpractice cases has occurred with respect to *gross* treatment errors (*grobe Behandlungsfehler*) by the doctor/hospital. Indeed, this comprises one of the most original and defining features of German medical malpractice law overall. The courts have here evolved rules to shift the risk of inability to prove causation from the patient to the doctor. In practice this development (allowing for a full reversal

[133] BGH, 13 February 1996, NJW 1996, 1589; BGH, 13 January 1998, NJW 1998, 1780.

[134] BGH, 13 January 1998, NJW 1998, 1780; BGH, 27 April 2004, NJW 2004, 2011.

[135] BGH, 6 October 1998, NJW 1999, 860 (861).

[136] Helbron, *Entwicklungen und Fehlentwicklungen im Arzthaftungsrecht* (n 125 above) 59 ff; S Heidelk, *Gesundheitsverletzung und Gesundheitsschaden: Ärztliche Verantwortung im Kontext des § 280 Abs. 1 BGB* (Berlin, Duncker & Humblot, 2005) 145. A simpler approach would be to find gross negligence in the failure to conduct the test, triggering the proof reversal from the outset.

of the burden of proof) has eclipsed the relaxations on causation discussed in (i)–(ii) above.[137]

The idea that, as regards an especially serious breach of duty, the onus to disprove causation might be put on the doctor originally surfaced in the late jurisprudence of the Imperial Court (*Reichsgericht*).[138] To begin with the approach was limited to situations involving subjective fault on the doctor's part, ie where he 'knowingly or recklessly' exposed his patient to a risk, which may have materialised and caused the injury.[139] Nonetheless, by the close of the 1950s the trigger for the reversal had become instead the objective presence of gross fault.[140] This would be satisfied if the doctor had 'seriously flouted the normal rules of medical practice, of which he must be taken to be aware'.[141]

In a leading decision from the 1980s, the BGH expressed the matter in the following terms:

> A mistake that, while amounting to a breach of duty, is of the type that may on occasion befall even a careful and conscientious doctor, is not sufficient; rather the mistake, while not necessarily subjectively inexcusable—eg if attributable to special factors affecting the particular doctor—must be one that, in terms of the training and qualifications objectively required of doctors, is no longer comprehensible—ie is a mistake of the sort that a doctor simply ought not to make.[142]

At the same time, it is recognised that the factors which make an error 'gross' will vary with the circumstances, and hence no conclusive or exhaustive definition of such an error is available.[143] In this context, the assessment of the medical experts will be of vital importance. A judge is not allowed to find that an error was 'gross' where the experts are divided or equivocal as to whether the mistake even amounted to ordinary negligence.[144] At the same time, though, the court should have regard to the overall history of treatment provided to the patient, and may treat a series of smaller errors, none of which individually could be considered gross, as having cumulatively attained this status.[145]

It appears that gross errors are just as likely to take a positive or negative form—ie they may be found not only in the active provision of faulty therapy, but also in misdiagnosis cases. As regards the latter, though, the BGH has counselled a measure of caution where the misinterpretation of test results is at issue. Given the ambiguity with which illnesses may present themselves, a court should only find

[137] Katzenmeier, *Arzthaftung* (n 21 above) 439; Giesen, *Arzthaftung* (n 121 above) para 174.

[138] RG, 17 May 1943, RGZ 171, 168. For a detailed account of the development of the case law in this area, see Helbron, *Entwicklungen und Fehlentwicklungen im Arzthaftungsrecht* (n 125 above) 23ff.

[139] BGH, 21 December 1955, VersR 1956, 499.

[140] BGH, 28 April 1959, VersR 1959, 598; BGH, 26 June 1962, VersR 1962, 960.

[141] BGH, 11 June 1968, NJW 1968, 2291 (2293); see also BGH, 16 June 1981, NJW 1981, 2513.

[142] BGH, 10 May 1983, NJW 1983, 2080 (2081).

[143] Laufs and Uhlenbruck, *Handbuch des Arztrechts* (n 5 above) § 110, para 5; Katzenmeier, *Arzthaftung* (n 21 above) 441ff.

[144] BGH, 27 January 1998, NJW 1998, 1782; BGH, 3 July 2001, NJW 2001, 2795.

[145] BGH, 29 May 2001, NJW 2001, 2792.

gross fault if there was a 'fundamental error'.[146] Less problematic (and more common) is such a finding following the doctor's failure to perform necessary diagnostic tests in the first place. Another area where gross errors are quite often found is with respect to errors at an institutional level.[147] For example, in one case the claimant, who was pregnant with twins, lost her second child following a delay in procuring delivery. The overnight CTG-monitoring of her pregnancy had been entrusted to an ordinary staff nurse and the urgency of her situation had not been recognised until it was too late. Here the court held that the deployment by the hospital of a non-specialist nurse had been grossly negligent in the context of a high-risk pregnancy such as the claimant's. Accordingly, the onus shifted to the hospital to prove that earlier delivery would not have saved the child.[148]

Importantly, however, besides the 'gross' nature of the error, there are two further conditions that need to be satisfied for the reversal of the burden of proof to operate. In the first place, the error must be one that is known to create a non-negligible risk of the injury in suit.[149] Thus, in a 1994 decision the BGH refused to countenance a reversal where the claimant was born severely premature (and with associated disabilities) after a doctor failed to administer drugs to try and forestall his mother's premature labour. Though such failure was grossly negligent, the overwhelming likelihood was that the birth would have been delayed by at most a few days (which would have made no appreciable difference to his disabilities).[150]

In certain decisions in the past the BGH went further by suggesting that the trial judge retained a general discretion to deny a formal reversal, to take account of the improbability that the error caused the harm. Rather he could apply a relaxation of proof short of this, as the equity of the case demanded. In this context, the court used to refer to 'relaxations up to and including full reversal of proof' (*Beweiserleichterungen bis zur Umkehr der Beweislast*).[151] However, it was never clear what form such relaxations might take,[152] and the BGH has now renounced this approach. Instead, as established in a decision from 2004, where the doctor's gross negligence created or added a more than minimal risk of the harm, the trial judge should apply a full reversal of the burden of proof.[153] The case in question concerned a failure to identify the claimant's fractured pelvis following a

[146] BGH, 23 March 1993, NJW 1993, 2375; BGH, 4 October 1994, NJW 1995, 778; E Steffen and B Pauge, *Arzthaftungsrecht—neue Entwicklungslinien der BGH-Rechtsprechung*, 10th edn (Cologne, RWS Kommunikationsforum, 2006) para 524.

[147] See Graf, *Die Beweislast bei Behandlungsfehlern im Arzthaftungsprozess* (n 5 above) 107 ff.

[148] BGH, 16 April 1996, NJW 1996, 2429.

[149] BGH, 12 March 1968, NJW 1968, 1185; BGH, 3 December 1985, NJW 1986, 1540. Thus in a case with facts such as in *Kay v Ayrshire and Arran Health Board* (see n 85 above) the burden would not be shifted.

[150] BGH, 4 October 1994, NJW 1995, 778. In such a case, it might equally be said that the doctor/hospital has succeeded in rebutting the presumption of causation.

[151] BGH, 21 September 1982, NJW 1983, 333; BGH, 28 June 1988, NJW 1988, 2949; BGH, 1 October 1996, NJW 1997, 796; Graf, *Die Beweislast bei Behandlungsfehlern im Arzthaftungsprozess* (n 5 above) 117 ff.

[152] Katzenmeier, *Arzthaftung* (n 21 above) 467 ff; Graf, *Die Beweislast bei Behandlungsfehlern im Arzthaftungsprozess* (n 5 above) 117.

[153] BGH, 27 April 2004, NJW 2004, 2011.

motorcycle accident. Here a reversal of proof was sanctioned (leading to a finding for the claimant) even though, according to the experts, it was only 10 per cent likely that proper treatment would have prevented her subsequent disability.

The second additional requirement for the burden of proof of causation to be reversed is that the doctor's conduct was *grossly* faulty with regard to the risk of the type of harm that actually occurred. In effect, a limitation based on '*Schutzzweck*' will apply. As discussed in chapter two, this restricts the application of a given rule (here that mandating a reversal of proof) by having regard to its protective purpose.[154] Thus the BGH refused in one case to sanction a reversal where the patient, who was discharged early from hospital after a heart-examination with a catheter, subsequently died of septicaemia. Although his discharge had been grossly negligent in virtue of certain other risks (which did not materialise), it was not so in relation to the remote chance of septicaemia. The court commented:

> The proof reversal finds its justification in the special difficulty of establishing a connection between a doctor's act or omission and its effect on the human organism in individual cases; here it appears equitable to relieve the patient of the at times insuperable burden of proof, insofar as the doctor committed a gross treatment error with the general propensity to cause the injury the patient suffered. However, these equitable considerations do not apply when it is clear that the risk, which it was grossly culpable for the doctor to run, was not the cause of injury; the possible causality of another risk bound up in the same treatment decision is immaterial where the latter risk involved merely ordinary negligence.[155]

Accordingly, the claimant (the deceased's widow) retained the burden of proving that, had he remained in hospital, the man would have been saved.

It follows too that the reversal of the burden proof will generally only apply to 'primary' harm allegedly resulting from the error, not 'secondary' (or ulterior) harm that is claimed to be its further consequence.[156] This is illustrated by the case referred to earlier, where—through gross organisational negligence—a contaminated disinfectant was used on the patient during her caesarian, which caused a skin reaction. That part of her claim relating to her kidney failure and lasting sensory disabilities (the alleged further consequences of the reaction and the drugs used to treat it), remained for her to prove.[157] However, where the further harm is closely associated with the initial harm, ie is a typical consequence of the latter, the proof reversal will extend to it.[158] A full reversal will also operate in 'eggshell skull' and multiple risk cases. Here (where the injury is a single, non-divisible event) it is immaterial that, besides the risk presented by the doctor's gross negligence, the

[154] See ch 2 pt III 2 (b).

[155] BGH, 16 June 1981, NJW 1981, 2513 (2514).

[156] BGH, 26 October 1993, NJW 1994, 801. Ie where the injury is divisible into different parts, the proof reversal will be limited to the part within the risk created by the grossly negligent aspect of the treatment.

[157] BGH, 9 May 1978, NJW 1978, 1683, discussed at n 124, above. As noted there, the proof in question only needed to be brought to the lower standard under § 287 ZPO.

[158] BGH, 28 June 1988, NJW 1988, 2948.

injury would not have occurred but for the presence of other unusual risk factors in the background causal set.[159]

As will be evident from the above discussion, the case law in this area is highly complex. At the same time, notwithstanding its longevity (stretching back over 60 years) it remains controversial, and in the view of many commentators, rests upon unsatisfactory foundations. Thus the courts have been criticised for an unwarranted departure from the normal civil proof rules provided for by the legislature, thereby trespassing on the latter's prerogative.[160] Moreover, a theoretical rationale for the reversal of proof requirements remains elusive. In particular, the justification sometimes ventured by the courts, namely that gross treatment errors are especially prone to create difficulties in proving causation, is perceived as tenuous. It is not clear how there could be a connection of this kind.[161] Instead, the true impulse behind the rule would seem to be one of 'practical justice', penalising the doctor for an especially flagrant error and the serious disappointment to the patient's expectations.[162] Further difficulty arises from the fluidity of the concept of a 'gross' error, especially as the courts have eschewed a fixed definition. Thus, it is hard to predict at the time of bringing proceedings whether the court will so qualify the doctor's conduct.[163] Since in practice the outcome of the proceedings will often turn on such a finding, this may well deter the patient from bringing proceedings. Nor, lastly, should the effect—in cases where the finding is made—on the doctor's professional reputation be forgotten (stigmatising his conduct as 'incomprehensible').[164]

Despite these misgivings, most commentators accept the courts' approach as a pragmatic response to the patient's proof difficulties, recognising that without it he would usually lose his case on causation and be sent away empty-handed.[165] In passing, it may be noted that one effect of it has been to pre-empt interest in allowing proportionate recovery for 'loss of chance'.[166] At any rate, this possibility has

[159] BGH, 1 October 1996, NJW 1997, 796; BGH, 27 January 1998, NJW 1998, 1782; BGH, 12 June 2000, VersR 2000, 1282; Müller, 'Beweislast und Beweisführung im Arzthaftungsprozeß' (n 40 above) 3052.

[160] See Katzenmeier, *Arzthaftung* (n 21 above) 454 ff.

[161] As discussed earlier, the degree of causal uncertainty in a given case turns on the number and plausibility of competing explanations for the injury in question, and is beyond the defendant's influence.

[162] Katzenmeier, *Arzthaftung* (n 21 above) 466–7; Graf, *Die Beweislast bei Behandlungsfehlern im Arzthaftungsprozess* (n 5 above) 123.

[163] Graf, *Die Beweislast bei Behandlungsfehlern im Arzthaftungsprozess* (n 5 above) 124; Heidelk, *Gesundheitsverletzung und Gesundheitsschaden* (n 136 above) 149–50. Arguably, the assessment of conduct as *grossly* unreasonable is inherently more uncertain than that it was (merely) unreasonable. Whereas the latter turns on a finding that the defendant took an unjustified risk, the former seems to add a subjective element (expressing the court's dismay).

[164] P Hanau, 'Anmerkung zu BGH, 11 June 1968' NJW 1968, 2291; Heidelk, *Gesundheitsverletzung und Gesundheitsschaden* (n 136 above) 150.

[165] Katzenmeier, *Arzthaftung* (n 21 above) 459 ff; Helbron, *Entwicklungen und Fehlentwicklungen im Arzthaftungsrecht* (n 125 above) 34–5.

[166] By contrast, in Austria and Switzerland where (in the context of a similar overall approach to that in Germany) the reversal of proof in gross error cases approach does not operate, the courts have flirted with loss of chance: see Kasche, *Verlust von Heilungschancen* (n 108 above).

not figured in the case law, and while there has been some academic discussion this does not approach the intense debate on the subject in the common law. Commentators who have considered the question are (like their English counterparts) divided on the question of how far this approach would be workable or desirable within the overall system of civil proof.[167] We shall return to this issue below, towards the end of the comparative assessment part.

IV. Comparative Assessment

As we have seen in this chapter, the rules of proof in relation to treatment malpractice cases under English and German law show a considerable divergence. As discussed, this reflects a broader systemic difference in the approach taken to fact-finding in private litigation, which may be traced to specific historic factors (in particular the use of jury trials in the common law, but less so in the civil law system). Whilst the proof of the relevant facts is under both systems usually for the claimant, one of the most telling divergences is with respect to the higher standard of proof in German private law as opposed to under the common law.

Applied to the context of treatment malpractice, where proof is unusually difficult relative to other private law actions, this difference attains particular force. Indeed in Germany, the effect of the default rules (requiring a standard close to certainty) without more is that the patient's claim would usually fail for want of sufficient proof. By contrast under the common law, the patient's difficulties of proof have not presented themselves as an autonomous problem to the same extent. There is—in the context of the 'balance of probabilities' standard—a less pronounced distinction between what the law requires by way of substantive elements to ground a claim and the issue of whether these were historically present.

Against this backdrop, the English judiciary has been reluctant to assist the patient over his proof difficulties. This may be seen as consistent with its general concern, adverted to in chapter two, to keep litigation against the NHS within manageable bounds.[168] By contrast, in Germany the precariousness of the patient's situation has been acknowledged and the courts, encouraged by constitutional norms, have developed a series of special modifications as a 'corrective'. In effect, these operate as a secondary tier of rules over and above the substantive

[167] Katzenmeier, *Arzthaftung* (n 21 above) 519 ff, remains sceptical as does H Stoll 'Schadensersatz für verlorene Heilungschancen vor englischen Gerichten in rechtsvergleichender Sicht' in E Deutsch (ed), *Festschrift für Steffen* (Berlin, de Gruyter, 1995) 465. By contrast Kasche, *Verlust von Heilungschancen* (n 108 above) 261 ff, takes a favourable view; see also N Jansen, 'The Idea of a Lost Chance' (1999) 19 *Oxford Journal of Legal Studies* 271.

[168] Consider eg the following remark of Brooke LJ (responding to the plea of *res ipsa loquitur*) in *Ratcliffe v Plymouth and Torbay Health Authority* [1998] PIQR P170 (CA) P176: 'The courts would be doing the practice of medicine a considerable disservice if in such a case, because the patient has suffered a grievous out turn from a visit to hospital, a careful doctor is ordered to pay him compensation, as if he had been negligent'.

rules looked at in chapter two (albeit in practice the rules function as an amalgam). As noted, the decisive point distinguishing the two types of rules is that the secondary rules owe their existence to the evidential uncertainty at the level of establishing substantive elements.[169] At the same time, this has added considerably to the complexity of the German law. There is an on-going need to refer to the secondary rules to check if a presumption has been triggered, altering the normal disposition of proof as to a claim's substantive elements.

As we saw, the relevant proof modifications have been developed in the course of an elaborate case law and may help the patient with various aspects of his claim, including the gathering of the primary facts (ie inferences drawn from missing documentation) and the presumption of fault in cases where the patient's injury arose from a risk deemed to be within the doctor's control (the doctrine of 'fully-masterable risks'). By contrast, the common law knows only the more general doctrine of *res ipsa loquitur*, which may (as with its German cousin, *Anscheinsbeweis*) allow a claimant—in the absence of another plausible explanation—to plead the fact of his injury as prima facie evidence of the defendant's negligence. Nonetheless, as we saw, in the treatment malpractice context there usually will be other explanations for the patient's injury, stemming from factors beyond the doctor's control.

This brings us to the issue which, both in England and Germany, typically gives rise to the greatest proof difficulties for the patient, namely factual causation. As noted, the patient is in this context required to prove that the risk created by the doctor's faulty treatment actually materialised—ie the fault was a necessary condition for the injury. The problem is that usually the patient was already at a significant background risk of injury from his underlying condition, allowing the doctor to argue that this rather than the faulty treatment was the cause. This argument may be difficult to refute, given the frequently opaque nature of the causal processes at work.

Here it is particularly interesting to compare the approaches of the English and German courts. As we saw, both countries have opted for an 'all-or-nothing' solution whose effect is that the party who carries the burden of proof (and thus the risk of causal uncertainty) loses, even where there is a significant degree of plausibility to his contentions. In England, insofar as the balance of probabilities threshold remains unsatisfied, this will be the patient. In Germany, it will sometimes be the patient (and here the uncertainty need only amount to a small doubt). However, quite often—ie following the finding of a 'gross error' shifting the burden of proof—it will be the doctor. In such cases, it is apparent that the doctor will be liable (in full) for the faulty creation of risk alone: the question of whether the risk actually materialised is left to one side.

As a corollary to the above, both England and Germany have thus far rejected the possibility (which presents itself particularly in misdiagnosis cases) of awarding proportionate damages for 'loss of chance'. As argued above, this may be

[169] Ie applying the 'omniscience hypothetical': see pt I above.

regarded as unfortunate.[170] In particular, such an approach is fairer (compared to all-or-nothing solutions) in reflecting the uncertainty in medical cases as to whether, individually, a patient would have benefited from the omitted treatment. Properly understood, it is consistent with traditional private law principles based upon corrective justice. As we saw, in *Gregg v Scott*, the House of Lords came close to introducing loss of chance into English law, and would arguably have done so, had it not been for the particular factual complexities of that case.[171] Its future adoption may now only be a matter of time.

By contrast, in Germany the position is complicated by the BGH's longstanding case law mandating a reversal of the burden of proof on causation in cases of gross treatment errors, which as noted, has pre-empted interest in loss of chance. A significant point here is that if loss of chance were adopted instead of the burden of proof-reversal approach, this would actually weaken the patient's ability to recover for treatment error. First, it would operate in fewer cases than those presently falling within the reversal rule, namely only where relevant statistics are available (usually misdiagnosis cases). Secondly, in those cases patients who currently recover 100 per cent damages—notwithstanding that their chance of benefiting from treatment was slim—would subsequently only receive proportionate damages. As we saw, despite the lack of a compelling theoretical basis to the gross negligence approach, the latter enjoys a high degree of acceptance within the German system and abandoning it would have something of a political character in terms of forsaking the patient's present advantages.

170 The English and German position may be contrasted with that in other jurisdictions. Such claims are recognised, inter alia, in Belgium, France, Holland, Greece, and many US States: see J Spier (ed), *Unification of Tort Law: Causation* (The Hague, Kluwer Law International, 2000) 154.

171 *Gregg v Scott* [2005] UKHL 2. See the discussion at n 102 ff, above.

4

Disclosure Malpractice

I. Introduction

AS WE SAW in chapters two and three, to obtain compensation for medical injury through an action for treatment malpractice, the patient in England or Germany must normally prove fault on the part of the doctor/hospital in the course of performing treatment (or the diagnosis preceding it). However, in the present chapter we shall consider a further route he may sometimes use to pursue compensation, namely an action for 'disclosure malpractice'. This offers itself where iatrogenic injury occurs through an inherent risk materialising during (carefully performed) treatment. In particular, in such a case, the patient may allege that the doctor did not warn him adequately about the risk in question. Here, the focus of the enquiry into the doctor's fault shifts back to his failure, prior to treatment, to obtain the patient's informed consent—a so-called 'disclosure-error' (*Aufklärungsfehler*).

Today, in both countries, arguments as to disclosure malpractice are raised in a significant proportion of medical malpractice litigation. As we shall see, this is especially true for Germany, where claims of this form have been estimated to arise—either as the main or a subsidiary line of complaint against the doctor—in between one-third and two-thirds of actions[1]; but in England too such claims have been growing in importance. Thus, in the recent House of Lords decision in *Chester v Afshar*, their Lordships' judgment made clear that compensation may here lie in a wider number of scenarios than had hitherto been supposed.[2] Such an argument is frequently used in the alternative in the course of an action for treatment malpractice. Thus the patient's primary allegation may be that injury occurred due to substandard performance of treatment; insofar as the doctor points to the inherent and unavoidable nature of the risk, the patient's retort will be that, in that case, he ought to have been told.

At the same time, it is evident that the contention of non-disclosure rests upon a different basis to the claim that the doctor should have taken greater care in carrying out the treatment. In a treatment malpractice claim the doctor's conduct

[1] U Thumann, *Reform der Arzthaftung* (2000) 204. For an insightful English discussion of this area of German law, see J Shaw (1986) 35 *ICLQ* 865.

[2] *Chester v Afshar* [2004] UKHL 41; see the discussion in pt IV 1 (a) below.

will be judged faulty insofar as it gave rise to an unjustified risk of injury: the desire to avoid injury was the reason for requiring care. By contrast, in a non-disclosure claim, it is usually conceded that the risk of injury was beyond the doctor's control—it was an inherent part of the treatment. The patient's argument is rather that, by denying him knowledge of the risk, the doctor usurped his right to choose whether to run it. In this regard, its foundations derive from the principle of patient autonomy.

In medical law, an autonomy-based approach, according primacy to the patient's informed decision-making in respect of his medical care, has become increasingly influential in England and Germany over the last century. In the process, it has supplanted the traditional ethic of 'paternalism' according to which it was for the doctor to decide—in the light of his view of the patient's 'best interests'—which treatment to employ and what to tell the patient.[3] This change can be linked to the appearance of a more individualistic, less deferential culture in Western society. Another factor has undoubtedly been the advances in medical science (producing the conditions for the patient to have choice between different therapies).[4] In legal terms, the autonomy principle has been accorded recognition through rules requiring consent to medical treatment; it is these that form the starting point in relation to actions based on the doctor's failure to disclose treatment risks.

II. Consent and the Disclosure of Treatment Information

In both England and Germany, it is a fundamental legal principle that, absent consent, medical treatment will be unlawful. This is so however well executed it might be and irrespective of the objective benefit to the patient.[5] The law in both countries agrees further that, in obtaining such consent, the doctor must provide the patient with treatment information. A person who submits 'blindly', without understanding what is to be done to him, does not meaningfully consent.[6] Nevertheless, the two systems diverge as regards the nature of information required, including the effect of its non-disclosure.

[3] See generally on the ethics of autonomy and paternalism, G Dworkin, *The Theory and Practice of Autonomy* (Cambridge, Cambridge University Press, 1988).

[4] It has been argued that the importance of consent was first recognised with the advent of modern anaesthetic medicine, which 'placed a caesura between consent and treatment': see D Voll, *Die Einwilligung im Arztrecht* (Frankfurt/Main, Peter Lang, 1996) 9.

[5] The assumption here is that the law is dealing with a competent (*einwilligungsfähig*) adult patient; in both countries special rules apply to certain categories of patients—eg children and the mentally disabled—allowing consent to be dispensed with. The latter are beyond the scope of this work.

[6] For a detailed account of the English law on consent, see A Grubb (ed), *Principles of Medical Law*, 2nd edn (Oxford, Oxford University Press, 2004) ch 3; for the principles that govern consent to treatment in Germany (*Einwilligung in die medizinische Behandlung*), see further Voll, *Die Einwilligung im Arztrecht* (n 4 above).

1. England: Battery *vs* Negligence

The rule that it is for the patient to decide which medical treatment he will and will not accept was recognised by the common law in the early years of the twentieth century. In the 1914 US case of *Schloendorff v New York Hospital*, Cardozo J famously declared that

> [e]very human being of adult years and sound mind has a right to determine what shall be done with his own body; and a surgeon who performs an operation without his patient's consent, commits an assault.[7]

Though such unequivocal judicial dicta only appear later in English decisions, this appears to have reflected the position there from around the same period.[8] In fact, in more recent years there have been numerous utterances by judges affirming the pre-eminence of autonomy, and the patient's right to refuse treatment even where this runs counter to his objective medical interests.[9] Thus in *Airedale NHS Trust v Bland*, Lord Goff remarked that

> the principle of self-determination requires that respect must be given to the wishes of the patient, so that if an adult patient of sound mind refuses, however unreasonably, to consent to treatment or care by which his life would or might be prolonged, the doctors responsible for his care must give effect to his wishes, even though they do not consider it to be in his best interests to do so[10]

The doctor, who does treat without consent, may in theory attract liability under the criminal law, in the form of a conviction for assault under the Offences Against the Person Act 1861. The reason, though, is not that non-consensual medical treatment qualifies as bodily injury, but because the failure to obtain consent renders it 'improper'. As Lord Mustill commented in *Airedale NHS Trust v Bland*,

> bodily invasions in the course of proper medical treatment stand completely outside the criminal law. The reason why the consent of the patient is so important is not that it furnishes a defence in itself, but because it is usually essential to the propriety of medical treatment. Thus, if the consent is absent, and is not dispensed with in special circumstances by operation of law, the acts of the doctor lose their immunity.[11]

Even so, this remains an academic point; in practice a prosecution for assault will not be brought against a bona fide doctor—this not being regarded as in the public interest.[12]

[7] *Schloendorff v New York Hospital* (1914) 211 NY 125, 126.

[8] See in this regard *Cull v Royal Surrey County Hospital* (1932) 1 BMJ 1195.

[9] See, eg *Re T (Adult: Refusal of Treatment)* [1992] 3 WLR 782 (HL) 786 (Lord Donaldson MR); *Re MB (Adult: Refusal of Treatment)* [1997] 2 FLR 426 (CA) 432 (Butler-Sloss LJ).

[10] *Airedale NHS Trust v Bland* [1993] AC 789 (HL) 864.

[11] *Ibid*, 891.

[12] This is a factor in a decision by the Crown to initiate criminal proceedings. By contrast, there have been cases of non-medically qualified person being convicted of assault, on the basis of carrying out 'treatment' on patients who believed them to be so qualified: see *R v Tabassum* [2000] Lloyd's Rep Med 404 (CA).

Instead such cases are left to private law to resolve, by allowing the patient to bring an action in the tort of battery (also known as 'trespass to the person'). As noted in chapter one, this tort confers protection from intentional, non-consensual touching that goes beyond what is acceptable 'in the ordinary conduct of daily life'. As Lord Goff noted in *Re F (a mental patient sterilisation)*, the 'ordinary conduct' exception concerns such matters as jostling in public places. By contrast,

> medical treatment, even treatment for minor ailments, does not fall within that category of events. The general rule is that consent is necessary to render such treatment lawful.[13]

In this context neither the doctor's lack of hostile motive, nor the beneficial character of his intervention will be relevant: it is enough that he acted in the knowledge that the patient did not sanction the procedure. In practice, battery liability is most likely in cases where the doctor makes no attempt to inform the patient of his intentions, thereby wholly failing to involve him in the treatment decision. Thus, a battery was assumed by the Court of Appeal in *Devi v West Midlands Regional Health Authority,* in which the patient consented to an operation to repair a tear in her uterus, but received a hysterectomy after the surgeon found the uterus to be in a worse condition than expected.[14] A fortiori, there will be such liability where a medical professional misleads the patient in bad faith: this was the case in *Appleton v Garrett,* where a dentist was found to have carried out unnecessary dental treatment on a number of patients for financial gain.[15]

Nonetheless, allegations of battery against doctors remain exceptional, and English judges have instinctively shied away from finding such liability. An underlying reason is the stigma that they perceive to attach to the tort, with its link to criminal assault. In ordinary speech, too, the verb 'to batter' is strongly pejorative, implying a sustained beating. In this context, Lord Scarman in *Sidaway v Board of Governors of the Bethlem Royal Hospital* signalled his agreement with an earlier High Court judge

> that it would be deplorable to base the law in medical cases of this kind on the torts of assault and battery.[16]

In the process, the judicial tendency has, whenever possible, been to find that the patient did, after all, provide sufficient consent to the doctor's intervention, and instead allow the patient a remedy—if at all—in the tort of negligence.[17]

[13] *Re F (a mental patient: sterilisation)* [1990] 2 AC 1 (HL) 73.

[14] *Devi v West Midlands RHA* (1981) (CA Transcript 491); the Court did not ultimately find it necessary to decide the question. See also *Potts v North West Devon RHA* (1983, unreported) where a patient who had consented to a rubella vaccination was injected with Depo-Provera, a contraceptive drug.

[15] *Appleton v Garrett* (1997) 8 Med LR 75 (QBD). Here a criminal law prosecution will also lie close to hand, albeit in that case one does not appear to have been brought.

[16] *Sidaway v Board of Governors of the Bethlem Royal Hospital* [1985] AC 871 (HL) 883, referring to the judgment of Hirst J in *Hills v Potter* [1984] 1 WLR 641.

[17] Sometimes even a complete failure to seek the patient's consent will be treated as merely involving negligence on the doctor's part: see *Williamson v East London and City Health Authority* [1998] Lloyd's Rep Med 6 (ChD). In that case it seems the doctor's motivation (to spare the patient distress) was regarded as telling towards the lesser form of liability.

Importantly, this attitude is reflected in the low hurdles that the law has set in terms of the treatment information needed for the patient's consent to be valid. In particular, the courts have distinguished between the failure by a doctor to provide *basic* information as to the 'nature and purpose' of treatment (which will negate consent and allow an action in battery), and the non-disclosure of collateral information, including the existence of risks and alternatives. As regards the latter, the patient will be limited to seeking redress in negligence. As Bristow J put it in *Chatterton v Gerson,*

> in my judgment once the patient is informed in broad terms of the nature of the procedure which is intended, and gives her consent, that consent is real, and the cause of the action on which to base a claim for failure to go into risks and implications is negligence, not trespass.[18]

The approach was subsequently endorsed by the House of Lords in *Sidaway v Board of Governors of the Bethlem Royal Hospital.*[19]

The distinction between basic and collateral information has not escaped criticism for a certain vagueness[20]; but in substance it distinguishes between those properties essential to the treatment—which manifest themselves every time it is given—and risks, which, though inherent (in the sense of unavoidable), only appear in a certain proportion of cases, and where the doctor's hope is that they will not do so on the occasion in question. In this regard the legal position in England accords with that elsewhere in the common law world, as initially adopted in the United States in the case of *Natanson v Kline.*[21] By way of conceptual justification, it has been argued that the doctor's general duty of care to the patient (in negligence) is here at issue; ie the doctor's duty to disclose a risk is analogous to his other duties carefully to diagnose and treat, etc. As Laskin CJ put the matter in the Canadian Supreme Court decision of *Reibl v Hughes,*

> [a]lthough such a failure [to disclose risks] relates to an informed choice of submitting to or refusing recommended and appropriate treatment, it arises as the breach of an anterior duty of due care, comparable in legal obligation to the duty of due care in carrying out the particular treatment to which the patient has consented. It is not a test of the validity of consent.[22]

Admittedly, this argument may be felt somewhat to 'beg the question', and to do less than full justice to the patient's distinctive autonomy interest. However, as discussed later, it serves to focus on the fact that, in bringing such an action, the

18 *Chatterton v Gerson* [1981] QB 432 (QBD) 443.

19 *Sidaway v Board of Governors of the Bethlem Royal Hospital* [1985] AC 871 (HL).

20 See further Grubb, *Principles of Medical Law* (n 6 above) paras 3.96–3.97; M Jones, *Medical Negligence*, 3rd edn (London, Sweet & Maxwell, 2003) para 6-037.

21 *Natanson v Kline* (1960) 350 P 2d 1093. Previously, there had been other US cases that suggested the appropriate action for failure to disclose medical risks was battery: see eg *Salgo v Leland Stanford Junior University Board of Trustees* (1957) 154 Cal App 2d 560; J Robertson, 'Informed Consent to Medical Treatment' (1981) 97 *LQR* 102 at 104–5.

22 *Reibl v Hughes* (1981) 114 DLR (3d) 1, 11.

patient's typical motivation is to recover compensation for iatrogenic injury.[23] In this regard, the analogy with cases of treatment malpractice, also dealt with in negligence, is arguably a persuasive one.

2. Germany: A Unitary Approach

In Germany the need for the patient to provide valid consent to medical treatment was first articulated by the *Reichsgericht* in 1894, in a case concerning a doctor's failure to obtain parental consent prior to carrying out a foot amputation on a child.[24] In its decision the court held that treatment amounted to prima facie unlawful bodily injury, which was for the physician to justify by showing consent. The courts have adhered to this approach consistently over the years. Following the Second World War, the importance of patient consent has gained added support from the enactment of the German Constitution (*Grundgesetz*), which enshrines the rights to dignity, free self-development and bodily integrity (in Articles 1 I, 2 I and 2 II, respectively).[25] The BGH adverted to these principles in its well-known '*Myom*-judgment' of 1957, where it stated:

> The right to bodily integrity guaranteed under Art. 2 II of the *Grundgesetz* must be respected even in the case of a person who refuses treatment that would serve to free him from a life-threatening illness. No one is entitled to assume the mantle of a judge in deciding under what circumstances another individual should be reasonably willing to sacrifice his bodily integrity in order to recover his health. This principle is also binding upon the doctor. It is true that the latter acts pursuant to the lofty imperative—and indeed legal duty—to do what is in his power to heal the sick; however, such imperative and duty are ultimately limited by the patient's right of self-determination over what is done to his body.[26]

As in England, the doctor who fails to gain consent may be liable both in criminal and private law. As to the criminal law, the treatment will amount to unlawful bodily injury (*Körperverletzung*) contrary to § 223 of the Criminal Code (*Strafgesetzbuch* (StGB)). This point has in fact given rise to academic criticism due to the counter-intuitiveness of classifying medical treatment as injury—at any rate where well executed and beneficial;[27] nonetheless the courts have remained unmoved. Indeed in the past, German prosecutors and judges appear to have had fewer inhibitions than their English counterparts in charging (and convicting) doctors of this offence—even where the latter's motives were benign. The *Myom*-judgment is a case in point. There the doctor, who, to spare the patient anxiety,

[23] See the discussion in pt VI below.

[24] RG, 31 May 1894, RSt 25, 375.

[25] See Voll, *Die Einwilligung im Arztrecht* (n 4 above) 10–11.

[26] BGH, 28 November 1957, NJW 1958, 267 (268).

[27] The debate is discussed in C Katzenmeier, *Arzthaftung* (Tübingen, Mohr Siebeck, 2002) 112 ff; see also Voll, *Die Einwilligung im Arztrecht* (n 4 above) 15 ff. As noted at n 11 above, in England the courts have side-stepped this problem; in the *Bland* case, Lord Mustill derived the doctor's potential liability (for assault) simply from the impropriety of proceeding without consent ([1993] AC 789 (HL) 891).

failed to tell her that surgery to remove an ovarian cyst might extend to a full hysterectomy, was held criminally liable for carrying the latter out. Admittedly, the tendency in criminal law has been to restrict liability in such circumstances. This has been achieved, inter alia, by stressing causal limitations—ie the non-disclosure must be shown to have affected the patient's decision to submit to the treatment.[28]

As regards the patient's private law remedies, non-consensual treatment will qualify as an unlawful injury to the patient's body and/or health within § 823 I BGB, giving rise to an action in tort. At the same time the doctor will be in breach of the contractual duties he owes to the patient.[29] In this respect, the relevant codal provisions are the same as in relation to claims for treatment malpractice. However, an important difference (in cases where lack of consent is at issue) is that, because the doctor's intervention per se counts as injury, the elements of unlawful and faulty bodily injury under § 823 I BGB are satisfied straightaway—unless, that is, the doctor demonstrates the fact of valid consent. In other words, the burden of proof will here rest upon him.

Admittedly, as in England, cases centering upon the doctor's total failure to seek consent are rare. There are a few cases where, having initially obtained consent to a given procedure, the doctor later exceeds its scope in the course of treatment, on the basis of clinical indication. The *Myom*-case was of this kind; a more recent example is a decision of the BGH from 1999, upholding the liability of two doctors, who carried out a sterilisation of the patient after performing a caesarean section. They did so, despite the patient's earlier rejection of this option, after forming the view during the caesarean that a further pregnancy could have life-threatening consequences for her.[30]

Far more common are situations where, in the course of acquiring consent, there is a failure to inform the patient as to a material aspect of the treatment (such as risks and alternatives). Crucially, however, in contrast to the common law, in Germany the two types of case are not treated as conceptually distinct. Rather, any wrongful failure to disclose information material to the patient's decision to undergo treatment, *including* the existence of treatment risks, will be regarded as invalidating consent, and thus turn the treatment into unlawful bodily injury.[31] This unitary approach to information disclosure reflects the absence of separate torts covering the intentional invasion of bodily integrity (with or without discrete injury) and the unintentional infliction of (bodily or other) injury. Rather, as noted in chapter one, § 823 I BGB applies to both types of situation in equal measure. Accordingly, the German courts, unlike their common law counterparts,

[28] See BGH, 29 June 1995, NStZ 96, 132; K Ulsenheimer, 'Die Entwicklung des Arztstrafrechts in der Praxis der letzten 20 Jahre' in A Laufs (ed), *Die Entwickung der Arzthaftung* (Berlin, Springer, 1997) 27, 33.

[29] K Geiß and H-P Greiner, *Arzthaftpflichtrecht*, 5th edn (Munich, Beck, 2006) para C2; E Deutsch and A Spickhoff, *Medizinrecht*, 5th edn (Berlin, Springer, 2003) paras 189–90.

[30] BGH, 4 October 1999, NJW 2000, 885.

[31] See Katzenmeier, *Arzthaftung* (n 27 above) 324 ff; Geiß and Greiner, *Arzthaftpflichtrecht* (n 29 above) paras C1–C5; E Steffen and B Pauge, *Arzthaftungsrecht—neue Entwicklungslinien der BGH-Rechtsprechung*, 10th edn (Cologne, RWS Kommunikationsforum, 2006) paras 321 and 329.

have not had to choose between more or less stigmatising actions against the less than informative doctor.

Admittedly, a number of academic commentators have argued that it would be preferable, in conceptual terms, for the law to qualify the failure to disclose information as an injury to the patient's right of personality, a residual protected interest (*sonstiges Recht*) under § 823 I.[32] This would banish the present reliance on the notion that careful and beneficial treatment amounts objectively to bodily injury, and would also restore the normal proof situation in respect of the codal paragraph; ie it would be for the patient to demonstrate inadequate disclosure. However, the courts have shown no inclination to re-conceptualise their jurisprudence in the suggested manner.

III. The Required Standard of Disclosure

As we saw in the last part, English and German law diverge in relation to the effect of a doctor's wrongful non-disclosure of treatment risks on the reality of the patient's consent. Another important difference is in their respective approaches to the standard or level of risk-disclosure required of the doctor, ie if he is to avoid being at fault.

1. England: From Accepted Practice to Informed Consent

As discussed, the doctor's duty to disclose treatment risks is positioned in the tort of negligence. Traditionally, the question whether the doctor who failed to disclose a given risk was thereby in breach of duty was determined—in common with his other duties of careful diagnosis and treatment—by reference to accepted medical practice. In short, the *Bolam* test was applied.[33] As Lord Diplock argued in the case of *Sidaway v Board of Governors of the Bethlem Royal Hospital*, the doctor's relationship with his patient was governed by,

> a single comprehensive duty [which] is not subject to dissection into a number of component parts to which different criteria of what satisfy the duty of care apply, such as diagnosis, treatment, advice (including warning of any risks of something going wrong however skilfully the treatment advised is carried out.).[34]

As to generally accepted practice among doctors, this, until fairly recently, was paternalistic in spirit. Doctors were prepared to conceal treatment risks—at least

[32] Katzenmeier, *Arzthaftung* (n 27 above) 118 ff; A Laufs, NJW 1974, 2025; D Hart '*Autonomiesicherung im Arzthaftungsrecht. Ein Beitrag zur Entkoppelung von ärztlicher Aufklärungspflicht und Körperverletzung*' in A Heldrich (ed), *Festschrift für Heinrichs* (Munich, Beck, 1998) 291.

[33] As to the *Bolam* approach, and its privileging of medical practice, see ch 2 pt II 3 (a) above.

[34] *Sidaway v Board of Governors of the Bethlem Royal Hospital* [1985] AC 871 (HL) 893.

if they saw these as minor and regarded treatment as objectively the best option. An illustration of this approach, and the courts' unwillingness to challenge it, is provided by Denning LJ's remarks in the 1954 case of *Hatcher v Black*, where the patient complained that the doctor had concealed the risk of laryngeal surgery paralysing her vocal cords:

> [The doctor] told a lie, but he did it because he thought that in the circumstances it was justifiable . . . the law does not condemn the doctor when he only does that which many a wise and good doctor would do.[35]

While in England the courts deferred thus to medical judgement, elsewhere in the common law world it was recognised earlier that there was here greater scope (relative to cases of treatment malpractice) for judges to take the lead in setting the relevant standard of care. In particular, in its landmark ruling in the 1972 case of *Canterbury v Spence*, the US Court of Appeals (District of Columbia Circuit) emphasised the link between information disclosure and patient autonomy. Robinson J commented that

> to bind the disclosure obligation to medical usage is to arrogate the decision on revelation to the physician alone. Respect for the patient's right of self-determination on particular therapy demands a standard set by law for physicians rather than one which physicians may or may not impose upon themselves.[36]

Accordingly, the court placed a duty upon the doctor to disclose 'material risks' of the treatment, namely those risks that

> a reasonable patient, in what the physician knows or should know to be the patient's position, would be likely to attach significance to [in deciding whether to have treatment].[37]

This approach has become known as 'informed consent', and has subsequently found favour in other common law jurisdictions. Thus the Canadian Supreme Court adopted it in *Reibl v Hughes*, as did the Australian High Court in *Rogers v Whitaker*.[38] Indeed, in the latter case, the court arguably went further than *Canterbury v Spence* by allowing for a subjective approach (based on the particular patient's informational needs rather those of the reasonable patient). As Mason CJ held,

> a risk is material if, in the circumstances of the particular case, a reasonable person in the patient's position, if warned of the risk, would be likely to attach significance to it or if the medical practitioner is or should reasonably be aware that the particular patient, if warned of the risk, would be likely to attach significance to it.[39]

[35] *Hatcher v Black* (QBD), *The Times* (2 July 1954), cited in Grubb, *Principles of Medical Law* (n 6 above) para 3.139.

[36] *Canterbury v Spence* (1972) 464 F 2d 772, 784.

[37] *Ibid*, 787.

[38] *Reibl v Hughes* (1981) 114 DLR (3d) 1; *Rogers v Whitaker* (1992) 109 ALR 625. By contrast, fewer than half of US States have followed the lead in *Canterbury* (the others preferring to retain accepted medical practice as their starting point): see Robertson, 'Informed Consent to Medical Treatment' (n 21 above) 108; J Healy, *Medical Negligence: Common Law Perspectives* (London, Sweet & Maxwell, 1999) 100 ff.

[39] *Rogers v Whitaker* (1992) 109 ALR 625, 634. See also *Rosenberg v Percival* (2001) 75 ALJR 734.

By contrast in England a more traditional approach (according a greater degree of discretion to the doctor) prevails, at least at first sight. There the leading authority remains the House of Lords' decision of *Sidaway v Board of Governors of the Bethlem Royal Hospital*, from the mid-1980s.[40] In that case the claimant sued in respect of partial paralysis following an operation to relieve neck pain. She alleged that the surgeon had failed to warn her that the operation carried a one to two per cent risk of damaging her spinal cord, which had materialised. Whilst unanimous in the result (dismissing the claim) their Lordships were divided as to the proper standard of risk-disclosure. For his part, Lord Scarman would have imported the informed consent approach into English law. As he commented,

> [i]f one considers the scope of the doctor's duty by beginning with the right of the patient to make his own decision whether he will or will not undergo the treatment proposed, the right to be informed of significant risk and the doctor's corresponding duty are easy to understand: for the proper implementation of the right requires that the doctor be under a duty to inform his patient of the material risks inherent in the treatment.[41]

However, this was a minority view; the rest of their Lordships preferred to adhere in varying degrees to the *Bolam* approach. For Lord Diplock a doctor's compliance with accepted practice (in not disclosing a given risk) would conclusively defeat an allegation of negligence.[42] For the others such practice formed the starting point, albeit it was subject to an exception for risks above a certain threshold: the latter ought always to be disclosed, irrespective of accepted practice. As Lord Bridge noted in his speech,

> even in a case where . . . no expert witness in the relevant medical field condemns the non-disclosure as being in conflict with accepted and responsible medical practice, I am of the opinion that the judge might in certain circumstances come to the conclusion that disclosure of a particular risk was so obviously necessary to an informed choice on the part of the patient that no reasonably prudent medical man would fail to make it. The kind of case I have in mind would be an operation involving a substantial risk of grave adverse consequences, as, for example, [a] ten per cent risk of a stroke[43]

Another situation where their Lordships were agreed that full information should be provided was in response to specific questioning by the patient.[44]

The House of Lords' decision in *Sidaway* has attracted criticism over the years in the academic literature, as well as from patient-support groups, for its lack of overall clarity and the at best half-hearted endorsement of patient autonomy.[45] Indeed, the failure of their Lordships to speak with one voice encouraged the Court of Appeal to adopt an even narrower approach to disclosure in some of its

[40] *Sidaway v Board of Governors of the Bethlem Royal Hospital*, [1985] AC 871 (HL).

[41] *Ibid*, 888.

[42] *Sidaway* [1985] AC 871 (HL) 888.

[43] *Sidaway* [1985] AC 871 (HL) 900.

[44] *Sidaway* [1985] AC 871 (HL) 895 (Lord Diplock); 898 (Lord Bridge).

[45] See IM Kennedy, *Treat me right: Essays in Medical Law and Ethics* (Oxford, Clarendon Press, 1988) 193 ff; Healy, *Medical Negligence: Common Law Perspectives* (n 38 above) 143 ff.

later case law. For example, in *Blyth v Bloomsbury HA*, the Court held—reversing the trial judge, and despite dicta in *Sidaway* to the contrary—that the doctor's duty to answer questions was also qualified by the *Bolam* test.[46] Arguably, the refusal to accord more weight to the patient's informational needs reflected the judiciary's own conservatism and attachment to paternalism as a value.[47] Indeed the courts' approach may be regarded as being of a piece with their reluctance to impugn accepted practice in cases of treatment malpractice. In the background lies the same sense of medicine as a public good, and a concern not to encourage additional litigation against the National Health Service.

Nevertheless, in the last decade or so English law has undeniably moved towards a greater acceptance of the patient's right to know. An important decision in this regard was *Pearce v United Bristol Healthcare NHS Trust*, where Lord Woolf MR remarked in the Court of Appeal that

> if there is a significant risk which would affect the judgment of a reasonable patient, then in the normal course it is the responsibility of a doctor to inform the patient of that significant risk.[48]

This dictum was subsequently cited with approval by Lord Steyn in the House of Lords in *Chester v Afshar*.[49]

At the same time, accepted medical practice has also shifted in the direction of greater disclosure. Thus the General Medical Council, in its 1998 guidance on obtaining consent, addresses doctors in the following terms:

> When providing information you must do your best to find out about patients' individual needs and priorities. For example, patients' beliefs, culture, occupation or other factors may have a bearing on the information they need in order to reach a decision. You should not make assumptions about patients' views, but discuss these matters with them, and ask them whether they have any concerns about the treatment or the risks it may involve. You should provide patients with appropriate information, which should include an explanation of any risks to which they may attach particular significance.[50]

In the light of the above, it is arguable that the dichotomy between the *Bolam*-yardstick of accepted medical practice (broadly endorsed by the majority in *Sidaway*), and the 'informed consent' approach, has disappeared. The failure, contrary to accepted practice, of a doctor to disclose risks that a reasonable patient

46 *Blyth v Bloomsbury Health Authority* (1993) 4 Med LR 151 (CA); see also *Gold v Haringey Health Authority* [1988] 1 QB 481 (CA).

47 See eg Lord Diplock's comments in the *Sidaway* case [1985] AC 871 (HL) 894–5, where he contrasted the position of a judge having treatment, who would naturally desire (and receive) all relevant information, with that of an ordinary patient.

48 *Pearce v United Bristol Healthcare NHS Trust* [1999] PIQR P53 (CA) P59.

49 *Chester v Afshar* [2004] UKHL 41, para 15. There the House of Lords dealt with the question of the standard of information disclosure quite briefly and obiter, as the doctor's breach of duty had been conceded in the courts below; instead the case dealt with issues of causation: see further pt IV 1 below.

50 General Medical Council, *Seeking Consent: the Ethical Considerations* (London, GMC, 1998) para 6. Lord Steyn referred to similar guidance by the Royal College of Surgeons in his speech in *Chester v Afshar* [2004] UKHL 41, para 26.

would wish to know about will amount to a breach of duty. In short, 'informed consent' (or something very close to it) has been transformed via the *Bolam* test into a legal requirement under English law.

One question that arises from this widening of the doctor's prima facie duty of disclosure is whether it may be qualified in certain circumstances by reference to considerations of 'therapeutic privilege'. In the past, when English law took the *Bolam*-based approach to determining the standard of disclosure, the issue did not present itself in a direct form (instead being subsumed within the doctor's general discretion not to disclose). Now though, this is relevant where the doctor is of the view that disclosing information (required to assist the patient in his autonomous choice) would cause the latter significant damage or distress. The existence of such a privilege was affirmed by the US Appeals Court in *Canterbury v Spence*, where Robinson J stated:

> It is recognized that patients occasionally become so ill or emotionally distraught on disclosure as to foreclose a rational decision, or complicate or hinder the treatment, or perhaps even pose psychological damage to the patient. Where that is so, the cases have generally held that the physician is armed with a privilege to keep the information from the patient.[51]

A similar attitude may be discerned in recent English judicial dicta. Thus, in *Pearce v United Bristol Healthcare NHS Trust*, Lord Woolf MR remarked as follows:

> Obviously the doctor, in determining what to tell a patient, has to take into account all the relevant considerations, which include the ability of the patient to comprehend what he has to say to him or her and the state of the patient at the particular time, both from the physical point of view and an emotional point of view. There can often be situations where a course different from the normal has to be employed.[52]

At the same time, the precise boundaries of the 'privilege' remain to be defined. It is, for example, uncertain whether it is the doctor or the patient who has the burden of proof in this regard. In *Sidaway*, Lord Scarman argued that the onus would be upon the doctor to show that the privilege applied.[53] However, this is hard to square with the fact that the issue concerns the doctor's alleged breach of duty in negligence, which ultimately is for the patient to prove. Another matter that remains unclear is how serious the potential damage to the patient (through disclosure) must be in order for the privilege to arise.[54]

A final question concerns the extent to which a doctor has a duty to divulge information as to his individual experience and success with a given procedure—or that of his hospital—relative to the success rate of other doctors/hospitals. This

[51] *Canterbury v Spence* (1972) 464 F2d 772, 789.

[52] *Pearce v United Bristol Healthcare NHS Trust* [1999] PIQR P53 (CA) P59. See also *Chester v Afshar* [2004] UKHL 41, para 16 (Lord Steyn).

[53] *Sidaway* [1985] AC 871 (HL) 888–9.

[54] See IM Kennedy and A Grubb, *Medical Law: Text, Cases and Materials*, 3rd edn (London, Butterworths, 2000) 701 ff, who note the danger that the therapeutic privilege exception, unless closely defined, may swallow the disclosure rule.

is a difficult question because of its connection to problems of resource allocation and regional variation in care.[55] Logistically too, it may create difficulty by focusing patient demand on a small group of doctors and hospitals. Nonetheless, the Kennedy Report (set up in the wake of the Bristol Royal Infirmary scandal) recommended that such information be made available,[56] and the Healthcare Commission (the independent monitoring body for health services) has, since 2005, been implementing this through 'league tables' of hospital performance.[57] There has not, though, so far been a suggestion of a duty in negligence to disclose information of this form. Rather, to the extent that treatment turns out to be substandard due to the individual shortcomings of a doctor or hospital, the patient's remedy will lie in an action for treatment malpractice.

2. Germany: Beyond Informed Consent

As we saw above, the rule requiring the patient's consent to medical treatment was first articulated by the *Reichsgericht* in 1894. Even so, originally it was only the doctor's complete failure to seek consent that qualified as faulty. He was not further required, when acquiring consent, to inform the patient about possible risks.[58] Indeed, in a case from 1912 the *Reichsgericht* rejected such a duty as inconsistent with good medical practice, on the basis that it might put patients off having needful treatment or might prejudice its success.[59] Nevertheless, from the late-1930s the courts began to demand that at least the most significant of the treatment's risks and side effects be disclosed. Thus, in a 1940 decision the *Reichsgericht* allowed recovery in a case where a doctor failed to advise the patient that the excision of a cyst would require the removal of her breast. In doing so it rejected an argument by the doctor based on his wish to avoid distressing her.[60] As we saw earlier, in the process the courts continued to treat such cases in the same way as ones where no attempt to obtain consent had been made: a wrongful failure to disclose information of any kind was seen as vitiating consent.[61]

In their case law after the Second World War, the courts rapidly heightened the standard of information disclosure required of doctors, so that an approach similar to the US 'informed consent' approach may already be discerned in BGH

[55] Another issue is the reliability of the statistics at issue, given that different doctors/hospitals often deal with different population groups.

[56] Kennedy Report, *Report of the Bristol Royal Infirmary Inquiry, Learning from Bristol: the report of the public inquiry into children's heart surgery at the Bristol Royal Infirmary 1984–1995* (Cm 5207) (2001) recommendations 102 and 155. As to the background to the inquiry, see ch 5 below, fn 71.

[57] See the Commission's website, http:/healthcarecommission.org.uk. Figures showing the success rates of individual specialist surgeons are also beginning to emerge under the Freedom of Information Act 2000, albeit their usefulness remains highly contested.

[58] Voll, *Die Einwilligung im Arztrecht* (n 4 above) 9; H Helbron, *Entwicklungen und Fehlentwicklungen im Arzthaftungsrecht* (Munich, Utz, 2001) 80.

[59] RG, 1 March 1912, RZ 78, 432.

[60] RG, 8 March 1940, RZ 163, 129.

[61] See the discussion at n 31 ff above.

decisions from the 1950s.[62] Here the figure of a reasonable patient (*verständiger Patient*) was used to identify those (rare) risks that did *not* have to be disclosed. Arguably this already went further than the 'informed consent' model, given that (in contrast to the latter) the approach began with a presumption in favour of unrestricted information disclosure. As the BGH stated in a decision from 1962,

> [t]he patient need not be informed of risks which are so rare—and whose appearance in the particular patient's case are thus so unlikely—that they would not carry any serious weight for the decision of a reasonable patient in his position as to whether to consent to the treatment.[63]

The Court went on to suggest that non-disclosure was also justifiable where the seriousness of the harm, were it to eventuate, would be significantly less than if the patient's condition were left untreated. In contrast, as the BGH made clear in a later case, if the treatment would strike a reasonable patient as less clearly therapeutically indicated, or wholly optional (such as cosmetic surgery), even very small risks of serious harm—eg of one or two in a thousand—needed to be divulged.[64]

Nonetheless, the above approach, and the use of the reasonable person yardstick, was subsequently found wanting. Specifically, it was criticised for failing to pay sufficient respect to the autonomy of the individual patient (including his right to be informed of risks that would not sway a rational person).[65] Moreover, as three judges pointed out in the 1979 medical malpractice decision of the *Bundesverfassungsgericht*, it gave rise to a danger that 'the sicker the patient, the more his right to know of risks is attenuated'.[66] Accordingly, in its jurisprudence over the last 25 years, the BGH has preferred a subjective standpoint in which it is the informational needs of the *particular* patient that provide the yardstick. The patient must be given information tailored to his own circumstances so as to allow him meaningful choice.[67] As the BGH held in a case from 1980,

> the patient's right to decide, which is paramount, also includes the right to make a decision that appears unreasonable from a medical point of view . . . This principle would be undermined . . . if, in determining whether the doctor should realise that the patient wishes to know of a given risk, too much emphasis is placed on the doctor's view as to what risks a reasonable patient would consider material . . . That would, in effect, allow the doctor to substitute his views for those of the patient.[68]

Following this newer approach, the doctor should disclose all risks specifically associated with a given treatment that could theoretically influence the particular patient's decision. This includes even very small risks if their materialisation would have serious repercussions for him as an individual. In a decision from

[62] For a detailed account of the development of the BGH's jurisprudence in this area, see Helbron, *Entwicklungen und Fehlentwicklungen im Arzthaftungsrecht* (n 58 above) 81 ff.

[63] BGH, 16 October 1962, NJW 1963, 393 (394); see also BGH, 9 December 1958, NJW 1959, 811.

[64] BGH, 16 November 1971, NJW 1972, 335.

[65] Helbron, *Entwicklungen und Fehlentwicklungen im Arzthaftungsrecht* (n 58 above) 90 ff.

[66] BVerfG, 25 July 1979, NJW 1979, 1925 (1931).

[67] Katzenmeier, *Arzthaftung* (n 27 above) 327–8.

[68] BGH, 24 June 1980, NJW 1980, 2751 (2752–3).

February 1984 the BGH stated that, where treatment was not urgent, a risk of one in 10,000–20,000 would normally need to be disclosed.[69] In another judgment, handed down on the same day, it held that a 0.15 per cent risk of paralysis from spinal radiotherapy should have been disclosed to a cancer patient, even though this treatment offered the only chance of curing her and the illness itself posed a risk of paralysis.[70] In fact, the tendency since then has been for the courts to ignore the statistical rarity of the risk as a relevant factor at all.[71] In a decision from February 2000, the BGH put the matter as follows:

> Determinative, as regards the doctor's duty to disclose, is not a given probability of a risk materialising, expressed in statistical terms. Rather, the decisive questions are how far the risk is particularly associated with the treatment and whether its occurrence would have a grave impact upon the patient's lifestyle . . . In principle this means that, on occasion, extremely rare risks may have to be disclosed.[72]

Indeed, in the case at hand, the relevant risk (of paralysis from a polio-vaccine), which the court held needed to be divulged, was just one in five million.

Even so the BGH has been prepared to temper the strictness of the legal disclosure rules in two respects. First, ordinary treatment risks, of which the patient can be taken to be aware, need not be disclosed. There is thus no obligation to inform the patient of the risk that an operation wound may become infected (in contrast to the need to do so in relation to possible infection following an injection).[73] Secondly, the court has stressed that it is usually enough for the patient to be told 'in general terms' (*im Großen und Ganzen*) about each discrete risk attaching to the treatment.[74] The doctor need not go into technical detail if doing so is simply likely to confuse the patient. Rather, the emphasis is on explaining what the occurrence of the risk could mean for that patient. In the case mentioned above, which concerned the doctor's failure to tell the patient of the risk of paralysis from spinal radiotherapy, the BGH commented that

> [t]he patient should receive a general idea of the seriousness of the intervention, and the dangers to which he will be exposed in the course of it . . . Here, for example, it would have sufficed if the defendant had told the patient the radiotherapy would entail inevitable stress to her spinal column, which might lead to symptoms of paralysis that in nearly all cases would be merely temporary . . . She would thus have known in general terms that the therapy involved risks of this kind and could then, if she had wished, asked the defendant for more details.[75]

[69] BGH, 7 February 1984, NJW 1984, 1395.

[70] BGH, 7 February 1984, NJW 1984, 1397. As discussed later, the BGH in the same case tightened the factual causation element, by requiring the patient to show a plausible basis for rejecting the treatment, if she had known of the risk: see n 129 below.

[71] Geiß and Greiner, *Arzthaftpflichtrecht* (n 29 above) para C43; Katzenmeier, *Arzthaftung* (n 27 above) 329.

[72] BGH, 15 February 2000, NJW 2000, 1784 (1785).

[73] BGH, 19 November 1985, NJW 1986, 780; BGH, 14 February 1989, NJW 1989, 1533.

[74] BGH, 26 February 1985, NJW 1985, 2192; BGH, 8 May 1990, NJW 1990, 2929; BGH, 15 February 2000, NJW 2000, 1784; M Gehrlein, *Grundriss der Arzthaftpflicht*, 2nd edn (Munich, Verlag Franz Vahlen, 2006) para C41.

[75] BGH, 7 February 1984, NJW 1984, 1397 (1398).

In this context, Geiß and Greiner suggest that there will be an inverse relationship between the urgency and likely efficacy of the treatment and the amount of detail in the exposition of risks, etc. Thus where treatment is urgent, but has a good chance of success, less detailed information is required. This contrasts with the proposed use of more speculative therapy. However, as they acknowledge, this is merely a rule of thumb and its application in determining a given case remains uncertain.[76]

In the course of an extensive jurisprudence, the German courts have considered further issues that have to date received little attention under the common law. One matter which has increasingly generated litigation is the doctor's duty to disclose alternatives. After all, the patent's lack of knowledge of these is arguably just as likely (as his ignorance of risks) to give him a false picture of the treatment he ends up having.[77] Here, as a starting point, the courts hold to the basic principle of the doctor's therapeutic freedom to choose between therapies. In so doing, and provided there is a broad equality between the two, he need not offer the patient information about the risks and side-effects of the discounted treatment.[78] As the BGH stated in a decision from 1988,

> [i]n general, a doctor does not need to discuss with the patient unasked every treatment method that theoretically comes into consideration, and the pros and cons of each, provided he selects a method that belongs to the current medical standard . . . The doctor is entitled as a rule to assume that the patient has confidence in his medical judgment, and does not expect a detailed discourse on matters of specialist interest.[79]

In this regard, the courts have adopted a more restrictive approach than with respect to arguments based on the non-disclosure of actual treatment risks.[80] A reason for this may be concerns as to the resource implications of demanding strict disclosure where newer and safer treatment options are as yet available only in a few specialist hospitals. Thus in one case the BGH refused to find consent invalidated where a patient died following a rare complication of an invasive neurological examination, and she had not been told of a newer, non-invasive method of performing it available at a handful of clinics.[81]

However, where the alternatives are in general use, then insofar as the risks attaching to each are distinct, the options should be discussed with the patient, for example where there is a choice between surgery and more conservative treatment.[82] Moreover, where one option is generally favoured by mainstream medical

[76] Geiß and Greiner, *Arzthaftpflichtrecht* (n 29 above) paras C8–C10.

[77] In England, there has been little judicial or academic consideration of the issue. However, it seems that a doctor need not enter into any detailed discussion of an alternative treatment with a patient, if he does not regard it as clinically appropriate: see *Pearce v United Bristol Healthcare NHS Trust* [1999] PIQR P53.

[78] See Katzenmeier, *Arzthaftung* (n 27 above) 331 ff.

[79] BGH, 22 September 1987, NJW 1988, 763 (764).

[80] D Giesen, *Arzthaftung*, 4th edn (Tübingen, Mohr, 1995) paras 218 ff.

[81] BGH, 28 February 1984, NJW 1984, 1810.

[82] BGH, 22 February 2000, NJW 2000, 1788; BGH, 15 March 2005, NJW 2005, 1718; Steffen and Pauge, *Arzthaftungsrecht* (n 31 above) para 381.

opinion this should also be made clear. Here it will be irrelevant that the other option, adopted by the doctor, turns out retrospectively to be medically justified. Thus, in one case a doctor advised a patient, with suspected ovarian cancer, to have an immediate hysterectomy rather than undergo further tests under local anaesthetic. The doctor's judgement was vindicated by the findings made during the operation, but unfortunately the patient suffered a stroke, allegedly due to the general anaesthetic. The BGH found the doctor in breach of his disclosure duty for failing to emphasise that the conservative option of further tests would have been the choice of most doctors.[83] In addition, if a proposed treatment method is novel, or where reputable voices in the medical world have expressed misgivings about it (due to its possibly unnecessary risks), the doctor will be obliged to disclose this.[84]

A detailed case law has also developed in relation to the background conditions for information disclosure to be effective, in particular with regard to its manner and timing. Thus, the courts have held that disclosure should take place in the course of an individual discussion: merely giving the patient an information sheet to read will not be sufficient, although the supplementary use of such sheets (with a direction that the patient may raise queries with a doctor) has been accepted.[85] As regards timing, the general rule is that the patient must receive the information sufficiently in advance of treatment, so as not to feel pressure to go through with it in any event. In the case of in-patients for surgery, disclosure should occur at least one day prior to the operation, and in cases of serious but finely balanced risks, it may well need to be earlier.[86] As a general rule, the lower the risks are, the later the permissible disclosure.[87]

As we saw earlier (in discussing the relevant English law), the common law courts have allowed for a possible exception to the normal disclosure rules under the heading of 'therapeutic privilege'. In effect, the doctor may justify non-disclosure if informing the patient would cause the patient significant distress or damage. A similar doctrine has also been recognised in Germany, and is referred to as the 'humanitarian principle' (*humanitäres Prinzip*). This terminology calls attention to the fact that it is not an indulgence to the doctor, but derives from the need to protect the patient's interests.[88]

In the context of the prescription of medicines with side-effects and risks attached, this principle has attained the force of statute. Thus, under the *Arzneimittelgesetz*, the need for informed consent may be dispensed with in grave cases, if the success of the treatment would be endangered by the information and there is no obvious desire on the patient's part to receive it.[89] Nonetheless, the

[83] BGH, 18 March 2003, NJW 2003, 1862. The BGH remitted the case to the appeal court on the issue of causation. For a critical comment on the decision, see C Wendehorst, *Lindenmaier-Möhring, Kommentierte BGH-Rechtsprechung 2003–6/2005* at 143.

[84] BGH, 21 November 1995, NJW 1996, 776; BGH, 13 June 2006, NJW 2006, 2477.

[85] BGH, 15 February 2000, NJW 2000, 1784.

[86] BGH, 7 April 1992, NJW 1992, 2351; BGH, 17 March 1998, NJW 1998, 2734.

[87] Katzenmeier, *Arzthaftung* (n 27 above) 343–4.

[88] Katzenmeier, *Arzthaftung* (n 27 above) 335.

[89] *Arzneimittelgesetz* § 41, nr 7.

BGH has taken a stricter line in relation to treatment risks generally, albeit the relevant dicta are obiter. Thus, it has been emphasised that, to avoid undermining patient autonomy, cases invoking the principle must remain the exception.[90] Here, the mere prospect of causing the patient emotional distress will not be enough; instead, as the BGH suggested in a decision from 1959, it is necessary that the patient's physical condition be compromised by the information.[91]

The generally strict approach of the German courts to the issue of information disclosure has met with resistance from doctors over the years, who have reacted unhappily to the encroachment upon their clinical discretion. Their perception is of duties imposed by medical laymen, which take little account of the patient's best interests (and that a cure may be jeopardised by too much information).[92] A further problem, noted by commentators, is the legal uncertainty generated by the highly subjective approach to the patient's information requirements. It is thus unclear for doctors in advance what standard of disclosure they will retrospectively be held to. In this regard, the law is, on the face of things, closer to a strict liability approach rather than one based on fault. At the same time, it has been mooted by some commentators that the courts at times decide the issue of disclosure malpractice according to whether they think the patient was in reality a victim of *treatment* malpractice. In other words, such claims may here serve as a 'fall back option' (*Auffangtatbestand*) in cases of probable *fault* in performing treatment, but where this cannot be shown to the high standard of proof set by German law.[93]

Finally, though, there is one area where German law, notwithstanding its generally strict insistence on patient autonomy, appears to be in agreement with the relevant English law. In particular, a doctor is not normally required to divulge his own (or his hospital's) unpromising track record with regard to the treatment. The view is that, where injury occurs through faulty execution of the therapy, the patient will be adequately protected by an action for treatment malpractice.[94] Similarly, a doctor need not normally advise the patient that another hospital has more advanced technical equipment. The position might be different if the risks were very much lower in one case than the other (and here, additionally, the decision of the doctor/hospital to undertake the treatment would itself amount to a breach of contractual and tortious duties).[95]

[90] BGH, 7 February 1984, NJW 1984, 1397.

[91] BGH, 16 January 1959, NJW 1959, 814.

[92] Katzenmeier, *Arzthaftung* (n 27 above) 350 ff; Helbron, *Entwicklungen und Fehlentwicklungen im Arzthaftungsrecht* (n 58 above) 84–5.

[93] See Katzenmeier, *Arzthaftung* (n 27 above) 350 ff; H-L Schreiber, 'Handlungsbedarf für den Gesetzgeber?' in A Laufs (ed) *Die Entwicklung der Arzthaftung* (1997) 342.

[94] Katzenmeier, *Arzthaftung* (n 27 above) 332.

[95] BGH, 22 September 1987, NJW 1988, 763; Katzenmeier, *Arzthaftung* (n 27 above) 333.

IV. Causation of Damage

In bringing a claim for disclosure malpractice, the patient typically wishes to recover damages for iatrogenic injury sustained during treatment. Here, the mere facts of the doctor's faulty conduct (in failing to disclosure a treatment risk) plus the injury will not be enough to generate the entitlement to compensation. Rather, as with the cases of faulty treatment discussed in chapter two, it remains essential that the fault and injury should stand in some form of causal relationship. At the same time, the divergent approaches of English and German law as to the effect of non-disclosure of risks on the patient's consent has important ramifications for the nature of the relationship required.

1. The Position in England

In England, as we saw, the patient will be required to bring a claim based on the doctor's failure to disclose risks in negligence. Here, the ordinary causation rules associated with that tort apply. As discussed earlier in relation to treatment malpractice, the causal enquiry may usefully be divided into a factual and a legal stage.[96]

(a) Factual Causation

As we saw in chapter two, factual causation entails that the defendant's faulty conduct was a necessary condition for the claimant's injury. In non-disclosure cases, this stage of the enquiry itself has two aspects. First of all, there is the requirement that the injury be physically connected to the treatment, ie the injury did not result from an independent risk connected to the natural progress of the patient's condition. Secondly, there needs to be a 'psychological' but-for link between the doctor's non-disclosure of the risk and the patient's decision to have the treatment: the court must be satisfied that if the patient had known of the risk he would not have gone ahead with the treatment.[97]

The first point is unlikely to pose difficulty. Typically the physical link will be conceded by the doctor in the course of his defence that the injury stemmed from an inherent risk of treatment (as opposed to malpractice in its execution). However, this may be subject to quantum arguments. Thus, if it is clear that, had the patient declined treatment, the same injury would have occurred later anyway,

[96] See ch 2 pt III.

[97] By contrast, it has been suggested that if iatrogenic injury were to occur in the course of a battery, the question whether the (informed) patient would have agreed to treatment will be irrelevant: see *Chatterton v Gerson* [1981] QB 432 (QBD) 442–3 (Bristow J, obiter). But see *Abbas v Kenney* (1996) 7 Med LR 47 (QBD) 50 where Gage J (again obiter) left the point open.

through his condition progressing, the actual treatment will merely have accelerated it. Here the patient's damages will be limited to the period for which he would have remained free of the injury.[98]

By contrast, the resolution of the psychological link issue is more problematic. In particular, it requires the court to make findings as to the patient's hypothetical conduct: how would he have reacted if he had been in possession of the information which the doctor improperly denied him? In assessing this, the courts in England have adopted a 'subjective' approach, which asks what the particular patient's response would have been. As Hutchison J noted in the case of *Smith v Barking, Havering and Brentwood HA*,

> both counsel invited me to accept that in the end the matter must be one for decision on a subjective basis. This must plainly as a matter of principle be right, because the question must be: 'If this plaintiff had been given the advice that she should have been given, would she have decided to undergo the operation or not?'[99]

This has also been accepted as the correct approach by the courts in Australia;[100] but may be contrasted with the 'objective' test favoured in the United States and Canada, which looks to the hypothetical response of a reasonable person in the patient's position.[101] The latter appears to be rooted in evidential and policy concerns—in particular, the fear (against the backdrop of a mounting medical malpractice crisis) that patients may deceive courts by giving false accounts as to how they would have proceeded if they had known of the risk.[102]

One scenario, which has only recently attracted attention, concerns the implications for the causation requirement of a case where the patient would have delayed the treatment (if properly informed of the risk), but not renounced it for all time. This issue arose in the Australian case of *Chappel v Hart*, in which the claimant sued for injury to her vocal cords and voice loss as a consequence of throat treatment. She could not show that, had she known of the risk of such injury, she would have declined treatment altogether; merely that she would have delayed it and sought the advice of a different surgeon. Ultimately, the High Court of Australia allowed her claim by a three to two majority.[103] Shortly afterwards the same point came before the English courts in the factually similar case of *Chester v Afshar*.[104] The latter case concerned the failure of the defendant neurosurgeon to advise a patient that surgery to relieve her progressive back-trouble carried a one-two per cent risk of causing caudal equina syndrome. She thereupon agreed to the

[98] *Smith v Barking, Havering and Brentwood Health Authority* (1994) 5 Med LR 285 (QBD); *Chester v Afshar* [2002] 3 All ER 533 (CA) para 42.

[99] *Smith v Barking, Havering and Brentwood Health Authority* (1994) 5 Med LR 285 (QBD) 288.

[100] *Rogers v Whitaker* (1992) 109 ALR 625; *Rosenberg v Percival* (2001) 75 ALJR 734.

[101] *Canterbury v Spence* (1972) 464 F 2d 772; *Reibl v Hughes* (1981) 114 DLR (3d) 1. The Supreme Court of Canada reaffirmed the use of the objective approach in *Arndt v Smith* [1997] 2 SCR 539.

[102] In particular, it appears to reflect a lack of confidence in the jury, which in the USA and Canada (unlike in England and Australia) decides such questions.

[103] *Chappel v Hart* (1998) 72 ALJR 1344.

[104] *Chester v Afshar* [2004] UKHL 41.

surgery and suffered severe injury when the risk materialised. Like the claimant in *Chappel*, she accepted that, while she would certainly have deferred the operation had she known of the risk (in order to seek a second opinion), she might well have submitted to it later.

On these facts, the English High Court found for the claimant. As the judge remarked,

> had [the patient] been adequately warned, the operation in question would not have taken place and she would not have suffered damage. In these circumstances, and without more, it seems to me that the necessary causal link is sufficiently established. I do not see how the fact that the claimant cannot prove that at no future time would she have undergone such an operation can break the causal link thus established.[105]

Instead, the possibility of the patient later suffering the same injury (from the hypothetical delayed treatment) would be relevant to the quantum of damages.[106] This reasoning was upheld by the Court of Appeal and ultimately by a majority of the House of Lords. Lord Steyn noted in his speech:

> [B]ut for the surgeon's negligent failure to warn the claimant of the small risk of serious injury the actual injury would not have occurred when it did and the chance of it occurring on a subsequent occasion was very small.[107]

Unfortunately, though, the House of Lords muddied the waters in *Chester* by failing to separate out clearly the issues of factual and legal causation.[108] The latter stage of the enquiry, which raises a special problem in the context of hypothetical delayed treatment, is examined below.

(b) Legal Causation

As discussed in chapter two, legal causation (or remoteness of damage) falls to be considered in negligence actions after factual causation has been established in the claimant's favour. At this point it operates to filter out certain injuries as being 'too remote'—and thus not to be attributed to the defendant—notwithstanding their sine qua non linkage to the latter's breach of duty. In particular, as we saw, the law is usually concerned to exclude liability for unforeseeable or coincidental events, ie cases where the defendant's conduct, though faulty in some respect, was not so in relation to the risk of harm that actually materialised. This is achieved by

105 *Chester v Afshar*, Judge Robert Taylor (QBD, unreported, 21 December 2000) para 81.

106 Ie as in cases where the patient shows he would have continued to refuse treatment, but his condition would later have progressed and caused the same injury. It is a moot point how far statistical evidence might be employed here, ie allowing damages to be discounted by the chance that later surgery would have caused the same injury.

107 *Chester v Afshar* [2004] UKHL 41, para 19.

108 For a trenchant criticism of the judgment, reaffirming the centrality of the factual *vs.* legal causation distinction in the law of negligence, see J Stapleton, 'Occam's Razor Reveals an Orthodox Basis for *Chester v Afshar*' (2006) 122 *LQR* 426.

requiring that the defendant's breach should have created or added to a reasonably foreseeable risk of the injury in suit.[109]

Nonetheless, this approach may run into difficulties in non-disclosure cases where (unlike other actions in negligence) the risk that directly leads to injury is outside the defendant's control, being inherent in the treatment.[110] Admittedly, the problem does not occur in cases where the patient, if told of the risk, would have declined the treatment: there the doctor has caused him to run a risk he would otherwise have avoided. However, matters are otherwise where the patient would merely have delayed treatment following proper disclosure, eg to seek a second opinion. In particular, although the risk there is clearly foreseeable (viz, the risk of iatrogenic injury from treatment), it cannot be said that the doctor's wrongful non-disclosure created or added to it. If the patient would later have had the same treatment, he would have been exposed to it in any event.

As we saw, this conundrum recently exercised the Australian and English courts, in *Chappel v Hart* and *Chester v Afshar*, respectively. On both occasions the doctor was ultimately found liable for the injury. In reaching this result the majority judges noted that a decision the other way would rule out compensation in a significant number of cases—namely whenever the patient could not show he would have continued to reject (equally risky) future treatment. Lord Hope commented in his speech in *Chester*:

> To leave the patient who would have found the decision difficult without a remedy . . . would render the duty [to disclose] useless in the cases where it may be needed most. This would discriminate against those who cannot honestly say that they would have declined the operation once and for all if they had been warned. I would find that result unacceptable. The function of the law is to enable rights to be vindicated and to provide remedies when duties have been breached.[111]

In effect, the usual rules of legal causation have here been relaxed to deal with an infringement of autonomy (through non-disclosure) that puts the patient in the path of a risk, which—while independent in nature—was the very subject of the disclosure duty.

Nonetheless, there remain other non-disclosure cases where liability might well be denied for want of legal causation. One situation is where the risk that injured the patient was entirely extraneous to the treatment. Thus in *Chappel v Hart*, it was implied that there would be no recovery for injury (following the non-disclosure of a risk which would have led the patient to decline treatment) resulting from

[109] *Chappel v Hart* (1998) 72 ALJR 1344, paras 27–29 (McHugh J, citing *Carslogie Steamship Co Ltd v Royal Norwegian Government* [1952] AC 292 (HL)).

[110] Analytically, this can be traced back to the fact that, as discussed in pt I above, the purpose of requiring disclosure is not to reduce the occurrence of injury, but to promote the patient's autonomy.

[111] *Chester v Afshar* [2004] UKHL 41, para 87. See also the Court of Appeal's judgment [2002] 3 All ER 552, para 47: 'If the doctor's failure to take that care results in her consenting to an operation to which she would not otherwise have given her consent, the purpose of that rule would be thwarted if he were not to be held responsible when the very risk about which he failed to warn her materialises and causes her an injury which she would not have suffered then and there'.

lightning striking the operating theatre.[112] More contentious are cases where the risk stemmed from the treatment, but from a *different* risk to that which was wrongly not disclosed (or from one that the patient was actually warned about). As we shall see shortly, this type of problem is well known to the German courts.[113] By contrast, there are few common law authorities in point, and these are not wholly consistent. In the Scottish decision of *Moyes v Lothian Health Board* the judge appeared (obiter) to accept that in such circumstances the doctor would remain liable.[114] However, the Court of Appeal's recent judgment in *Thompson v Bradford* would suggest otherwise.[115]

Ultimately, much is likely to turn upon the judge's intuitive view as to the comparability of the risks at issue. Where they appear similar, the courts, in keeping with their overall approach to legal causation in negligence, may well refuse to draw fine distinctions, and the upshot will be liability.[116] This is especially likely when the doctor's failure to disclose is perceived to involve arrogance or high-handedness. Support for this proposition may be found in the High Court decision of *Hepworth v Kerr*, where a doctor over a period of years experimented with a novel anaesthetic procedure on patients without ever submitting it to proper trials or informing patients of its untested status. In doing so, he knew of the significant risk of causing a cerebral stroke. In the event, one of his patients suffered a spinal stroke, and though this particular risk had not been foreseeable, the court had no hesitation in holding him liable.[117]

2. The Position in Germany

In Germany, the causation issue in disclosure malpractice cases falls to be approached from the starting point that the doctor, by not obtaining valid consent, has unlawfully invaded the patient's bodily integrity. In this context, it remains necessary for there to be a physical causal link between the (unlawful) treatment and the injury. The doctor will not be liable if the injury stemmed instead from a risk associated with the natural progression of the patient's disease.[118] However, the 'psychological' link (ie how would the patient have decided, if he had known of the risk?) was traditionally less important: the direct cause of injury was the unlawful treatment; the circumstances leading up to the treatment could generally be ignored. Instead the main focus, as a potential means of limiting the doctor's liability, was on legal causation arguments—in particular as to scope of duty (*Schutzzweck der Norm*).

[112] *Chappel v Hart* (1998) 72 ALJR 1344, para 118 (Hayne J). See also Gummow J's comments at paras 66–7.

[113] See the discussion in pt IV 2 (a) below.

[114] *Moyes v Lothian Health Board* (1990) 1 Med LR 463 (Ct of Session (OH)) 467 (Lord Caplan).

[115] *Thompson v Bradford* [2005] EWCA Civ 1439; the facts case are discussed in ch 2 above, fn 139.

[116] See ch 2 pt III 2 (a).

[117] *Hepworth v Kerr* (1995) 6 Med LR 139 (QBD). The case was not primarily dealt with as one of non-disclosure. Rather the use of such a risky procedure was held to be treatment malpractice.

[118] BGH, 23 October 1984, NJW 1985, 676.

Admittedly, in more recent years—in the face of an upsurge in disclosure malpractice claims—the psychological factual causation link has been accorded greater prominence in the form of a defence for the doctor of 'hypothetical consent' (*hypothetische Einwilligung*). Even so, since analytically this plea only arises after arguments based on legal causation have failed to exculpate the doctor, we shall examine the latter first.

*(a) Legal Causation (*Schutzzweck der Norm*)*

As we have seen, the doctor's wrongful failure to disclose information to the patient prior to undertaking treatment renders the latter unlawful in its entirety. As noted, conceptually each case is thus akin to battery under the common law. Here, as a starting point, it is clear that where the risk that materialises is that which the doctor wrongly failed to warn the patient about, the doctor will be liable. This includes cases where the same treatment would later have taken place in any event (ie the scenario that occurred in *Chester v Afshar* in England): the doctor is not allowed to argue that his default did not add to the risk of harm, as the patient would subsequently have been exposed to an identical risk. Rather, he would need to show the risk (from the hypothetical later treatment) would actually have materialised and caused the same injury—usually an impossible task.[119]

Nonetheless, sometimes it may be less clear how far the patient's injury should be fairly imputed to the doctor. Problematic in particular are cases where the doctor wrongfully withholds information as to one risk (risk x), and the patient is injured when a *different* risk (risk y) materialises, which it was not necessary to disclose (or indeed was disclosed). Here some commentators have argued for a general limitation of liability in line with *Schutzzweck* considerations. The rule requiring disclosure did not encompass, and hence was not designed to give the patient the opportunity (by declining treatment) to avoid the risk of injury that occurred.[120] This view initially commanded some judicial support. Thus, in a case from 1984 the BGH denied liability where the doctor wrongly failed to warn of the risk of pain during the performance of a rectoscopic examination, and the patient instead suffered a perforated bowel (the remote risk of which did not need to be disclosed).[121] There the court regarded the two risks as incommensurable, the one going to temporary discomfort, the other to bodily health. However, it expressly

[119] See BGH, 13 December 1988, NJW 1989, 1541; Katzenmeier, *Arzthaftungsrecht* (n 27 above) 350. In short, the doctor would have to show 'alternative causation'. As suggested in ch 2 above, text at n 120, this argument may be regarded, strictly, as going to quantum rather than causation.

[120] A Laufs and W Uhlenbruck (eds), *Handbuch des Arztrechts*, 3rd edn (Munich, Beck, 2002) § 67, paras 5 ff; E Deutsch, 'Schutzbereich und Beweislast der ärztlichen Aufklärungspflicht' *NJW* 1984, 1802; see further E Steffen, 'Haftung des Arztes für Fehler bei der Risikoaufklärung—Zurechnungsbeschränkungen oder *versari in re illicita*?' in V Beuthien (ed), *Festschrift für Medicus* (Cologne, Heymann, 1999) 637, 639 ff.

[121] BGH, 7 February 1984, NJW 1984, 1395.

left open whether a similar *Schutzzweck* limitation would apply where both risks at issue concerned the patient's health.[122]

The BGH subsequently had occasion to consider this point in a decision in 1989 and there prima facie rejected such a limitation. Rather, the doctor's liability would extend in the first instance to *all* injuries flowing from the treatment:

> Consent to medical treatment is something that can only be given or refused in its entirety . . . Accordingly, where there is a deficit in disclosure, the treatment as a whole is unlawful, regardless of whether the risk that materialised was itself disclosable or not; to the extent that the lack of disclosure involved fault on the doctor's part, he will thus be liable in principle for all of the treatment's injurious consequences.[123]

As a justification, the court pointed to the central importance of protecting the patient's autonomy and bodily integrity. However, at the same time it acknowledged a residual role for *Schutzzweck* arguments. In particular, these would be relevant where, notwithstanding the doctor's failure to divulge all legally disclosable information, there was at least a 'basic disclosure' (*Grundaufklärung*)—ie the patient was told of the most serious risks that might occur. Here, provided further that the (non-disclosable) risk that eventuated was very rare and 'lay in a different direction' to the risk whose non-disclosure made the treatment unlawful, the doctor would escape liability.[124] By contrast, in cases where there is no *Grundaufklärung* the doctor will remain liable. Thus, in a case from 1996, the BGH imposed liability where the patient was not warned that her treatment (a myelography) could, in rare cases, result in paralysis. This risk—whose disclosure the court regarded as within the *Grundaufklärung*—did not materialise, but she suffered a permanent neurological deficit when a different (non-disclosable) risk did.[125]

At first sight, the distinction revolving around the presence or absence of a *Grundaufklärung* may strike the comparativist as having parallels with that between basic and collateral information, underpinning the battery-negligence divide in common law. However, on closer examination the two ideas have little in common. Thus, as noted, the German distinction goes to the discrete risks bound up with a given treatment; it does not involve distinguishing information as to the treatment's 'nature and purpose' from its risks. Moreover, whereas the common law distinction underlies the conceptualisation of the whole area of disclosure malpractice, the role of the *Grundaufklärung* is more peripheral: it is merely one precondition for the doctor to run a limiting argument (relevant at most in a minority of cases) that the injury in suit fell outside the scope of his disclosure duty.

[122] *Ibid*, 1396. See further the discussion in Helbron, *Entwicklungen und Fehlentwicklungen im Arzthaftungsrecht* (n 58 above) 95 ff.

[123] BGH, 14 February 1989, NJW 1989, 1533 (1535).

[124] *Ibid.* See also BGH, 12 March 1991, NJW 1991, 2346; Geiß and Greiner, *Arzthaftpflichtrecht* (n 29 above) paras C156–C157; Katzenmeier, *Arzthaftung* (n 27 above) 345 ff.

[125] BGH, 14 November 1995, VersR 1996, 195. The decision is translated and discussed (as case no 1) in M Faure and H Koziol (eds), *Cases on Medical Malpractice in a Comparative Perspective* (Vienna, Springer, 2001).

More recently, a further limitation on liability—again stemming from *Schutzzweck* considerations—has been applied in cases where the risk of the injury in suit had in fact been disclosed. In this context, the BGH dismissed an action brought by a mother, who, in consenting to a vaccination on behalf of her child, had been told of the risk of injury that actually occurred, but not of certain other risks she ought to have been.[126] In such a case, it does not matter if the patient received a *Grundaufklärung*: it is sufficient that he was put in the picture with respect to the risk of the actual injury. This, however, is subject to an exception where, besides the injury stemming from the risk that was disclosed, the patient simultaneously suffers injury through another risk that was wrongly not disclosed. Thus, in a case from 2001, the patient suffered both nerve damage (leading to lameness) and impotence following spinal surgery. The doctor, who had wrongly failed to warn of the second risk, was held liable for *both* consequences—the issue of whether he had told the patient about the first risk was treated as irrelevant.[127]

(b) The Defence of Hypothetical Consent

As noted earlier, in the past the defence of hypothetical consent (*hypothetische Einwilligung*) was rarely used. However, because of the problem of very wide potential liability in disclosure malpractice cases—following both from the onerous duties of disclosure and the relative lack of *Schutzzweck* limitations—the courts have increasingly had recourse to it in the last 25 years.[128] In a leading decision from 1984, the BGH commented that

> in cases where the patient seeks to derive a compensation claim from a deficit in risk-disclosure, he too may come under a duty to substantiate his claim . . . This is at any rate so when, in the light of the gravity of his illness and the success to be expected from the therapy (as against the relatively slight disadvantages normally bound up with it), it is not on the face of it clear why the patient should have rejected it . . . Only thus can the misuse of the rules relating to risk-disclosure be prevented, viz their use retrospectively to bolster claims that are in reality about obtaining compensation.[129]

In conceptual terms, the argument is an instance of a more general defence under German law, namely that of *rechtmäßiges Alternativverhalten* (lawful alternative conduct). Potentially this is available in cases where the law categorises conduct as unlawful per se (ie irrespective of whether it results in harm), because then, insofar as harm occurs, it may be queried whether the feature making the

[126] BGH, 15 February 2000, NJW 2000, 1784.

[127] BGH, 30 January 2001, NJW 2001, 2798. See further the commentary by C Wendehorst in *Lindenmaier Möhring* § 823 (Dd) BGB (Nr 27).

[128] See eg BGH, 1 October 1985, NJW 1986, 1541; OLG Karlsruhe, 3 March 1993, VersR 1994, 860; OLG Stuttgart, 15 May 1997, VersR 1998, 1111.

[129] BGH, 7 February 1984, NJW 1984, 1397 (1399). This case was that of the spinal radiotherapy treatment: see n 70 above.

conduct unlawful was implicated (as a necessary condition) in the harm.[130] In the present context, it is clear that injury flowed physically from the doctor's unlawful treatment. Nevertheless the latter's argument would be that, even if he had acted lawfully (by disclosing the risks), such injury would have occurred, as in that case, too, the patient would have agreed to the treatment.

Admittedly, there has been some debate in the academic literature as to how far the doctor should be permitted to run such a defence.[131] In this regard it has sometimes been suggested that its availability represents an unjustifiable weakening of patient autonomy, as safeguarded by the underlying disclosure rule. Indeed, Giesen argued that the court, in second-guessing the patient's hypothetical choice (in the course of applying the defence), becomes complicit in the deprivation of autonomy.[132] However, as other commentators have pointed out, the right to choose was in truth lost when the doctor failed to make proper disclosure. Furthermore, it has been noted that not to allow the defence would favour patients who would have run the risk (but were not told of it) over those who did run the risk, having been told of it.[133] In the main, the general academic view today is supportive of the BGH's approach, seeing the defence as allowing a reasonable compromise between the different interests at stake—the patient's autonomy on the one hand, and the need to avoid making it too easy for him to secure fortuitous recovery against the doctor on the other.[134]

In this regard, the patient's interests are seen as adequately protected by the fact that, as noted, hypothetical consent is a defence, which the doctor must raise. Failing this, a court is precluded from enquiring into the matter of its own motion.[135] To the extent that the question is before the court, the latter (like the English courts) employ a subjective perspective: the doctor will be required to prove that the particular patient (possessed of the information) would still have agreed to the treatment.[136] As we shall see below, in rebuttal the patient need do

130 See Geiß and Greiner, *Arzthaftpflichtrecht* (n 29 above) para C137. This type of argument is known to the common law in the context of breaches of statutory duty. A case in point is *The Empire Jamaica* [1957] AC 386 (HL), where an uncertificated, but experienced ship's officer caused a collision: the decision is discussed by HLA Hart and AM Honoré, *Causation in the Law*, 2nd edn (Oxford, Clarendon Press, 1985) *Preface: lviii–lix.*

131 See Katzenmeier, *Arzthaftung* (n 27 above) 367.

132 Giesen, *Arzthaftung* (n 80 above) para 234; see also H Koziol, 'Rechtmäßiges Alternativverhalten—Auflockerung starrer Lösungsansätze' in J Ahrens (ed), *Festschrift für Deutsch* (Cologne, Heymann, 1999) 179, who argues (at 186–7) that the defence's availability should turn on an overall assessment of how flagrantly the doctor violated the patient's autonomy, by failing to disclose information.

133 Katzenmeier, *Arzthaftung* (n 27 above) 368; K Nüßgens, 'Zwei Fragen zur zivilrechtlichen Haftung des Arztes' in E von Caemmerer (ed), *Festschrift für Hauß* (Karlsruhe, VVW, 1978) 287, 293.

134 Katzenmeier, *Arzthaftung* (n 27 above) 368.

135 BGH, 14 June 1994, NJW 1994, 2414; Geiß and Greiner, *Arzthaftpflichtrecht* (n 29 above) para C 139.

136 BGH, 22 January 1980, NJW 1980, 1333; Steffen, 'Haftung des Arztes für Fehler bei der Risikoaufklärung' (n 120 above) 643.

no more than show that the information would have placed him in a 'significant dilemma', not that he would necessarily have refused.[137]

V. Proof Issues

The divergent approaches in England and Germany to the substantive legal rules in this area carry over into the proof rules that supplement them. In England the rules assume little autonomous significance: the patient's situation in respect of a non-disclosure action is similar to that if he were claiming for treatment malpractice. By contrast, in Germany, the distinctive structure of this type of action is attended by considerable proof advantages for the patient (compared to an action for treatment malpractice).

1. England: Parallels with Treatment Malpractice

In England, the same proof rules apply as for the tort of negligence in general. That is to say, the patient has the burden of proving both the doctor's breach of duty and factual causation on the balance of probabilities.[138] As regards the first element, this means that—before any question of legally evaluating the doctor's conduct arises—the patient must satisfy the court that the doctor in fact failed to warn him of the relevant risk. Here, the court will proceed as in any other factual dispute, doing its best to reconstruct events in the light of all the evidence now available.

Insofar as the patient signed a consent form acknowledging that he was informed of the risk, this, while supportive of the doctor's position, will not be conclusive. In this context, Bristow J in *Chatterton v Gerson* commented that getting the patient to sign such a form

> should be a valuable reminder to everyone of the need for explanation and consent. But it would be no defence . . . if no explanation had in fact been given.[139]

As this implies, the court might decide on the balance of other evidence available that the patient signed the form 'blindly', without receiving the information. In doing so, it will take account of his personality and concerns, as reflected eg in previous consultations, and whether this squares psychologically with a decision to submit to the treatment despite the risk (ie were the consent form to be accepted as an accurate record).[140]

[137] See the discussion at n 153 ff, below.

[138] See ch 3 pt II 1. In the (rare) case of an alleged battery, it remains uncertain whether the patient or doctor has the burden of proving the absence/presence of consent. The few authorities are divided on the question: see Jones, *Medical Negligence* (n 20 above) para 6-015.

[139] *Chatterton v Gerson* [1981] QB 432 (QBD) 443.

[140] See the Court of Appeal's judgment in *Chester v Afshar* [2002] 3 All ER 533, para 17.

Conversely, the doctor's failure to document what he told the patient will not automatically lead to an adverse inference being drawn. As with cases where treatment malpractice is alleged, the court will be prepared to admit evidence as to the doctor's normal practice with regard to risk-disclosure as an indicator of what probably occurred in the case at hand. This was the position, for example, in *Sidaway v Board of Governors of the Bethlem Royal Hospital*, where the surgeon had died prior to the case coming to trial.[141]

Moving on to the issue of factual causation, as discussed earlier, this involves the need to show both a 'physical' and 'psychological' link between the non-disclosure and the injury. In terms of the former, the court must be satisfied on the balance of probabilities that the injury was physically connected to the treatment. This is unlikely to be in point as a basis for denying liability altogether—as noted earlier, the doctor will usually concede such a connection. Nonetheless, he may sometimes seek a reduction in the quantum of damages by arguing that treatment merely accelerated an injury which (had the patient rejected it) would have materialised a short time later due to the progression of his medical condition. This argument will be for the doctor to raise and prove.[142]

Secondly, as regards the psychological link, the focus will be upon the particular patient's personality and concerns. As discussed above, the substantive issue is how the latter would have reacted to the information: would it have affected his decision to have the treatment? By the nature of things, the only direct evidence will come from the patient, and he has a vested interest in answering the question affirmatively. It is this point which underlies the American and Canadian courts' preference for an inquiry based on what a hypothetical reasonable patient would have done.[143] However, where a judge is trying the issue, that approach appears superfluous. As Kirby J noted in the Australian High Court in *Chappel v Hart*,

> these dangers [ie that patients might deceive the court] should not be overstated. Tribunals of fact can be trusted to reject absurd, self-interested assertions.[144]

In this context, Hutchison J in the English High Court decision of *Smith v Barking, Havering and Brentwood Health Authority* suggested that

> [i]f everything points to the fact that a reasonable plaintiff, properly informed, would have assented to the operation the assertion from the witness box, made after the adverse outcome is known, in a wholly artificial situation and in the knowledge that the outcome of the case depends upon that assertion being maintained, does not carry great weight unless there are extraneous or additional factors to substantiate it.[145]

In other words, the court will be guided evidentially by the likely conduct of a hypothetical reasonable patient. If the claimant testifies that his conduct would

[141] *Sidaway v Board of Governors of the Bethlem Royal Hospital* [1985] AC 871 (HL).

[142] The same will apply if the doctor wishes to argue that the patient would later have had the treatment and the same risk would then have eventuated: see n 106 above.

[143] See the text at n 101 above.

[144] *Chappel v Hart* (1998) 72 ALJR, para 91 (Kirby J).

[145] *Smith v Barking, Havering and Brentwood Health Authority* (1994) 5 Med LR 285 (QBD) 289.

have deviated from the norm, the court will require this to be supported by extra reasons. Examples of these could include 'religious or some other firmly held convictions; particular social or domestic considerations'.[146]

2. Germany: A Distinct Framework

As we have seen, analytically, the patient's consent to treatment provides a defence to conduct that would otherwise qualify as an unlawful bodily injury. Accordingly, the burden of proof as to showing consent rests upon the doctor. Furthermore, since under German law this presupposes the adequate disclosure of risks and alternatives (not just—as under the common law—basic knowledge about the treatment), it follows that the doctor must prove the patient received all such relevant information.[147] The evidence that the doctor tenders in this respect will fall to be assessed by reference to the onerous standard of proof under § 286 of the Code of Civil Procedure (*Zivilprozessordnung*—ZPO).

In this regard, the fact that the patient signed a consent form acknowledging that various risks were disclosed will not be enough by itself: it must be shown that a discussion of the relevant risks with the patient actually took place.[148] At the same time, the courts have taken note of the potential difficulties for doctors in cases where the patient flatly denies there was any discussion. Thus, the BGH has stated:

> If at least some evidence is to hand, showing the doctor conscientiously informed the patient as to the risks, the doctor should in cases of doubt be believed that the requisite information was provided in the case at hand . . . Written documentation recording the discussion—at least in its essentials—is helpful and strongly to be recommended. However, the lack of such evidence should not be treated by itself as meaning that the doctor has failed to discharge his burden of proof.[149]

Indeed, the court in the same case observed that the relationship between doctor and patient should remain free as far as possible from 'the bureaucratic formalism of insisting strictly upon the patient's signature'.[150]

As regards the physical causation link between the treatment and injury, the burden of proof will remain on the patient: ie he must show that the injury occurred through the materialisation of a treatment risk. Nonetheless, the relevant standard of proof will be the lower one (under § 287 ZPO). This is because, in terms of the distinction between *haftungsbegründende* and *haftungsausfüllende Kausalität* ('liability-grounding' and 'liability-completing' causation), looked at in chapter two, the injury qualifies as secondary, flowing from the primary wrong of

[146] *Smith v Barking, Havering and Brentwood Health Authority* (1994) 5 Med LR 285 (QBD) 289.
[147] Geiß and Greiner, *Arzthaftpflichtrecht* (n 29 above) para C131.
[148] Katzenmeier, *Arzthaftung* (n 27 above) 498.
[149] BGH, 8 January 1985, NJW 1985, 1399 (1399).
[150] *Ibid.*

non-consensual treatment.[151] As noted in discussing the English law, the physical link as such will normally not be in dispute. However, sometimes the doctor may try to reduce the damages payable by arguing that without treatment, the same injury would have occurred later. In such cases, the burden of proving the existence of such alternative causation (*hypothetischer Kausalverlauf*) will be on the doctor, and to the high standard of proof under § 286 ZPO.[152]

Lastly, with respect to the psychological factual causation link (involving the defence of hypothetical consent), this, as noted above, will also be for the doctor to raise and prove. Nonetheless, once he shows that, objectively, a refusal of consent would have been very much against the patient's interests, the tactical burden will shift to the latter. At this stage, the patient is not, though, required to show how he would actually have decided: such a question is regarded as inherently speculative and uncertain. Rather, it is sufficient for him to demonstrate that he would have faced a significant dilemma (*ernsthafter Entscheidungskonflikt*).[153] The BGH stated in a case from 1990:

> A precise answer from the patient as to how he would actually have chosen cannot be demanded, and indeed would set him an impossible task, given the difficulty . . . in reconstructing the situation that then faced him. The most that he can and should be asked to show is that full information as to the pros and cons of the treatment would have led him seriously to question whether he should agree to it or not.[154]

The conclusion that there would have been no dilemma and the patient would have consented anyway will need a clear foundation in the actual circumstances and character of the patient. In this regard, the trial judge will be required to hear the patient in person.[155] The BGH has cautioned against an unduly strict approach in assessing the testimony in question. Thus, in the 1990 decision cited above it was prepared to accept that, had the patient known the treatment involved a high risk of hepatitis, he would have hesitated between it and the amputation of his hand. This again may be seen to be consistent with the onerous standard of proof under § 286 ZPO, by which any reasonable doubt will be fatal to the doctor's contention. However, where there appears to be no plausible basis at all for a dilemma on the patient's part, the court will find the doctor's defence made out.[156]

[151] BGH, 13 January 1987, NJW 1987, 1481; Geiß and Greiner, *Arzthaftpflichtrecht* (n 29 above) para C147. As to the distinction between primary and secondary harm, see ch 2 pt III 1 (b).

[152] BGH, 15 March 2005, NJW 2005, 1718; BGH, 5 April 2005, NJW 2005, 2072.

[153] Geiß and Greiner, above n 29, paras C138 ff.

[154] BGH, 11 December 1990, NJW 1991, 1543 (1544).

[155] BGH, 4 April 1995, NJW 1995, 2410.

[156] BGH, 7 February 1984, NJW 1984, 1397; BGH, 1 October 1985, NJW 1986, 1541; OLG Karlsruhe, 3 March 1993, VersR 1994, 860.

VI. Comparative Assessment

As in the case of proof issues examined in chapter three, the comparison of the way English and German law deal with claims for disclosure malpractice has revealed some striking differences of approach. These manifest themselves at various stages of the legal inquiry, beginning with the categorisation of the medical duty to disclose information about treatment (and the implications for consent). Here, as we saw, English law has—in common with other common law systems—taken a bifurcated approach. On the one hand, there is 'basic information' as to the nature and purpose of the treatment, failing the disclosure of which consent is invalid and the patient has an action in battery; and on the other hand, 'collateral information' (including risks and alternatives). The failure to divulge the latter does not affect consent, instead going at most to liability in negligence. German law, by contrast, adopts a unitary approach, under which the wrongful failure to disclose risks will—as in the case of more basic information—vitiate consent and render treatment unlawful.

On one level, as we saw, this difference rests on a structural divergence in the tort law of the two countries: English law distinguishes historically between intentional and unintentional invasions of a person's bodily interests (covered by battery and negligence, respectively); by contrast, German law places both types of invasion under a single codal provision, in § 823 I BGB. Here, a key factor motivating common law courts to find consent, despite the patient's ignorance of treatment risks, is in order to sidestep the need to address such claims in battery, a motive absent within the context of the German scheme. At another level, though, the difference arguably betrays distinct views as to what such claims are really 'about'. The common law, by placing them in negligence, assimilates them to other cases involving compensation for personal injury: the patient is required to get over the same hurdles as his counterpart suing for treatment malpractice. By contrast, in Germany, such claims have been conceptually disengaged. The focus is there upon the injury to the patient's autonomy in not receiving the information he was due. This is the primary object of complaint, with the additional personal injury that accrues a corollary to be made good usually as a matter of course.[157]

Also striking is the divergent standards used in each country to determine when the doctor will be at fault, ie When ought a given risk to have been disclosed? In England the courts in the past accorded considerable discretion to the doctor to withhold information as to risks, where this conformed to 'accepted practice'. In this regard English law lagged behind the common law norm, as reflected in the 'informed consent' approach of many US States, Canada and Australia. In holding

[157] As noted, and further discussed below, in practice the difference is watered down. Thus in Germany too there will be causal limitations placed on the patient's ability to recover for personal injury even though it flowed directly from the invasion of his autonomy.

to it, the courts (as in cases involving treatment malpractice) accorded primacy to the doctor's judgement and discretion, in this case over the patient's interest in participating as an intelligent subject in treatment. Admittedly, this restrictive approach has softened in recent years. However, this is arguably due less to progressive judicial decisions than changes in the attitudes and practice of the medical profession.[158]

Even so, English law remains a good way behind the German disclosure standard, which has sometimes required risks calculated in minute fractions to be divulged. On the face of it, the German case law appears maximally protective of patient autonomy.[159] However, as noted, it has by no means found universal acceptance. In particular, it has been criticised for imposing an exaggerated and uncertain standard, which in practice is impossible to meet. Indeed the courts' approach may be regarded as one of de facto strict liability: the doctor is liable simply on the basis of the injurious treatment outcome. As noted earlier, there is a suspicion that such claims here serve as a fall-back option to redress the evidential difficulties patients encounter in alleging fault in the treatment. In this context, the contrast with a doctor who fails to disclose his (or his hospital's) ex ante inability to satisfy the required standard of care is arguably revealing. There—where treatment malpractice will subsequently be relatively easy to establish—German law appears to be no stricter as to the relevant disclosure duties than the law in England.[160]

Moving on to the causal connection required between the doctor's wrongful non-disclosure and the patient's injury, the English and German approaches here again differ markedly. This can again be linked to the different sense of what is at stake. As we have seen, the assumption in both systems is that the doctor was not to blame in relation to the actual materialisation of the injurious risk, but rather in not disclosing its existence (so denying the patient the opportunity to avoid it). In England, where the legal focus is on the resulting injury, it remains for the patient to show he would have used the opportunity, by deciding against treatment.[161] This accords with the principle of corrective justice, which, as argued in chapter two, reserves compensation for cases where an agent's faulty conduct actually altered events, leading to injury where otherwise there would have been none. It is apparent, though, that in the process the common law gives imperfect expression to patient autonomy: there is no sanction for the breach of the patient's right to know where he would not have acted on the information.

[158] As to the doctors' own professional guidance on the disclosure of risks, see GMC, *Seeking Consent: the Ethical Considerations* (n 50 above).

[159] Albeit it might be queried how far knowledge of negligible risks is really required by the autonomy principle; on one view this is more likely to encourage whimsical choices than mature decision-making in line with the actor's life-plan. For the conception of autonomy, see Dworkin, *The Theory and Practice of Autonomy* (n 3 above) 108 ff.

[160] See the text at n 94 above.

[161] As noted, following the decision in *Chester v Ashfar* [2004] UKHL 41, the patient must still show that he would at least have delayed the treatment (ie not undergone the operation when he did).

By contrast, the approach in Germany places greater stress upon the usurpation of autonomy: the doctor's failure to provide the information makes the treatment unlawful, and it is enough that the injury occurred as a physical consequence. At the same time, as we saw, a factual causation limitation has increasingly been recognised in German law in the form of the defence of 'hypothetical consent'. Though this remains for the doctor to prove (to a high standard), it can be argued that the law has thereby drawn closer to the common law approach. Indeed, as we saw, in developing the defence the BGH has acknowledged that the motivation of patients in bringing non-disclosure claims is not so much to vindicate autonomy, but to recover damages for iatrogenic injury.[162]

Secondly, as we saw, there remains at the stage of deciding legal causation the question how far the risk that materialised must be one of the risks whose non-disclosure rendered the doctor's conduct faulty. German law has—in the light of the weaker role played by factual causation as a filter—had more occasion to consider this point than the common law. On the whole, as we saw, the courts have adopted an expansive approach, refusing to apply *Schutzzweck* considerations to limit recovery. Under the common law, it is likely that a similar approach would prevail, not allowing the doctor to escape liability on the basis of small discrepancies in the risks at issue, but arguably doing so where they are radically different. Even so, this problem arises comparatively rarely: the patient's injury will in most cases derive straightforwardly from a risk the doctor ought to have disclosed.

Lastly, as we saw, the general conceptual divergence in the two countries' approach to disclosure malpractice claims has radical implications for issues of proof. Whereas in negligence under the common law the burden remains on the patient, in Germany it is the doctor, who must prove as a defence (to what will otherwise be unlawful bodily injury) that he disclosed sufficient information about risks to render consent valid. In the light of the problems that patients there often have in treatment malpractice cases due to the high civil standard of proof, this is of great importance, and has contributed to the popularity of non-disclosure actions. Notwithstanding academic criticisms, the German courts have held steadfastly to their 'treatment as bodily injury' approach, rationalising a shift in proof from the outset, without the need (in contrast to treatment malpractice cases) to develop elaborate exceptions to the normal rules.

[162] See BGH, 7 February 1984, NJW 1984, 1397.

5

Reforming Medical Negligence Law

I. Introduction

IN THE FOREGOING chapters we have examined the legal rules in England and Germany that govern claims by patients in respect of medical injury—both in terms of the substantive elements required for such claims to succeed and the proof aspects relating to the same. In both countries, as we saw, the courts have developed the rules in question within the context of private law, in which a central role has been taken by the fault principle: the patient will generally only be entitled to compensation where he can show that his injury resulted from faulty (ie substandard) conduct on the doctor or hospital's part.[1] By contrast, the present chapter has a broader focus, placing the bilateral obligations between doctor and patient in the wider social context, where the costs of upholding the fault principle may appear unreasonably high. In this regard, it will consider proposals from outside the courts that have been mooted in both countries over the years, and have aimed to replace or supplement the existing legal mechanisms for addressing medical injury claims.

Undoubtedly, a key stimulus in promoting critical reflection about how the law deals with medical malpractice claims has been the increase in such litigation. Since around 1950, prior to which such claims appear to have been restricted in both countries to a handful per year, the rise has been exponential. In England, there are today over 10 times as many claims (5,000–7,000 per annum) as the 500 per year that the Pearson Report estimated for the mid-1970s[2]; in Germany, where the increase began earlier (in the late-1950s), there were by the end of the 1970s already around 6,000 claims per annum. Since then, this figure has further multiplied to at least 20,000 (though it may in fact be a good deal higher).[3] During the

[1] As noted, in Germany, liability is in practice increasingly strict, eg as in cases involving the non-disclosure of risks, looked at in ch 4.

[2] Chief Medical Officer (Sir Liam Donaldson) *Making Amends: A consultation paper setting out proposals for reforming the approach to clinical negligence in the NHS* (London, Department of Health, 2003) 58 ff; R Lewis, A Morris and K Oliphant, 'Tort Personal Injury Statistics: Is there a Compensation Culture in the United Kingdom?' (2006) 2 *Journal of Personal Injury Law* 87 at 92 ff.

[3] See C Katzenmeier, *Arzthaftung* (Tübingen, Mohr Siebeck, 2002) 39 ff, who notes lack of reliable figures for Germany, but puts the figure (based on reports to liability insurers) at between 20,000 and 35,000 per year; A Ehlers and H Broglie (eds), *Arzthaftung*, 3rd edn (Munich, Beck, 2005) 3, posit a figure anywhere between 20,000 and 100,000.

same period the costs of dealing with such claims have also risen dramatically, with a sharp increase discernible in both legal costs and the amount of compensation paid out. Thus, in England the total expenditure on negligence by the NHS rose from £6.33m (at 2002 prices) in 1975 to £446m in 2001–02.[4] In Germany, the average expenses per insurer per claim (including those that are abandoned or settled) trebled from 1981–2001; in some sub-areas the rise has been more than six-fold.[5]

Admittedly, as noted in chapter one, the above developments are part of an overall trend towards increased 'claims-consciousness' in society. In fact, considered as a proportion of overall litigation for personal injuries, the incidence of medical malpractice claims remains low. Thus, in England such claims still only make up 1.5 per cent of claims for compensation for personal injury (compared to 0.2 per cent at the end of the 1970s).[6] This point is reinforced when their number is set against the millions of treatment decisions taken each year for patients in healthcare: the risk, for an individual doctor, of being sued is fairly small.[7] In this regard commentators in England and Germany agree that a US-style malpractice crisis has not occurred in either country, and is unlikely to do so.[8] Even so, the increase in litigation in this field has generated a disproportionate amount of concern compared to that provoked by other types of compensation claim.

II. Dissatisfaction with Private Law in Medical Injury Claims

1. Criticisms of the Fault-Based Approach

Dissatisfaction with the present system of private law as a response to claims for medical injury has a number of aspects. First, there is a perception that the fault principle, underpinning private law, sits uneasily with the special nature of the doctor-patient relationship. As previously noted, the rationale for the principle, in terms of the underlying ideal of corrective justice, is that in one case the claimant's injury is attributable to a wrong—the defendant's unjustified risk-taking—and in the other it is not: the injury is simply 'fateful'. However, while this model is plausible in terms of self-interested risk-taking by a defendant (furthering their

[4] See Lewis, 'Tort Personal Injury Statistics' (n 2 above) 95 ff; CMO, *Making Amends* (n 2 above) 60.

[5] Katzenmeier, *Arzthaftung* (n 3 above) 42. In gynaecology, costs increased six-fold in the decade between 1981 and 1991: see G Fischer and H Lilie (eds), *Ärztliche Verantwortung im europäischen Rechtsvergleich* (Cologne, Heymann, 1999) 22.

[6] CMO, *Making Amends* (n 2 above) 59.

[7] Ehlers and Broglie, *Arzthaftung* (n 3 above) 3.

[8] Katzenmeier, *Arzthaftung* (n 3 above) 43 ff; M Brazier, 'The Case for a No-Fault Compensation Scheme for Medical Accidents' in SAM McLean (ed), *Compensation for Damage: an international perspective* (Aldershot, Dartmouth Publishing, 1993) 51 at 52.

interests while taking insufficient account of those of the claimant), it arguably transfers less well to the medical setting of primarily altruistic risk-taking. Effective medical care involves on-going interventions by the doctor on behalf of the patient. The doctor is required to take finely calculated risks, involving skill and judgement aimed at (and generally succeeding in) conferring benefits upon the patient. Here, a single error may set at nought weeks or months of supererogatory care. As Mustill LJ commented in the English Court of Appeal in *Wilsher v Essex Area Health Authority*,

> [the medical staff] safely brought [the claimant] through the perilous shoals of [his] early life. For all that we know, they far surpassed on numerous occasions the standard of reasonable care. Yet it is said that for one lapse they . . . are to be held liable in damages . . . Has not the law taken a wrong turning if an action like this is to succeed?[9]

In this context it has been argued that the prospect of litigation in the event that something goes wrong undermines from the outset the trust and confidence that are so important to the therapeutic relationship. This is often coupled with doubts as to whether the fault principle here achieves the positive effects claimed for it in other areas, in the form of prevention/deterrence and accountability.[10] Indeed, it has been suggested that the prospect of liability may produce perverse incentives, leading to the practice of 'defensive medicine' (where treatment measures are aimed at avoiding litigation more than benefiting the patient). The latter is admittedly a difficult phenomenon to substantiate, and some commentators query its existence. Thus, Jones has observed that it is unclear how 'doing something that is potentially harmful to patients can be a sensible strategy for avoiding litigation'.[11] A response may be that doctors are overly willing to expose patients to procedures that are 'harmful' in a non-actionable sense (eg inconvenient, time-consuming and uncomfortable) in order to ward off the remote risk of actionable injury. Be that as it may, there is a widespread assumption in both England and Germany that the practice exists.[12]

A second major concern relates to the high costs of litigation itself in this area, deriving from the complexity and uncertainty of many claims. This is an issue that

[9] *Wilsher v Essex Area Health Authority* [1987] QB 730 (CA) 746. Mustill LJ put this point in the mouth of an imaginary critic, as opposed to expressing it as his own view.

[10] There is an extensive literature here, with some commentators expressing doubt as to whether—in the context of tort liability as a whole—the fault principle really achieves these effects: see generally, P Cane, *Atiyah's Accidents, Compensation and the Law*, 6th edn (London, Butterworths, 1999) 361 ff. As regards the specific question whether fault-based liability achieves them in the medical context, the consensus seems to be that such effects are unclear: see eg Brazier, 'The Case for a No-Fault Compensation Scheme for Medical Accidents' (n 8 above) 59 ff; A Merry and A McCall Smith, *Errors, Medicine and the Law* (Cambridge, Cambridge University Press, 2001), 50 ff; Katzenmeier, *Arzthaftung* (n 3 above) 249 ff; U Thumann, *Reform der Arzthaftung in den Vereinigten Staaten von Amerika* (Cologne, Heymann, 2000) 206.

[11] M Jones, *Medical Negligence*, 3rd edn (London, Sweet & Maxwell, 2003) para 1-052.

[12] See CMO, *Making Amends* (n 2 above) 76; Brazier, 'The Case for a No-Fault Compensation Scheme for Medical Accidents' (n 8 above) 63–4; H-L Schreiber, 'Handlungsbedarf für den Gesetzgeber?' in A Laufs (ed), *Die Entwicklung der Arzthaftung* (Berlin, Springer, 1997) 343; H Radau, *Ersetzung der Arzthaftung durch Versicherungsschutz* (Karlsruhe, VVW, 1993) 115. An underlying concern is also the financial cost of such a strategy.

affects medical injury claims probably more than any comparable form of action. One reason, as we saw in chapter two, is that medical negligence requires expert evaluation to determine if there was fault—frequently a contested question, given the fluidity and scope for variant practices in medical science. Above all, though, it is difficulties of proof that make such claims so hard to predict. As discussed in chapter three, it is often difficult, especially for the patient, to reconstruct events so as to provide an adequate basis for a finding of fault against the doctor. In the light of this there has been some discussion in both England and Germany as to whether doctors should be under a 'duty of candour' to tell patients when negligence occurs.[13] So far, though, a duty of this kind does not exist as a matter of law. Moreover, it would provide only a partial solution, as it leaves untouched the evidential problems in deciding if fault, where found, caused the patient's injury.

It remains true that—as with other private law actions—only a small minority of claims ultimately reach court, most being settled or abandoned well before that point: figures for England, cited by the Chief Medical Officer (CMO) suggest that 60–70 per cent of claims do not proceed beyond initial contact with a solicitor. Of those that continue, around 95 per cent will be settled before trial.[14] In Germany, too, most actions do not proceed beyond the early stages, with ultimately fewer than 10 per cent going to court.[15] Nonetheless, for the reasons cited, they invariably consume significant investigative resources. In his Report, the CMO estimated for England that the legal and administrative costs of settling claims exceeded money paid out in the majority of claims worth under £45,000.[16] Similarly, in both countries it is not uncommon for cases, especially where appealed, to drag on for years. In Germany, it appears proceedings take on average more than three years to go to trial and—in the case of final appeals—over 10 years to reach the BGH.[17] Unsurprisingly the costs and strain involved will often deter the patient from bringing a notionally valid claim to begin with (or lead him to settle it on unfavourable terms). This appears to be borne out by international studies, suggesting that only a fraction of patients injured by medical negligence commence legal proceedings: the upshot is the denial of practical justice in many instances.[18]

[13] See the remarks of Sir John Donaldson MR in *Lee v South West Thames Regional Health Authority* [1985] 1 WLR 845 (CA) 850–51; for Germany, see H Prütting, 'Gibt es eine ärztliche Pflicht zur Fehleroffenbarung?' in B-R Kern (ed), *Festschrift für Laufs* (Berlin, Springer, 2006) 1009. In his Report, *Making Amends*, the Chief Medical Officer recommended such a duty should be introduced (backed by protection to the doctor from disciplinary sanctions): CMO (n 2 above) 125. However, this has not yet occurred.

[14] CMO, *Making Amends* (n 2 above) 60.

[15] GH Schlund, 'Bestandaufnahme: Gutachter- und Schlichtungsstellen' in A Laufs (ed), *Die Entwicklung der Arzthaftung* (n 12 above) 333.

[16] CMO, *Making Amends* (n 2 above) 69; see for Germany Radau, *Ersetzung der Arzthaftung durch Versicherungsschutz* (n 12 above) 80 ff.

[17] Radau, *Ersetzung der Arzthaftung durch Versicherungsschutz* (n 12 above) 81.

[18] Cane, *Atiyah's Accidents, Compensation and the Law* (n 10 above) 170 ff. As Brazier notes in 'The Case for a No-Fault Compensation Scheme for Medical Accidents' (n 8 above) at 60, this also feeds back negatively on the accountability issue.

For the doctor too, though, the disadvantages of the present system should not be forgotten. It is true he need not directly fear the financial impact of liability—this being borne by his insurer or employer. However, where an action is brought, he is likely see his professional reputation as being under attack, and this may be a source of great stress. In his recent Report, *Making Amends*,[19] the Chief Medical Officer, noted evidence that a substantial number of doctors who are the subject of a negligence claim will suffer clinical depression as a consequence. He went on to note:

> Although this consideration must always be secondary to the trauma experienced by the injured patient and their family, it is nevertheless doubtful whether the destruction of self-confidence and morale of clinical teams around the country is an additional price that should have to be paid in circumstances where the harm resulted from an honest mistake.[20]

Insofar as there is an arguable basis for denying liability, the doctor is likely to defend himself vigorously, with the effect that (even where some damages are eventually paid) proceedings become acrimonious and further drawn out. Ironically, where negligence is clear, there is the converse temptation to 'hush things up', by settling the claim quickly on secret terms. This may help the individual patient, but prevents wider lessons being learnt as to how a similar mistake may be avoided in the future.[21]

2. The No-Fault Option—the New Zealand and Swedish Models

In the light of the above concerns, there have, during the last 30 or so years, been various proposals in both England and Germany, directed to reforming the present system of medical malpractice liability. A frequently discussed option is to remove such claims from the ambit of private law altogether in favour of compensation through a collective insurance fund. Payouts under such a scheme would then follow on a 'no-fault' basis, requiring simply that the patient show 'medical injury', it being immaterial whether this occurred through negligence or not.

Here, reformists and commentators in both countries have been able to draw upon the experiences of other jurisdictions with such an approach, in particular those of New Zealand and Sweden. As regards New Zealand, medical injury has since 1974 been subject to no-fault recovery as part of that country's public insurance scheme (Accident Compensation Corporation—ACC), covering accidental injury in general. Under this, claimants who suffer personal injury in accidents

[19] CMO, *Making Amends* (n 2 above).

[20] CMO, *Making Amends* (n 2 above) 43. For the expression of similar concerns by a German commentator, see Radau, *Ersetzung der Arzthaftung durch Versicherungsschutz* (n 12 above) 114–15.

[21] In England, the failure of the tort system to contribute sufficiently to future accident-prevention in the health care sector has been a major theme in recent years, as highlighted in the Kennedy Report into *Bristol* and the CMO's Report, *Making Amends*: see further the discussion in pt III 1 (b)–(c) below.

(including patients injured in the course of medical treatment) no longer have an action against the injurer, but apply instead for compensation to an administrative tribunal. The scheme was enacted originally by the Accident Compensation Act 1972, but has been subject to various amendments since, which have varied the eligibility criteria for recovery. These have been motivated both by dissatisfaction as to their original clarity and effect, and the desire to reduce costs.

As regards medical injury claims, a distinct approach was initially signalled by the Accident Rehabilitation and Compensation Insurance Act 1992, which introduced provisions to delimit those injuries for which compensation was recoverable under the Scheme. In this regard, the 1992 Act distinguished between 'medical mishap'—comprising iatrogenic injury due to the materialisation of an inherent treatment risk—and 'medical error'.[22] In the former case compensation was awarded on a no-fault basis, albeit subject to qualifying thresholds in terms of the injury's rarity and severity.[23] In other cases—of iatrogenic injury outside the thresholds, as well as harm (in terms of the lost benefit) from non-treatment following misdiagnosis—the patient was required instead to show a 'medical error'. Here the scheme reverted to a fault-based approach. Such an error was defined as

> the failure of a registered health professional to observe the standard of care and skill reasonably to be expected in the circumstances.[24]

Nevertheless, in 2005 further, major reforms were made to the medical injury part of the New Zealand scheme, which have abolished the above distinction.[25] In doing so a key motive was to excise the residual element of fault from the system, and thereby increase the willingness of practitioners to report and learn from mistakes.[26] Following this, compensation is now available across the board for 'treatment injury', defined as personal injury caused by treatment, which was not a necessary part or ordinary part of the same, taking into account all the circumstances including the person's underlying health condition and the clinical knowledge at the time it was provided.[27] In this regard, 'treatment' is drawn widely to encompass initial diagnosis, as well as the decision as to what treatment to give. This includes cases of delay or omission in its provision.[28] At the same time, a significant exclusion under the new approach is that compensation will not

[22] Accident Rehabilitation and Compensation Insurance Act 1992 s 5.

[23] To qualify as 'rare' the risk of injury had to be less than 1 %, judged ex ante; in terms of severity the injury needed to involve significant disability and/or hospitalisation for at least 14 days, or death.

[24] Accident Rehabilitation and Compensation Insurance Act 1992 s 5(1).

[25] The changes have been implemented by the Injury Prevention, Rehabilitation, and Compensation Amendment Act (No 2) 2005, amending the Injury Prevention, Rehabilitation, and Compensation Act 2001; see further K Oliphant, 'Beyond Misadventure: Compensation for Medical Injuries in New Zealand' (2007) 15 *Medical Law Review* 357.

[26] Oliphant, 'Beyond Misadventure' (n 25 above) 369 ff. The qualifying thresholds in terms of an injury's rarity and severity were also perceived as arbitrary.

[27] Injury Prevention, Rehabilitation, and Compensation Act 2001 (as amended), s 32(1).

[28] Injury Prevention, Rehabilitation, and Compensation Act 2001 (as amended) s 33(1). Also covered is the doctor's failure to obtain informed consent.

be paid for injury 'wholly or substantially caused by a person's underlying health condition'.[29]

Insofar as the patient shows a relevant injury under the scheme, he will be entitled to damages assessed by a tribunal. Nonetheless these have been capped since 2002 at a maximum of NZ $100,000 (around £50,000). They are thus much lower than awards under private law. Indeed, according to a survey carried out for the CMO in England, the average payment appears to be just NZ $7,419 (or £3,115).[30] The general consensus among commentators is that the scheme's success, as a means of dealing with medical injury cases, has been equivocal—though critics concede it has not been helped by the frequent changes made over the years. In this context the full effect of the 2005 reforms must remain to be seen, including whether they succeed in banishing fault considerations from the healthcare arena.[31]

Turning next to the Swedish no-fault scheme, this was initially established in 1975 by means of a concordat between the communes (responsible for the provision of healthcare) and the major insurance companies. Unlike the New Zealand scheme, it does not formally replace private law: the patient remains free to pursue an action in tort (though in practice this hardly ever occurs).[32] However (again, unlike New Zealand), the scheme was from the outset aimed specifically at medical injury and was carefully designed to take account of the features of such claims. Initially, its terms were set out in the concordat mentioned above. However, more recently the scheme has been placed on a statutory footing by the *Patientskadelag* (Patient Damages Act) of 1996. The eligibility criteria for bringing a claim are set out in § 6 of the Act, and allow for compensation for personal injury in a number of closely defined circumstances.[33] These include iatrogenic injury suffered by a patient during treatment (including medical examinations and after-care) if, judged after the event, this could have been avoided by the use of an alternative, less risky method. This will not apply, though, if the treatment was necessary to save the patient's life or prevent serious disability.[34] Also covered by the scheme is injury (through the progress of the patient's underlying illness) following a mistaken diagnosis, provided that an experienced specialist in the relevant field would have reached a proper diagnosis.[35] In all cases, though, the injury must pass a severity threshold—namely incapacity for 30 days, hospitalisation for 10 days, permanent disability, or death.[36]

29 Injury Prevention, Rehabilitation, and Compensation Act 2001 (as amended) s 32(2)(a).

30 CMO, *Making Amends* (n 2 above) at 106.

31 Commentators have expressed scepticism as to this: see Oliphant, 'Beyond Misadventure: Compensation for Medical Injuries in New Zealand' (n 25 above) 383 ff; S Todd, 'Twenty years of professional negligence in New Zealand' (2005) 21 *Professional Negligence* 257 at 260–61. See further the discussion in pt IV below (text at n 134 ff below).

32 See generally L Wendel, 'Compensation in the Swedish Health Care Sector' in J Dute, M Faure and H Koziol (eds), *No-Fault Compensation in the Health Sector* (Vienna, Springer, 2004) 367.

33 The relevant provisions are complex; for a detailed analysis, see Wendel, 'Compensation in the Swedish Health Care Sector' (n 32 above) 372 ff; Katzenmeier, *Arzthaftung* (n 3 above) 219 ff.

34 Patient Damages Act 1996 § 6 I 1 and § 7.

35 Patient Damages Act 1996 § 6 I 3 and § 6 II.

36 CMO, *Making Amends* (n 2 above) 99.

As in the case of New Zealand, payments under the Swedish scheme are in no way comparable to awards in medical malpractice cases in England and Germany (made on the full restitution basis under private law). Thus, average payouts are in the region of £7,000 and serve to top up generous social security payments.[37] Another point about the scheme is that claims based on the lack of informed consent do not have independent status, being subsumed within claims for iatrogenic injury. The patient's right to respect for autonomy therefore does not receive specific protection.[38] Nonetheless, the Swedish scheme is generally perceived as a success, particularly in reducing tensions between doctors and patients, and it has since been imitated in the other Scandinavian countries.[39]

III. Reform Initiatives in England and Germany

As noted above, in both England and Germany, there has over the years been interest in adopting a no-fault approach in medical injury cases. However, this has not found favour as a general response to such injury. Instead, the focus has increasingly been on improving and supplementing the existing private law system of liability to address its most significant defects in relation to medical malpractice litigation.

1. Developments in England

(a) Pearson and the General Rejection of No-Fault

In England, medical negligence litigation was first placed on the reform agenda by the Royal Commission on Civil Liability and Compensation for Personal Injury, whose report appeared in 1978.[40] The Government had set up the Commission under the chairmanship of Lord Pearson in 1972 in response to growing unease at the way in which tort law functioned as a compensation system.[41] This had been expressed in academic works, criticising the fault principle for its alleged failure to achieve a just distribution of risks in modern society. It was argued that the risk of accidental injury should instead be socialised and covered by the welfare state.[42] At

[37] CMO, *Making Amends* (n 2 above) 105–6.

[38] Wendel, 'Compensation in the Swedish Health Care Sector' (n 32 above) 381.

[39] Schemes based on the Swedish model were introduced in Finland in 1986, Norway in 1988 and Denmark in 1992 (in Denmark's case, restricted to injury during hospital treatment).

[40] Pearson, *Report of the Royal Commission on Civil Liability and Compensation for Personal Injury*, (Chairman: Lord Pearson) Cmnd 7054 (London, HMSO, 1978).

[41] For the background to Pearson, see Cane, *Atiyah's Accidents, Compensation and the Law* (n 10 above) 395 ff.

[42] T Ison, *The Forensic Lottery: a Critique on Tort Liability as a System of Personal Injury Compensation* (London, Staples Press, 1967), PS Atiyah, *Accidents, Compensation and the Law* (London, Weidenfeld & Nicolson, 1970).

the same time, public concern was brought to a head by the Thalidomide disaster, in which catastrophic injury occurred to thousands of babies around the world whose mothers had ingested a pharmaceutical drug during pregnancy, in the absence of provable fault by the drug manufacturers.

Against this background, the Pearson Commission was given a broad remit to look at options for reforming tort liability in personal injury claims, either by replacing it with a no-fault compensation scheme or through other changes. As this implies, its concern was much wider than injury (allegedly) caused by medical negligence. Indeed, at that time such claims were in England scarcely recognised as posing a distinct problem. As noted earlier, the Commission in its research into the operation of the tort system estimated that just 500 medical malpractice claims were commenced each year (0.2 per cent of personal injury litigation in total).[43] Nonetheless, the Pearson Commission noted their potential to become problematic in the future and devoted separate attention to them.[44] It commented:

> The employment of new techniques and the development of medical science have increased the ability of the doctor to attempt the treatment of severe diseases and to effect a cure, but at the same time have widened the area in which medical accidents may occur. This trend of greater risks for greater gain is likely to continue.[45]

In its discussion, the Commission noted the particular difficulties facing patients in proving their claims. Interestingly, given our examination in chapter three of the German approach to the matter, one option it considered was of reversing the burden of proof. It noted that doctors—with their ready access to medical records and expert opinions—were arguably 'in a better position to prove absence of negligence than patients were to establish liability'.[46] However, ultimately it rejected this idea due to concern that such a reversal would lead to a large increase in the number of claims made and, 'although many would be groundless, each one would have to be investigated and answered'.[47] The Commission also rejected for similar reasons a general approach imposing strict liability on the doctor.[48]

In addition the Pearson Report considered the more radical option of introducing a scheme of no-fault compensation for medical injury. Here it noted the existence of the Swedish and New Zealand schemes, but suggested these had been in operation for too short a time to permit a useful appraisal.[49] Moreover, as well as again raising practical concerns as to the costs and possible increase in the level of claims, the Commission recorded the opposition voiced by the medical profession,

[43] See n 2 above.
[44] Pearson Report (n 40 above) vol 1, ch 24.
[45] Pearson Report (n 40 above) vol 1, ch 24, para 1349.
[46] Pearson Report (n 40 above) para 1336.
[47] Pearson Report (n 40 above) para 1336.
[48] Pearson Report (n 40 above) para 1337 ff. Here, in contrast to 'no fault', the patient would still sue the individual doctor, but would need merely to demonstrate the fact of the treatment's harmful outcome.
[49] Pearson Report (n 40 above) para 1359.

which was concerned that such a scheme could lead to a loss of clinical autonomy.[50] Above all, though, it was impressed by the problems it foresaw in designing the scheme to achieve a sensible demarcation of injuries covered by it (as opposed to ones for the patient to bear). In this regard it argued that

> there would be difficulty in distinguishing medical accident from the natural progression of a disease or injury, and from a foreseeable side effect of treatment . . . Even rare side effects such as vaccine damage not caused by negligence are often foreseeable in the sense that they are well known to medical science. If such injuries were to be included in a no-fault scheme, where would the line be drawn between them and the accepted risks of treatment?[51]

Accordingly, the Commission rejected the option of a no-fault scheme for medical injury, and affirmed the continued use of negligence for dealing with such claims.[52]

In fact, subsequent to the publication of the Pearson Report, the issue of law reform in respect of personal injury compensation declined in impetus generally. One reason was the change in political climate following the election in 1979 of the Conservative Government of Margaret Thatcher, preaching a philosophy of personal responsibility and self-reliance. There was no longer much interest in expensive collective schemes for sharing the risks of accidental injury.[53] However, one limited pocket of no-fault liability relevant to the area of medical injury was introduced by the Vaccine Damages (Compensation) Act 1979, which provided for the payment of compensation to persons severely disabled through vaccination. This Act set up a tribunal to authorise payment if satisfied that the applicant had been severely disabled and that a vaccine was the cause. Payment in an individual case was initially limited to £10,000 (though this has since been raised to £100,000).[54] Subsequently, a regime of strict liability of sorts has developed in respect of medicinal products, as part of the overall scheme of liability for defective consumer products under the Consumer Protection Act 1987.[55] Under this, rather than having to show fault in the product's design or manufacture, the injured patient need show only that the product was defective in objective terms. According to section 3 of the 1987 Act, there will be such a defect if 'the safety of a product is not such as persons generally are entitled to expect'.

Admittedly, these developments are relevant only at the periphery of medical malpractice. The alleged faulty conduct of a doctor is not at issue, but rather the

[50] Pearson Report (n 40 above) para 1342. The Commission expressed some scepticism as to this argument.

[51] Pearson Report (n 40 above) paras 1365–6.

[52] Pearson Report (n 40 above) para 1370–71.

[53] Cane, *Atiyah's Accidents, Compensation and the Law* (n 10 above) 396. The more radical of Pearson's recommendations (such as a proposed no-fault scheme for road accidents) were shelved and, to this day, have not been acted upon.

[54] See M Brazier, *Medicine, Patients and the Law*, 3rd edn (London, Penguin Books, 2003) 218 ff.

[55] The 1987 Act stemmed from initiatives at EC level—transposing the Product Liability Directive 85/374/EC into domestic law.

propensity of medicinal drugs (or other products), when properly prescribed and administered, to do harm. As regards the 1987 Act, its impact in this area has been modest. While its definition of 'defect' (in section 3) will catch manufacturing errors—involving an unplanned deviation of a particular unit of the product from the norm, eg through contamination—it does not appear to cover cases of an otherwise beneficial medicine producing an adverse reaction in a tiny minority of cases. A second feature, tending against liability, is the availability of the so-called 'development risk' defence under section 4(1)(e) of the Act. Indeed this was allowed for by the parent EC Directive specifically because of lobbying from the pharmaceutical industry. It permits a manufacturer to escape liability for defects that were not foreseeable in the light of scientific knowledge at the time the product was put into circulation. In the result, the Act has, to date, seldom been relied upon to sue in medical injury cases.[56]

(b) Developments in the 1980s and 90s

Returning to the issue of liability for faulty treatment by a doctor, it was during the 1980s that—fuelled by the rapid rise in medical negligence actions—dissatisfaction with this area of law became pronounced. This was felt on the side of both doctors and patients. Thus, in 1987 the British Medical Association, worried by the sharp increase in insurance premiums paid by its members, dropped its earlier opposition to no-fault compensation (as expressed to Pearson), and began campaigning for the introduction of such a scheme.[57] Indeed, insurance premiums with the Medical Defence Union (one of the two major medical liability insurers) escalated from £40 per annum in 1978 to £1350 in 1989.[58]

In the event, the Government responded in 1990 by establishing a scheme of 'NHS Indemnity', under which the negligence liability of doctors working within the NHS was covered centrally rather than each doctor taking out individual insurance.[59] However, while this assuaged the most immediate concerns of doctors, patients continued to feel poorly served by the existing law, and by the process of litigation as a prelude to compensation. This was a system bedevilled by cost and delay, where the injured patient often encountered a wall of silence in trying to discover what had happened. In substantive legal terms too, the doctor held most of the trumps—epitomised by the courts' routine incantation of the *Bolam*

[56] An exception is *A and others v National Blood Authority* [2001] 3 All ER 289 (QBD), involving a successful class action by haemophiliacs who contracted Hepatitis C from contaminated blood products. Here the High Court interpreted the development risk defence narrowly, holding that it did not apply once the defendant was aware of the risk, even though there was nothing—given the prevailing state of scientific knowledge—it could do to eliminate it.

[57] Report of the *BMA Working Party on No Fault Compensation* (London, British Medical Association, 1987).

[58] See Brazier, 'The Case for a No-Fault Compensation Scheme for Medical Accidents' (n 8 above) 52.

[59] Brazier, *Medicine, Patients and the Law* (n 54 above) 176–7. The body charged with managing the indemnity, the NHS Litigation Authority, initiated the recording of statistics revealing the overall costs to the system of settling malpractice claims: see n 66 below.

test to deny liability. During this period too, interest groups began to emerge, giving voice to the concerns of patients injured during treatment.[60]

Although reform to substantive law remained off the political agenda, medical negligence litigation as it operated in practice was the subject of attention and criticism by Lord Woolf in his review of the civil justice system in England and Wales in the mid-90s. In his Report '*Access to Justice*',[61] Lord Woolf devoted an entire chapter to problems in this area. He wrote:

> [E]arly in the Inquiry it became increasingly obvious that it was in the area of medical negligence that the civil justice system was failing most conspicuously to meet the needs of litigants in a number of respects.[62]

His Lordship proceeded to identify, as specific defects, the disproportionality between costs and damages in such cases, the protracted pursuit of unmerited claims or defence of clear-cut claims, the lower success rate (relative to other personal injury claims) and the fact that,

> the suspicion between the parties is more intense and the lack of co-operation frequently greater than in many other areas of litigation.[63]

Accordingly, as part of his general recommendations for modernising civil procedure, Lord Woolf made a number of proposals specific to medical negligence. These were aimed at increasing the expertise of the lawyers and judges (eg through specialist courts), and encouraging greater use of mediation. Formal litigation was to be seen as 'last resort'.[64] As yet the latter proposals have not been implemented, but the general Woolf reforms (including stricter pre-trial management and more incentives to settle claims) appear to be having a positive impact on medical litigation. Thus there has been some reduction in costs, and an increase in claims settled.[65]

Nevertheless, wider anxieties with respect to this area of litigation have persisted, not least in the light of new data on the overall costs of medical accidents to the NHS. Statistics collated by the NHS Litigation Authority—the body set up (in 1995) to manage the NHS Indemnity scheme—showed total payments by the NHS in respect of medical negligence (in settlements, awards, and lawyer's fees) to be £235 million in 1996–97; by 2004–05 this figure had doubled once more to £500 million.[66] Equally, it has been recognised that claims brought are merely the tip of iceberg relative to the actual number of 'preventable adverse events' that occur in the health sector. On the basis of international studies (including the 1990

[60] The best known group is AVMA (Action for Victims of Medical Accidents), a charity founded in 1982; it is now known as 'Action against Medical Accidents'.

[61] Lord Woolf, *Access to Justice: Final Report to the Lord Chancellor on the Civil Justice System in England and Wales* (London, HMSO, 1996).

[62] *Ibid*, ch 15, para 2

[63] Woolf, *Access to Justice* (n 61 above) ch 15, para 2.

[64] See the CMO's analysis of the impact of the Woolf Reforms on medical claims: CMO, *Making Amends* (n 2 above) 90 ff.

[65] CMO, *Making Amends* (n 2 above) 91.

[66] Lewis, Morris and Oliphant, 'Tort Personal Injury Statistics: Is there a Compensation Culture in the United Kingdom?' (n 2 above) 95.

Harvard Medical Practice Study in the US), it has been estimated that 850,000 adverse outcomes occur in the NHS annually, of which around half are 'preventable'.[67] Indeed the number of extra 'bed days' alone (ie extra care required for patients involved in such events) has been estimated to cost the NHS £2 billion annually—ie four times as much as it pays out in respect of negligence claims.[68]

This has stimulated a growing interest in risk management strategies aimed at accident prevention. Thus in 2001, following a Department of Health Consultation Paper, '*An Organisation with a Memory*',[69] the Government established the National Patient Safety Agency to oversee a national safety programme. In doing so, it acknowledged that accidents often stem from flawed system design at an institutional level, where the 'faulty' conduct of a particular doctor is merely the last link in the chain of events.[70] In terms of this broader focus on prevention, there has been a renewed sense that negligence liability may be counterproductive by concentrating the enquiry unduly on that last link (the 'smoking gun'). Moreover, as noted earlier, instead of conducing to an open investigation, the loss of reputation associated with fault-based liability is apt to encourage denial and dissembling by the medical team. These concerns were highlighted by the public inquiry, set up in response to the revelations of deficient practices in children's heart surgery at the Bristol Royal Infirmary.[71] In his Report, Professor Sir Ian Kennedy drew attention to a culture of paternalism and repeated mistakes. His recommendations included the introduction of a no-fault scheme to remove the cloak of legal secrecy over clinical negligence.[72]

(c) Making Amends *and the NHS Redress Act 2006*

Against this background, the Government in July 2001 commissioned a wide-ranging consultation paper from its Chief Medical Officer, Sir Liam Donaldson, to consider afresh the options for compensating for medical injury in the NHS. In his Report, '*Making Amends*',[73] which appeared in June 2003, the CMO identified at the outset a number of key goals that an alternative to the present system of

[67] CMO, *Making Amends* (n 2 above) 32. Other research has suggested that typically around a quarter of adverse medical outcomes are attributable to negligence—still a striking number overall: see Cane, *Atiyah's Accidents, Compensation and the Law* (n 10 above) 179.

[68] *Ibid.* There is also a recognition that, if the figures quoted in the previous footnote are correct, the number of claims has the potential to rise considerably further.

[69] Department of Health, *An Organisation with a Memory: Report of an Expert Group on Learning from Adverse Events in the NHS* (London, DoH Consultation Paper, 2000).

[70] For a discussion of the psychology of errors, with particular reference to the provision of medical treatment, see Merry and McCall Smith, *Errors, Medicine and the Law* (n 10 above).

[71] Kennedy Report, *Report of the Bristol Royal Infirmary Inquiry, Learning from Bristol: the report of the public inquiry into children's heart surgery at the Bristol Royal Infirmary 1984–1995* (Cm 5207) (2001). The Inquiry, into the deaths of 29 babies during heart surgery, found surgeons had persisted over a number of years in carrying out such surgery despite knowing that their mortality rates were well above the national average.

[72] Kennedy Report, *ibid*, recommendation 119.

[73] CMO, *Making Amends* (n 2 above).

medical litigation should incorporate. These included: the need to encourage medical staff to report medical errors and near misses (to enhance patient safety); the provision of fair and efficient compensation for injury where it does occur; and ensuring that the compensation process does not undermine the doctor-patient relationship.[74]

In the light of these objectives, the Report examined various reform options, including, once again, the possible introduction of a no-fault compensation scheme. In the event, the CMO favoured the introduction of no-fault in one area, namely for claims by severely neurologically impaired babies whose impairment occurred during birth in an NHS hospital. Here, he was impressed by the special difficulties in proving such actions, and the fact that, under the current system, huge damages are awarded in one case, and nothing in another when the boundary between the two may appear slight. Indeed, as he observed, there is continuing disagreement among the world scientific community as to how far birth-related asphyxia (as opposed to genetic predisposition and infection) are causative of such injury.[75]

However, the CMO's Report rejected a general shift to no-fault liability in medical injury cases, and for reasons similar to those previously adumbrated by the Pearson Commission. These were principally the difficulty of demarcating the injuries to be covered by any scheme and concerns about the potential financial costs. As regards the latter, his Report considered evidence from the Swedish and New Zealand schemes, noting that

> England has fewer clinical negligence claims per 100,000 population, and the proportion of successful claims is lower. However, the average compensation award in England is far higher than the average in the New Zealand and Sweden schemes.[76]

In this context, a study he commissioned for the Report suggested there would be a significant increase in the overall number of claims (as well as the proportion among them resulting in awards), so that if compensation were calculated on traditional tort principles, the costs would be unmanageable. Indeed it suggested the total cost of a no-fault scheme to the NHS (even with a 25 per cent reduction in the size of awards and where only 28 per cent of eligible claimants applied) would be over £4 billion, ie nearly 10 times the total costs of the negligence-based system.[77]

Instead, the CMO's preferred solution lay in what he christened the '*NHS Redress Scheme*'. This initiative, which he described as 'a composite package of reform', was to embody the following features: an investigation of the incident leading to the alleged harm; an explanation to the patient of what had happened and action proposed to prevent repetition; and the development and delivery of a

[74] CMO, *Making Amends* (n 2 above) 30.

[75] CMO, *Making Amends* (n 2 above) 46 ff. As he noted, two American States—Florida and Virginia—currently operate limited no-fault schemes in relation to children disabled at birth.

[76] CMO, *Making Amends* (n 2 above) 106.

[77] CMO, *Making Amends* (n 2 above) 112. This has been queried by some commentators: see P Fenn, A Gray and N Rickman, 'The Economics of Clinical Negligence Reform in England' (2004) 114 *The Economic Journal* F272 (putting the total cost at £2.1 billion).

package of on-going care (including remedial treatment) to be provided by the NHS.[78] In addition, the CMO proposed that where (causative) fault was found, in the form of 'serious shortcomings in the standards of care',[79] compensation of up to £30,000 could be authorised directly by the body administering the scheme. This would provide an alternative to formal litigation by the patient in lower value claims, where the costs of litigation are often in excess of damages awarded.[80]

These proposals have recently formed the basis for an Act of Parliament, the NHS Redress Act 2006, which received Royal Assent in November 2006. The Act is an enabling statute, which lays down the framework of the Redress Scheme, while leaving much of the detail to be fleshed out in regulations to be made by the Secretary of State for Health. Indeed, at present the details are subject to a lengthy on-going consultation process, so that (as of late 2007) it remains unclear exactly when the Scheme will become operative, albeit a date some time in 2008 has been mooted.[81] However, the Act gives effect to the CMO's intention that lower value medical negligence claims should be dealt with outside the courts. Such claims will be referred to the NHS Litigation Authority, which will manage the Scheme, for investigation and, in cases where substandard treatment and care is found, it may offer redress (including financial compensation). The latter is intended to be roughly equivalent to the award a court might order if the matter went to trial. The patient is not required to accept the offer, but if he does he will be asked to sign a waiver, to prevent him from bringing subsequent legal proceedings.[82] The Scheme will apply only to claims arising from hospital care within the NHS, not private healthcare. Also excluded (by section 1(6) of the Act) are 'primary care' provided by general practitioners, and dental services.

As is apparent, the Redress Scheme is intended to supplement, not replace, the existing private law mechanism for determining liability, and indeed builds heavily on the latter. Thus the need for a breach of duty in order to trigger an offer of redress has been made explicit in the 2006 Act.[83] It remains to be seen how effective the Scheme will be in practice. Indeed, some commentators have expressed concern that the patient's interests are insufficiently protected. This stems from the lack of an independent overseer of the scheme, and the lack of an appeal procedure.[84] Nonetheless, as noted, besides being designed to relieve

[78] CMO, *Making Amends* (n 2 above) 115. In the event that the NHS were unable to provide the care in question, the patient would receive the monetary value of obtaining it privately.

[79] CMO, *Making Amends* (n 2 above) 120.

[80] CMO, *Making Amends* (n 2 above) 120. A ceiling of £20,000 is currently favoured—a figure that would still cover awards in 75 per cent of actions against the NHS (based on records from 2001–2004): see A-M Farrell and S Devaney, 'Making Amends or Making Things Worse? Clinical Negligence Reform and Patient Redress in England' (2007) 27 *Legal Studies* 630 at 638.

[81] Farrell and Devaney, 'Making Amends or Making Things Worse? (n 80 above) 631.

[82] NHS Redress Act 2006 s 6(5).

[83] NHS Redress Act 2006 s 1(4). By contrast, the limited no-fault scheme proposed by the CMO in respect of neurologically impaired babies has not been taken up in the 2006 Act.

[84] See Farrell and Devaney, 'Making Amends or Making Things Worse? (n 80 above) 642 ff. For a critical analysis of the CMO's proposals, prior to their partial enactment in the 2006 Act, see Jones, *Medical Negligence* (n 11 above) I-054 ff.

pressure on the legal system in cases where litigation is most uneconomic, the Scheme has, as another crucial goal, the furtherance of risk-management and learning from mistakes. In this regard the 2006 Act provides that each case investigated should be the subject of a written report, and requires members of the Scheme (ie NHS hospitals) to

> prepare and publish an annual report about cases involving the member that are dealt with under the scheme and the lessons to be learnt from them.[85]

2. Developments in Germany

(a) The General Rejection of No-Fault

In Germany, where the rise in medical negligence litigation began some 20 years earlier than in England, suggestions as to the desirability of reform in this field may already be found in legal literature from the early 1960s.[86] As in England, the system of dealing with medical injury cases in private law was criticised for its damaging effect on the doctor-patient relationship, and the difficulty on the patient's side in proving a good cause of action (particularly in the light of the high standard of proof).[87] At the same time, reform initiatives in this area—particularly in the 1970s—formed part of a wider search for alternatives to private law in cases of personal injury. In this regard the Thalidomide disaster had a profound impact on public and political opinion in Germany as well.[88] Indeed, a no-fault scheme specifically to compensate Thalidomide victims was established by the *Contergangesetz* of 1971. This provided for compensation from a fund financed by a lump-sum contribution by the federal government and the drug manufacturers.[89]

Subsequently, the disaster also led to the enactment in 1976 of the Pharmaceutical Products Act (*Arzneimittelgesetz*—AMG). This provides in § 84 for liability against pharmaceutical manufacturers in cases where a medicinal product, used as prescribed, causes injury that, in the light of the overall level of medical scientific development, may be regarded as unacceptable.[90] In fact the relevant provisions of the AMG are complex, and have rarely been invoked before the courts.[91] In particular the Act will not assist an individual injured by an adverse reaction to the drug (in its normal form), where the drug fulfilled an important

[85] NHS Redress Act 2006 ss 6(3) and 10(3).

[86] Katzenmeier, *Arzthaftung* (n 3 above) 215.

[87] Katzenmeier, *Arzthaftung* (n 3 above) 217 ff; Radau, *Ersetzung der Arzthaftung durch Versicherungsschutz* (n 12 above) 83 ff and 114 ff.

[88] In Germany this episode is known as the 'Contergan-Katastrophe' after the drug's German name.

[89] See C Wendehorst, 'Compensation in the German Health Care Sector' in J Dute, M Faure and H Koziol (eds), *No-Fault Compensation in the Health Sector* (Vienna, Springer, 2004) 261 at 270 ff.

[90] See E Deutsch (ed), *Kommentar zum Arzneimittelgesetz*, 2nd edn (Berlin, Springer, 2007) 672 ff.

[91] Problems in relation to the proof of claims under the AMG led to reforms to § 84 in 2002: for a detailed discussion, see G Wagner, 'Die Reform der Arzneimittelhaftung im Entwurf eines Zweiten Schadensrechtsänderungsgesetzes' *VersR* 2001, 1334.

medical need and alternative treatment was not available. Thus the liability of the manufacturer is not strict 'causal' liability (for each actual injury), but turns instead on an overall cost-benefit analysis. On the other hand, in order for liability to arise it is sufficient that the product was objectively unnecessarily dangerous (given the availability of other safer options): the manufacturer—in contrast to under the general (EC-based) regime governing consumer products—is not able to rely on a 'development risk' style defence.[92]

As regards liability for injuries from medical treatment more generally, the discussion in Germany of replacing private law by a no-fault scheme, reached its peak in 1978, the same year the Pearson Report appeared in England. That year, a debate was held on the future of malpractice litigation at the *Deutscher Juristentag* (DJT), an annual conference of legal academics and practitioners, whose recommendations are influential with respect to legislative reform. This took as its starting point an Expert Report (*Gutachten*) prepared by Hans-Leo Weyers, a Professor at Frankfurt University, which considered a number of options, including strict liability and the introduction of no-fault compensation.[93] There, besides assembling data on the growing incidence of medical malpractice litigation in Germany, Weyers looked at the new no-fault compensation scheme for medical injury in Sweden, noting that the early evidence as to its effects appeared positive. At the same time, he recognised that the absence of empirical data made predicting the costs of a similar approach for Germany highly uncertain. In addition, like the Pearson Report in England, he was impressed by the difficulty that would be posed in demarcating the injuries to be appropriately covered by such a scheme.[94] These doubts were shared by the medical law section of the DJT, which voted heavily against the motion recommending reform to the existing private law in this area.[95]

In the years after the 1978 DJT the question of radical reform of medical malpractice law remained largely off the agenda. As noted in chapter one, one initiative that was pursued in the early1980s was to codify the case law of the BGH in the area into a number of new paragraphs in the BGB. However, this idea—which concerned the source of the relevant law rather than its substance—was later dropped.[96] Also noteworthy in this context is the fate of the (partial) no-fault scheme of 'additional support for victims of medical injury' in the former German Democratic Republic.[97] This had operated against the backdrop of § 334 of the

[92] See the discussion of the defence in relation to the English Consumer Protection Act 1987 in the text at n 56, above. In Germany, § 84 AMG retains priority over the general development risk defence found in the *Produkthaftungsgesetz* (the German statute transposing EC Directive 85/374/EC) in line with the *lex specialis* rule.

[93] H-L Weyers, 'Empfiehlt es sich, im Interesse der Patienten und Ärzte ergänzende Regelungen für das ärztliche Vertrags- (Standes-) und Haftungsrecht einzuführen?' *Gutachten zum 52. DJT* (Wiesbaden, DJT, 1978).

[94] *Ibid*, A 62 ff, A 94 ff.

[95] 23 votes in favour; 101 against; 9 abstentions: 'Deutscher Juristentag in Wiesbaden: Der Tagungsverlauf' NJW 1979, 2185 (2193).

[96] See ch 1 above, n 30.

[97] *Anordnung über die Erweiterung der materiellen Unterstützung der Bürger bei Schäden infolge medizinischer Eingriffe*, GBl I 1975 Nr 3 S.59.

Zivilgesetzbuch-DDR, which (while retaining a fault-based starting point) put the burden of proof in iatrogenic injury cases on the treating side to show that injury was unavoidable. In cases where the doctors succeeded in doing so, it allowed compensation if injury was severe and in gross disproportion to the seriousness of the condition being treated. Nonetheless, following German reunification, the scheme was no longer regarded as socially justified. It was ultimately wound up in 1994 by an Act of the Federal Parliament (the *Unterstützungsabschlussgesetz*).[98]

By contrast, one new limited pocket of no-fault liability (in addition to the earlier scheme for Thalidomide victims) was created in 1995 to cover patients infected with HIV as a result of receiving contaminated blood.[99] This was introduced by the *HIV-Hilfegesetz* in response to difficulties—especially in relation to matters of proof—that such patients had encountered in using § 84 of the *Arzneimittelgesetz* to bring their claims.[100]

(b) The System of Medical Arbitration Boards

At the same time as adopting its sceptical stance on radical reform, the DJT in 1978 welcomed a recent development in Germany supplemental to the existing law, in the form of special 'arbitration boards' set up to deal with medical malpractice disputes. This initiative began in 1975 at the instigation of the regional medical councils (*Landesärztekammern*), which were concerned at the increase in malpractice actions and the climate of distrust engendered between doctors and patients—including accusations of partiality in the medical evidence offered at trials.[101] By establishing the boards, the medical profession hoped to defuse these tensions, and demonstrate openness. In particular, they would assist the patient in making good well-founded claims, while encouraging the abandonment of unmerited claims. Another aim was to reduce the tendency for patients—frustrated by lack of knowledge—to report doctors to the police, leading to criminal investigations into negligent or intentional bodily injury.[102]

In the intervening years, and in cooperation with the association of personal injury insurers (*HUK-Verband*), 12 such boards (annexed to the regional medical councils) have been set up in regions across Germany. Their general remit is to offer an expert report (*Gutachten*) outside the formal process of litigation, as to whether there was faulty treatment causative of injury. Typically a claim will be assessed by expert panels of between three and five members, one of whom is legally

[98] For further discussion, see Katzenmeier, *Arzthaftung* (n 3 above) 229 ff, who locates the scheme's justification in the context of the duty of GDR citizens to seek treatment to safeguard their economic productivity.

[99] See further Wendehorst, 'Compensation in the German Health Care Sector' (n 89 above) 266 ff.

[100] See Wagner, 'Die Reform der Arzneimittelhaftung (n 91 above).

[101] In a number of cases the courts acknowledged the justified nature of such allegations: see eg BGH, 22 April 1975, NJW 1975, 1463; see also the discussion in ch 3 pt II 2.

[102] I Weizel, *Gutachterkommissionen und Schlichtungsstellen für Arzthaftpflichtfragen* (Hamburg, Kovaç, 1999) 13 ff. As to the doctor's criminal law liability for bodily injury, see ch 1 above, text at n 21.

qualified and the others doctors (including one from the relevant specialty).[103] The majority of boards, known as *Gutachterkommissionen*, will confine themselves to issuing a report. Others—termed *Schlichtungsstellen*—will also seek to mediate a settlement in appropriate cases.[104] There is considerable variation in the size and geographical coverage of the boards. Thus the state of Baden-Würtemberg alone has four boards. By contrast, a single board, the *Schlichtungsstelle für Arzthaftpflichtfragen der Norddeutschen Ärztekammern* (based in Hanover) deals not only with claims across North Germany, but also from Berlin and the states of the former GDR. There are also differences of composition and procedure between the boards, eg some have an appeal mechanism, but others do not.

Three general principles have been identified as underpinning the work of the arbitration boards. The first is that submitting to their adjudication is voluntary. Patients thus remain free to commence legal proceedings straightaway. The doctor, too, is not required to agree to the board's investigation—though in practice the great majority are happy to do so.[105] Secondly, the proceedings are cost-free to the patient, being financed by the medical councils, with contributions from the relevant hospital authorities (though if the patient wishes to be legally represented, he will need to pay for that).[106] In the third place, the board's decision as to whether there was a faulty treatment error is not legally binding on the parties. The boards are not surrogate courts, and will avoid contentious points of fact or law.[107] Instead, they reach their findings upon a limited review of largely agreed evidence (typically the patient's medical records and affidavits from the patient and doctor). Thus where there is a factual disagreement—eg as to what was said in a non-disclosure case—they will not adjudicate.[108] As a rule it takes around 8–14 months for them to reach their decision.

The take-up on the arbitration boards has shown a steady increase over time. Statistics published on the website of the Federal Medical Council (*Bundesärztekammer*), the umbrella organisation for the regional medical councils, show that in 2006 a total of 10,280 new applications were made (some 3,000 more than in 1990, though marginally fewer than in 2005).[109] While this represents less than half of the total number of cases that begin in Germany each year, it probably accounts for a majority where the claim is genuinely arguable.[110] On

[103] See further Ehlers and Broglie, *Arzthaftung* (n 3 above) 137 ff; Weizel, *Gutachterkommissionen und Schlichtungsstellen für Arzthaftpflichtfragen* (n 102 above) *ibid.*

[104] In practice, the difference is not great; in both cases, the expert opinion is focus of efforts: Thumann, *Reform der Arzthaftung in den Vereinigten Staaten von Amerika* (n 10 above) 209.

[105] Ehlers and Broglie, *Arzthaftung* (n 3 above) 143.

[106] Ehlers and Broglie, *Arzthaftung* (n 3 above) 137. In practice, around half of patients pay for such representation.

[107] Thumann, *Reform der Arzthaftung in den Vereinigten Staaten von Amerika* (n 10 above) 210.

[108] Schlund, 'Bestandaufnahme: Gutachter- und Schlichtungsstellen' (n 15 above) 336.

[109] Bundesärztekammer, *Statistische Erhebung der Gutachterkommissionen und Schlichtungsstellen* (2006).

[110] See E Deutsch and A Spickhoff, *Medizinrecht*, 5th edn (Berlin, Springer, 2003) para 434. As noted at the outset of this chapter, most of the 20,000 plus medical malpractice claims originating each year will be abandoned or settled at an early stage.

average the boards identify treatment malpractice as the cause of injury in around a quarter of cases they investigate. The 2006 statistics published by the Federal Medical Council show this was the finding in 1,562 of some 6,750 determinations that year.[111] In such cases the patient will be able to take the report to the doctor's liability insurer and in some 70 per cent of cases the latter will then settle the action. Thus, according to a 1990 survey of the *Nordrhein Gutachterkommission*, in the 218 claims that year (from a total of 657) where the board found substandard treatment, the patient pursued matters in 167 cases; of these, the doctor's insurer settled 117 straightaway. Conversely, where no error is found, most patients will abandon their claim. The same survey recorded that, of the 439 cases where substandard treatment was not found, the patient proceeded to litigate in just 64.[112]

It appears that the arbitration boards have, at least in less complex cases, played a useful role in facilitating settlements or inducing discontinuation of unmerited actions.[113] In the course of their work, they have won a reputation for neutrality, and their decisions enjoy high acceptance rates. Another important positive effect the boards have been credited with is in relation to quality control and risk-management—their reports, where errors are found, being passed onto the relevant regional medical council so appropriate action can be taken.[114] On the other hand, a degree of scepticism remains, particularly on the side of patients' lawyers, who not infrequently advise their clients instead to bring immediate legal proceedings.[115] This is due to the fact that, as noted, the board's investigation is largely conducted by agreed written testimony, with little opportunity to persuade panel members to reconsider a negative finding. This is added to by worries that a subsequent legal action may thereby be prejudiced. Moreover, in cases where the claim's success turns upon the application of one or other of the special proof modifications fashioned by the courts, it will be doomed from the start.[116]

(c) Current Initiatives

The state of medical malpractice litigation in the new united Germany, as well as possible options for reform were examined at a two-part symposium organised by the German Medical Law Association (*Deutsche Gesellschaft für Medizinrecht*) in 1995–96. At its conclusion it published a set of observations and recommendations: these included some criticism of the relevant case law, both for its complexity and the de facto imposition of strict liability (particularly in cases of disclosure

[111] Bundesärztekammer, *Statistische Erhebung der Gutachterkommissionen und Schlichtungsstellen* (n 109 above). This figure excludes Bavaria, for which data was not available.

[112] Ehlers and Broglie, *Arzthaftung* (n 3 above) 153 ff.

[113] See Weizel, *Gutachterkommissionen und Schlichtungsstellen für Arzthaftpflichtfragen* (n 102 above); Ehlers and Broglie, *Arzthaftung* (n 3 above); but see Deutsch and Spickhoff, *Medizinrecht* (n 110 above) para 436, who point to a lack of data for directly comparing cases dealt with by the boards and those reaching court.

[114] Thumann, *Reform der Arzthaftung in den Vereinigten Staaten von Amerika* (n 10 above) 212–13.

[115] See W Hempfing, *Aufklärungspflichten und Arzthaftung* (Starnberg, Schulz, 2000) 97–8.

[116] Thumann, *Reform der Arzthaftung in den Vereinigten Staaten von Amerika* (n 10 above) 213.

malpractice).[117] Nonetheless the Association expressed serious doubts as to putting a no-fault scheme in its place. Here it suggested a number of stringent preconditions that would need to be fulfilled, including a workable demarcation of the injuries to be covered, the retention of some judicial control over medical conduct (to preserve a deterrent effect), and the provision of on-going and sustainable financing.[118] Instead it saw greater promise in more modest steps, including pre-litigation non-judicial mechanisms. In this regard, it proposed that the use of the arbitration boards should be made compulsory; at the same time their procedures should be put on a more uniform footing, and each assessment panel should be presided over by a qualified judge.[119]

As noted by Katzenmeier, one feature that has handicapped serious discussions in this area is the lack of relevant empirical data in Germany, both as to the existing levels of litigation and the potential increase in it (and attendant costs) that the move to a no-fault scheme might bring.[120] While, against this background, the debate remains open, majority opinion, both among academics and politicians, is currently against radical reform.[121] In this regard it is significant that recent general reforms to the BGB and ZPO have left the area of medical malpractice pretty much untouched.[122] Here, the operation of the overall civil litigation system in Germany, and availability of the cost-free arbitration boards, appears to have ensured a reasonable level of access to justice for injured patients.[123] This has pre-empted some of the concerns in this regard identified in England by the Woolf Report.[124]

Recently, increasing attention has also been devoted to quality assurance and risk-management processes designed to prevent accidents in healthcare, matters where private law liability alone arguably fails to provide sufficient incentives for improvement. In this regard it has, as in England, been recognised that actions litigated are only a minority of cases where avoidable medical injury occurs. In Germany too there have been high profile cases of systemic failure in particular hospitals, leading to deficient care over a period of years; the best-known example—with parallels to the Bristol Royal Infirmary Scandal—is the

[117] A Laufs (ed), *Die Entwicklung der Arzthaftung* (Berlin, Springer,1997) 349 ff.

[118] *Ibid*, 351.

[119] A Laufs (ed), *Die Entwicklung der Arzthaftung* (n 117 above) 352. This proposal has not attracted political support.

[120] See further the discussion in Katzenmeier, *Arzthaftung* (n 3 above) 266 ff.

[121] Katzenmeier, *Arzthaftung* (n 3 above) 266 ff. Supporters of no fault liability include Radau, *Ersetzung der Arzthaftung durch Versicherungsschutz* (n 12 above), who outlines a possible scheme, based on the Swedish model; see also Schreiber, 'Handlungsbedarf für den Gesetzgeber?' (n 12 above) 343–4; Thumann, *Reform der Arzthaftung in den Vereinigten Staaten von Amerika* (n 10 above) 201 ff.

[122] Reforms to the ZPO (in 2002) have changed the rules of civil appeal procedure and are likely to lead to a decline in such claims going all the way to the BGH; otherwise their impact in this area has been modest: see K-O Bergmann, 'Die Reform der Zivilprozessordnung und ihre Auswirkungen auf den Arzthaftungsprozess' in T Ratacjzak and C-M Stegers (eds), *Arzthaftungsrecht—Rechtspraxis und Perspektiven* (Berlin, Springer, 2006) 1 ff.

[123] Generally the relevant legal costs appear lower in Germany. A reason may be that, as noted in ch 3, patient lawyers receive more help from the court, and hence require less expertise than in England.

[124] For discussion of the Woolf Report, see the text at n 61 ff above.

'*Barmbek/Bernbeck* case', which concerned an eminent doctor at a Hamburg hospital who continued to practise when no longer competent.[125] Unlike the Kennedy report into Bristol, the subsequent committee of enquiry, set up by the *Hamburg Landesparlament*, did not identify the system of private law litigation (in encouraging cover-ups) as a contributory factor; rather the finger was pointed at the strong hierarchies and collegiality at the hospital.

In this context, an important statutory provision promoting patient safety is § 137 in Book V of the *Sozialgesetzbuch* (SGB), which requires hospital authorities to implement measures directed at quality assurance.[126] Subsequently, the Federal Ministry for Health also put forward a central quality assurance initiative, *Maßnahmen der medizinischen Qualitätssicherung in der Bundesrepublik Deutschland* (1994). This is supplemented by rules at state level, as well as in the detailed provisions of the contracts between hospitals and the public health insurance companies.[127] Though, the breach of such rules will not of itself give rise to liability, it may result in disciplinary or contractual sanctions. Furthermore it will be an indicator of a negligent breach of duty in the context of a particular action brought by an injured patient.[128]

IV. Comparative Assessment

In comparing the history of reform proposals in England and Germany, as well as their character, various similarities are apparent. However, so too are differences. First, as we saw, there is agreement that the existing system of private law liability is not necessarily the optimum means of compensating for medical injury, and this rests on similar sorts of concern. In particular, there is a perception that the doctor-patient relationship is undermined by fault-based liability, as well as the recognition of the high secondary costs of litigation in this area. As regards the various alternatives proposed in both countries, these too have much in common: namely, on the one hand, reform aimed at replacing private law by awarding damages on a no-fault basis from collective funds; and on the other, schemes that, while leaving the underlying law intact, aim to counteract its main defects. Indeed, a certain chronological parallelism is also evident, with the more radical proposals being aired in the 1970s, to give way to more modest initiatives in later years.

Here, the doubts in both countries telling against radical change to a no-fault approach show much common ground. In the main these centre upon the financial implications, as well as the conceptual and practical problems of framing such a scheme so as to draw principled and clear distinctions between injuries to be

[125] See B Beyerle, *Rechtsfragen medizinischer Qualitätskontrolle* (Heidelberg, Müller, 2004) 11.
[126] *Ibid*, 6 ff.
[127] See Deutsch and Spickhoff, *Medizinrecht* (n 110 above) para 441.
[128] Deutsch and Spickhoff, *Medizinrecht* (n 110 above) para 447.

compensated for and not.[129] To some extent these matters are linked: the more widely drawn the scheme, the more it will cost. However, there is also the point that the number of claims will automatically increase, due to the absence of inhibiting effects stemming from adversarial litigation (ie a higher proportion of people with notionally valid claims will apply for compensation). This may not in itself be regarded as a bad thing, but is undoubtedly a significant practical worry in the light of the data noted above as to the true numbers of avoidable errors in healthcare.[130]

As we saw, in terms of assessing these matters, English and German reformers have had the examples of the Swedish and New Zealand schemes, which have both now existed for over 30 years. First, as regards costs, experience in those countries suggests that this indeed is likely to remain a major stumbling block. In particular, as the CMO noted in his Report in England, far more claims for medical injury are brought pro rata there than under the private law in England and Germany, which especially in New Zealand has created problems.[131] Conversely, damages paid out are much lower than the level of compensation under private law. In those countries, this solution is evidently acceptable, but this arguably reflects special aspects of society there, in which there is a shared sense across fairly small and homogenous populations that health is a common public good (and where damages augment generous social security provision for disability).

As to the design issue, the New Zealand and Swedish experiences show that no-fault liability is most straightforward in iatrogenic injury cases. Here one can take the statistical rarity of the injury (as formerly in New Zealand), or its ex post facto avoidability (as in Sweden), as the initial basis for compensation. This may be buttressed by the requirement that the injury in question attains a certain threshold of severity (perhaps in conjunction with its disproportionality to the gravity of the condition being treated). The Swedish scheme adopts this approach, as did the scheme of additional support for victims of medical accidents that operated in the former GDR.

Here the main difficulty is one of principle, namely that, absent the use of fault with its appeal to corrective justice, the basis for making an award remains obscure. Certainly the fact that serious injury should have materialised in his case makes the patient unlucky relative to (most) other patients for whom it does not; but then a person who contracts a rare and from the outset untreatable illness has been equally unlucky compared to the majority of the population, who do not.[132]

[129] Compare the discussion in Jones, *Medical Negligence* (n 11 above) 1-039 ff, with that in Katzenmeier, *Arzthaftung* (n 3 above) 242 ff.

[130] See n 67 above. Here, the need to show fault acts as a brake in forcing down the level of claims; this is at least in part because of secondary costs and proof problems associated with litigation, but it may also reflect a reluctance by the public to call doctors to account for bona fide mistakes in the context of overall beneficial care: see further the data in the CMO's Report, *Making Amends* (n 2 above) 75 ff.

[131] Oliphant, 'Beyond Misadventure: Compensation for Medical Injuries in New Zealand' (n 25 above) 361–2.

[132] Interestingly, in this context, the New Zealand scheme was in the early 1980s extended to allow awards for heart-attacks and strokes, but this was later discontinued due to financial considerations: see Merry and McCall Smith, *Errors, Medicine and the Law* (n 10 above) 226.

This is added to by 'line-drawing' problems in deciding if, in a given case, the risk was sufficiently rare, the patient's injury reached the required severity, etc. Here, patients who fall on the wrong side of the line may feel justifiably aggrieved (in terms of considerations of distributive justice). The same criticism can incidentally be made of the limited 'pockets-based' no-fault schemes operative in England and Germany, which restrict recovery to injury connected to a narrowly defined source of risk.[133] Even so, an approach of the above kind—collectivising the risk of iatrogenic harm—arguably conduces to greater social welfare and appears relatively workable in practice. It will be yet more persuasive if, at the same time, some of the disadvantages associated with private litigation can be successfully removed.

However, this still leaves the other large sub-class of medical injury cases, in which the patient's 'injury' consists in the natural progress of his condition following misdiagnosis and/or inadequate treatment. Here the patient's harmful outcome itself will not do for identifying cases for compensation: illness and death will always have the final word over the doctor. Instead, the harm must have been avoidable given appropriate care. This, though, raises the question of what *is* 'appropriate care', ie what standard of diagnosis and treatment are patients notionally entitled to? The higher this is pitched, the more patients will be covered. Nonetheless (unless an entirely ex post facto approach is taken, compensating for every diagnosis that turns out to be wrong) the enquiry will inevitably bear a strong resemblance to one into fault. This is already so under the Swedish model, employing the standard of a skilled specialist; and if—as formerly in New Zealand—the scheme uses a lower (financially more workable) standard based on the diagnostic skill and care of a careful doctor, the difference evaporates entirely.

As noted earlier, since 2005 the New Zealand scheme has been radically altered so that it now encompasses unplanned injury across the board, provided that this is attributable mainly to the treatment rather than the patient's underlying condition.[134] In doing so the new approach attempts to do away with the division posited above between iatrogenic harm and misdiagnosis cases (including the use, for the former, of arbitrary qualifying thresholds). Instead all of the work—in demarcating the injuries to be covered and excluded—is to be done by asking whether treatment or illness was the 'substantial cause'. This notion, though, remains very slippery: in practice it will require the decision-maker to assign a weighting to the various factors that contribute (each as a necessary condition in an overall causal set) to injury in a given case. As Oliphant argues, the most plausible basis for doing this involves assessing the overall regularity of connection between each factor in isolation and the type of harm at issue. The greater a given

[133] See M Jones's criticism of birth-injuries schemes (covering severe neurological disability related to a child's birth, but excluding 'congenital disabilities': *Medical Negligence* (n 11 above) 1-050. Arguably an exception applies to treatment agreed to (in part) altruistically—this was the justification for the Vaccine Damages Payment scheme in England.

[134] See the text at n 25 ff, above.

factor's propensity under normal conditions to produce the harm, the more 'substantial' it will be.[135] Thus,

> [w]hen a patient suffering from heart disease has a heart attack as a result of treatment that does not ordinarily carry that risk, the additional injury could well be described as substantially caused by the underlying condition on the basis that it was a more regular consequence of the disease than of the procedure in question.[136]

By the same token, however, the conclusion in other cases (be they of iatrogenic harm or missed diagnosis) that *treatment* was the substantial cause may well imply a finding of fault: 'the [underlying] condition would not normally produce the injury because one would not normally expect negligent treatment'.[137] In sum, whilst it is too early to pass a concluded judgement, there is a suspicion that, in seeking to devise a uniform approach removing reference to fault in misdiagnosis cases, the latest New Zealand reforms have in fact reintroduced a wholly fault-based approach (ie also in relation to iatrogenic harm), albeit this has been screened behind causal metaphor.[138]

Returning to England and Germany, as we saw, both countries have for their part renounced a general no-fault approach to compensating for medical injury, instead putting faith in more modest reforms to the underlying, fault-based private law. It is at this juncture that a divergence (or at least a different *dynamic*) between the two jurisdictions becomes apparent. In particular, in Germany there has generally been less pressure in terms of reform, and such proposals that have emerged have been of a less centralised and political character, compared to England. Here a major factor in easing tensions in Germany has arguably been the stance of the courts, which have developed the relevant private law in a patient-friendly direction. Unlike the NHS-conscious English judiciary, they have seemingly been undeterred by fears of escalating costs. Rather, there appears to be a tolerance of malpractice litigation as a natural corollary of complex medical care. This should be viewed too in the context of the greater ease of access to civil justice in Germany, in terms of lower legal fees. Thus, where patients have suspected negligence on the doctor's part, it has been easier for them to instigate a claim. In addition, as we saw, extra-legal initiatives (notably, the system of arbitration boards set up by the regional medical councils) have helped to take pressure off the legal system.

In England, following a series of centralised reviews (most recently by the Government Chief Medical Officer), the system of NHS Redress currently being introduced could be seen as having features in common with the German arbitration

[135] Oliphant, 'Beyond Misadventure: Compensation for Medical Injuries in New Zealand' (n 25 above) 384, citing HLA Hart and AM Honoré, *Causation in the Law*, 2nd edn (Oxford, Clarendon Press, 1985) 233.

[136] Oliphant, 'Beyond Misadventure' (n 25 above) 384.

[137] Oliphant, 'Beyond Misadventure' (n 25 above) 384–5.

[138] This is separate from the evidential problems that (as with fault-based private law) will remain in any case with respect to factual causation; eg the need in a misdiagnosis case to establish that non-treatment was a factor at all in the injury—was the illness treatable ab initio? See ch 3 pt III 3, above.

boards.[139] In both cases, a cost-free mechanism, which remains outside the formal litigation process, has been established with the object of leading to a relatively swift resolution of more straightforward, lower-cost claims. Nonetheless, while in Germany the boards have an intermediate role—providing the patient with a report to submit to the doctor's insurers—in England the NHS Litigation Authority will be directly responsible for offering settlements in cases where it deems this appropriate. In Germany, as we saw, the fact that the arbitration boards, even where their Report is favourable towards the patient, cannot dictate the terms of (any) settlement is one reason why patient lawyers remain sceptical about them. In this regard, it will be interesting to see if the model proposed by the NHS Redress Act fares better.

Finally, as we saw, in both countries there is an increasing emphasis (quite apart from questions of legal liability) upon improving safety in healthcare. Here a 'wake-up call' has been provided by international surveys revealing the true extent of preventable adverse outcomes in modern mass systems of healthcare, most of which never lead to legal action. In this regard, it has been recognised that, while it may suppress the number of claims for compensation, the litigation system does not by itself do enough to promote accident prevention.

[139] There is no evidence, though, that the German model influenced the Redress Scheme. The arbitration boards were briefly considered by the Pearson Report (n 40 above) vol 3, para 510, but are not referred to by the CMO.

6

Conclusions

THIS STUDY HAS focused on a defined area of English and German law, namely that dealing with compensation for medical injury, and has sought to describe and analyse it in some detail. In doing so the aim has primarily been theoretical—seeking an understanding of why the respective legal rules have developed as they have. Medical malpractice law has offered a rich basis for a micro-comparative study of this kind. England and Germany have societies at a similar stage of development and with broadly similar values. In each country the mass provision of healthcare is taken for granted, and the individual citizen's access to a reasonable level of treatment seen as a social right. The law too can be seen in both countries to proceed from a common starting point in allocating medical injury cases to private law (and under the aegis of the fault principle). Nonetheless, the detailed rules regulating the provision of compensation when treatment goes wrong or fails to work differ markedly. In this regard, the two systems have developed independently from one another in the context of different legal traditions: there has been little sign of the two seeking to learn from one another, let alone copy from each other's rules or approaches.[1]

In the first chapter we saw how certain underlying systemic differences between English and German medical malpractice law that initially appear significant have in practice only a limited impact upon the concrete legal rules. This is true in the first place of the common law/civil law divide between the two countries. Here, quite apart from the general debate as to how far those approaches are 'converging', we saw that within the German civil tradition, too, medical malpractice law is judge-made law, which for present purposes can be regarded as operating in the same way as the English common law tradition. Secondly, we found that the divergent classification of medical malpractice claims, in tort in England and contract in Germany, is of little import. Such claims have a hybrid quality: the patient agrees to be treated by the doctor (and the doctor gains his mandate to treat) on account of the hoped for benefit; at the same time there is the risk that the intervention—especially if unskilful—may make things worse. In view of this there has,

[1] There are scarcely any German decisions in the field of medical malpractice that refer to English authorities, or vice versa. Exceptions, where the issue concerned liability in principle for a particular form of injury, are BGH, 18 January 1983, NJW, 1371 (which referred to *McKay v Essex Area Health Authority* [1982] 1 QB 1166 (CA) in rejecting a claim for 'wrongful life') and, conversely, *McFarlane v Tayside Health Board* [2000] 2 AC 59 and *Rees v Darlington Memorial Hospital* [2003] UKHL 52, where the House of Lords briefly alluded to the German approach in wrongful conception/birth cases.

in both countries, been a merging of those two private law institutions. The same key interests (which certainly include the patient's bodily integrity and health) are protected under both.

As discussed in chapter two, English and German law go on to adopt similar starting positions as to the circumstances when a patient may recover damages for injury arising in respect of medical treatment. Here, both systems distinguish between injuries on the one hand that are attributable to fault on the doctor's part, and on the other those that are not, and will be for the patient to bear as 'fateful'. As noted, the 'fault principle' may be regarded as privileging the abstract 'equal freedom' of the parties. The activity of the doctor is not to be penalised simply on account of an adverse outcome of treatment (a matter partly beyond his control), but only where his conduct fell below the standard of a reasonably skilled doctor, thus exposing the patient to an unjustified risk of harm. Moreover, the risk in question must also materialise: there is no duty to compensate if, quite apart from anything the doctor did or failed to do, the same injury would have occurred.

Nevertheless, as Zweigert and Kötz observe, the choice between fault-based and stricter approaches to liability is not a straightforward dichotomy, but admits of degrees.[2] In the first place, the law in assessing the doctor's conduct may take a variety of stances in determining when he took the legally required care. In this regard, as we saw, the English courts traditionally allowed doctors significant latitude in their treatment practices. Thus, provided the doctor showed he complied with a practice endorsed by other doctors at the time, he would generally escape an imputation of fault. The courts were reluctant to go behind an accepted practice to ask if the practice itself involved unjustified risk-taking. Though in more recent years the courts have reasserted their ultimate authority to determine the issue, in practice—given their caution in second-guessing the opinions of the medical experts—the effect has not been great. By contrast, the German courts' approach has from the outset been more sceptical of doctors' conduct and clearer in the need to subject it to scrutiny. This is true both as regards their greater hesitation in exculpating the defendant on the basis of favourable testimony from other doctors, and in their use of the doctrine of 'fully-masterable risks'. As noted, under the latter doctrine, the burden in the case of injury from risks deemed within the doctor's sphere, will be placed on the defence to show that every possible precaution was taken.

A second, very significant way in which the German system exhibits a more 'patient-friendly' stance than that in England concerns the greater ease—against the background of evidential uncertainty—with which causative negligence may be shown as a question of historical fact. As discussed in chapter three, this has occurred somewhat paradoxically from the starting point of more difficult prima facie rules. Here it is as if the sharper contrast between the substantive law elements, and the ancillary rules establishing their presence, has forced the German

[2] K Zweigert and H Kötz, *Introduction to Comparative Law*, 3rd edn (trans T Weir) (Oxford, Clarendon Press, 1998) 649 ff.

courts into an explicit choice: one they have made in favour of the patient. Thus, in derogation from the normal position in matters of civil proof, they have developed a number of special concessions, casting the burden upon the defendant doctor in respect of a given question. This includes, as we saw, presumptions as to the primary facts underlying the claim, as well as defining circumstances where the doctor has the onus of explaining how, consistently with due care, certain forms of iatrogenic injury could occur.[3]

In this regard, one of the most striking aspects of German law is the reversal of proof as to causation applied in cases of 'gross negligence'. Here the result is not to promote strict liability as such: ex hypothesi the doctor's conduct was faulty. Instead, the effect has been to chip away at the second main plank of corrective justice, viz factual causation. The defendant doctor is singled out because he created a (grossly) unjustified risk to the patient, and this suffices for liability even though in many cases the injury did not stem from that risk, but would have occurred anyway.[4] By contrast, in England the courts have consistently rejected arguments for reversing the burden of proof of causation in medical malpractice cases. In doing so, they have adverted to the potential costs to the National Health Service. In the result, the German system can be seen to generate more 'false positives', and the English system more 'false negatives' (relative to whether the doctor's fault really played a necessary part in the harm). Interestingly, in this context, where both countries agree is in rejecting the alternative possibility (in misdiagnosis cases) of proportionate recovery based on the loss of the patient's statistical chance of a cure.[5]

A third, important area where German law is more helpful to the patient than the equivalent English law is in relation to claims for 'disclosure malpractice'. Here, as we saw in chapter four, the differences between the two systems that conduce to this result are two-fold. In the first place, divergent views are taken of the failure by a doctor to divulge risks (that subsequently materialise and cause iatrogenic injury). In Germany this renders the patient's consent invalid and the entire subsequent treatment unlawful. In England (and other common law systems) the treatment remains lawful, and the patient instead has at most a claim for negligent breach of duty. This has significant implications in terms of the structure of such actions: in Germany this form of claim brings with it notable advantages for the patient in matters of causation and proof; by contrast in England, though recognised as a separate category, disclosure malpractice is dealt with in a similar manner to a treatment malpractice claim.

In the second place the question of what amounts to fault in this context (or in other words, what risks the doctor was legally obliged to disclose) receives different answers. In England, the law has moved laboriously towards recognising the

[3] Ie the evidential aspect of the approach based on fully-masterable risks.

[4] As noted, liability was mandated in one case where, on the evidence, it was 90 % probable that proper treatment would not have helped the claimant: see BGH, 27 April 2004, NJW 2004, 2011.

[5] Given the different starting points just outlined, were English law to adopt the latter approach this would tend towards a widening of liability; in German law its tendency would be a narrowing.

patient's right to know of those risks that would matter to a reasonable person. By contrast, in Germany a highly subjective approach is taken, stressing the importance of the patient's individual autonomy and at times requiring the disclosure of utterly negligible risks. The upshot, as we saw, is that in the latter country such claims have become a distinct and popular avenue of redress, allowing the patient to circumvent many of the proof difficulties in showing treatment malpractice (in respect of the same injury).

Unsurprisingly, as we saw in chapter five, the different attitude of the English and German courts to medical malpractice claims has had an impact upon the reform dynamic in the respective systems. Here we identified a common rejection of the option of no-fault liability in the medical treatment context, based both on the potential financial costs and the difficulties in designing an effective scheme. Otherwise, though, there has been greater dissatisfaction in England with the operation of private litigation in this sphere. In particular, the perception has been of a failure to give sufficient weight to the patient's interests. By contrast, in Germany the latter is better provided for. Not only is a higher rate of claiming evidently seen as acceptable, but the chances (for the individual patient) of obtaining damages are higher.[6] Overall, it appears that significantly more resources have been invested there into compensating for medical accidents. In this regard, we saw too a key extra-legal initiative in the form of the arbitration boards, established by the medical profession and its insurers to help investigate and settle claims. In England, following the recommendations of the Chief Medical Officer, an initiative with some similarities to that scheme is to be introduced following legislation by the government, albeit of a more formal and centralised character.

In making sense of the differences chronicled above, it is helpful to distinguish issues of outcome—that is, the tendency for the law to impose liability or no liability—from ones of doctrine (affecting the way the elements of a claim are categorised and ordered). First, as regards outcome, we have seen that German law is more disposed to mandate findings in favour of the injured patient than English law, which for its part is more protective of the treating side. In seeking an explanation for this, it is plausible to begin with the different way the healthcare systems are organised in the two countries. Under the National Health Service system used by the bulk of the population in England, healthcare has been collectivised: the scheme, including both the costs of treatment and external overheads (such as compensation for injury) is financed directly out of central taxation.

Against this background, the communal public good dimension of healthcare has arguably impressed the courts there more than in Germany. Judges have been mindful implicitly (and sometimes explicitly) of the overall pressure on healthcare resources—the sense that the more money is paid out to victims of medical negligence, the less will be left for treating other patients. By contrast, in the devolved German system, where the costs of liability are borne by liability insurers, the link

[6] Though comparative data is not available, this would seem a necessary implication of the more favourable substantive and procedural law rules in Germany, as discussed in chs 2–4 of this work.

is less immediate. The settlement of medical injury claims will be reflected in an adjustment in the premiums paid by doctors, which in turn impacts on the fees they charge for their services (to the health insurance funds).[7] However, such effects will not be felt until some time after the event; and certainly in the past there seems to have been an implicit assumption that the necessary resources would be available.

At a conceptual level, the above difference may be analysed in terms of the interaction of corrective and distributive justice concerns. As regards the former, it was noted earlier that the fault principle, underpinning the law in both countries, strikes a balance between the ex ante interests of the parties to an injurious interaction: the defendant is liable where he causes injury by failing to act as a reasonable person, but not otherwise. In this regard, the principle has an intuitive appeal in regulating the relations of private actors, viewed as abstract pre-social entities.[8] Nonetheless, in the empirical social world injury represents a tangible setback to the claimant's flesh and blood interests. A previously fit person can no longer earn a living, with serious consequences for himself and his family and knock-on effects for society. By the same token, the impact of a liability finding upon the defendant may need to be considered, eg if ordering damages for a venial slip will reduce the latter to poverty.

It is at this point that distributive justice concerns enter the picture, and may require a departure from the formal demands of corrective justice. Importantly, though, the practical expression of such concerns will turn on the organisation and resources of a particular society. As Bix has argued, in the related context of discussing JS Mill's harm principle,

> [t]he line between actions which harm others and those that do not has strong intuitive appeal: 'if my actions don't harm anyone, they are nobody else's business'. But in societies where insurance is pervasive (and/or compulsory)—where the government may run the health service / provide health care and social services to the destitute—there may no longer be actions that are purely self-regarding . . . Such facts, which of course vary from country to country, undermine some of the persuasive power of Mill's dividing line.[9]

Thus, under one set of arrangements (eg where the putative injurer carries liability insurance) it may appear expedient to order him to make reparation whether or not the claimant's injury was really attributable to fault. Here the pendulum will swing from fault-based liability towards strict liability. Conversely, though, considerations based on social welfare could move it the opposite way towards a

[7] See H-L Schreiber, 'Handlungsbedarf für den Gesetzgeber?' in A Laufs (ed), *Die Entwicklung der Arzthaftung* (Berlin, Springer, 1997) 343; A Merry and A McCall Smith, *Errors, Medicine and the Law* (Cambridge, Cambridge University Press, 2001) 212.

[8] Admittedly this is to ignore proof issues, ie that the court must be persuaded of the factual presence of the elements grounding the claim. The fact that the burden of proof rests on one side—usually the claimant—who carries the risk of evidential uncertainty, detracts in practice from the fault principle's neutrality: see P Cane, *Atiyah's Accidents, Compensation and the Law*, 6th edn (London, Butterworths, 1999) 176.

[9] B Bix, *Jurisprudence: Theory and Context*, 4th edn (London, Sweet & Maxwell, 2006) 158.

denial of liability notwithstanding fault and causation. This would be so if it were thought better to use a scarce public resource for the on-going benefit of the majority (eg persons requiring future medical care), than to compensate the minority injured in the past.[10] In the context of medical malpractice litigation, the English courts have in their judgments tended in the second direction. It is true, they have not accepted shortages in resources as an explicit basis for a reduction in care; nor, though, have they been prepared actively to set standards. Above all, judges have refused to be swayed by the patient's practical difficulties in vindicating his rights (due to evidential uncertainties). By contrast, the German courts have been influenced by distributive justice considerations in the first direction, towards a spreading of the risks of medical injury.[11]

There are, though, other subtle differences in values (stemming from historical and constitutional factors) that arguably colour the different legal approaches in the two countries. One matter, noted in chapter four in respect of disclosure malpractice cases, is that the German courts have invoked considerations of patient autonomy more readily than the courts in England. Not only have they imposed far-reaching disclosure duties, but there has been a down-playing of factual causation in such cases. From a pure corrective justice standpoint the effect of the German rules leads to over-compensation: the doctor will be liable even where it is at best doubtful that his faulty non-disclosure made any difference to the patient's decision to have the injurious treatment. Admittedly, it is ultimately difficult to be sure in such cases how far protection of autonomy is the guiding consideration. This is because the courts' approach is at the same time consistent with (and explicable in terms of) their previously identified disposition to spread the risks of medical injury.

At a more diffuse level, it is interesting to speculate how far differences in the perception and prestige of the medical profession in England and Germany may have had an influence upon the incidence of liability findings. This is a difficult argument to substantiate, but the *Bolam* test in England (in its pre-*Bolitho* guise), seems to have stemmed at least in part from an instinctive judicial deference to medical skill, according doctors a degree of latitude not shared by other professionals. Similarly, as we saw, English judges have reacted strongly against the possibility of doctors being held to account in battery. By contrast, in Germany, a less sanguine view of medical professionals appears to prevail.[12] As noted in chap-

[10] Noteworthy, in this context, is the suggestion by the moral philosopher, John Harris, that victims of medical negligence in the National Health Service should take their place in a queue for resources (in terms of compensation and remedial treatment) alongside persons requiring on-going and future care: see Harris, 'The Injustice of Compensation for Victims of Medical Accidents' (1997) 314 *British Medical Journal* 1821. This idea has attracted little support—arguably because of its neglect of the corrective justice perspective.

[11] See further A Laufs, 'Delikt und Gefährdung—Von der Schadenszurechnung zur Schadensverteilung?' in Laufs, *Die Entwicklung der Arzthaftung* (n 7 above); C Katzenmeier, *Arzthaftung* (2002) 169–70.

[12] This may possibly have its roots in the role of certain doctors in iniquitous programmes during the National Socialist era. In England, a shift in the perception of doctors has arguably occurred in the

ter one, it is by no means rare for them to be charged with criminal offences in respect of bona fide, faulty treatment of patients—something almost unthinkable in England.

So far we have been concerned with differences relevant to divergent outcomes reached in medical malpractice cases in England and Germany. However, as noted above, other key differences are of a doctrinal nature—going to the structure of the relevant rules in each county. Indeed it can be argued that differences of this type are more far-reaching than those of outcome. Thus, it seems clear that the outcome of a claim based on the same underlying facts would often be the same in both countries. It is only comparatively rarely that, say, an injured patient would obtain damages in Germany, where in identical circumstances, he would fail in England.[13] By contrast, differences of doctrine are all-pervasive and will indeed usually be the first thing to strike the comparative observer.

Unlike differences of outcome these differences are less amenable to an explanation in terms of divergent societal values. Instead, they stem from the nature of positive law as an historically conditioned, dynamic system of rules. Thus we may begin by noting that there are often high-level differences in the way legal phenomena are organised in different systems, reflecting divergent traditions—eg the fact consideration is required in English but not German contract law, or that English law has developed separate torts of battery and negligence, for intended touchings and unintended harm, respectively. It is also apparent that, in developing the sub-rules in a certain area, such as medical malpractice, the courts will try to ensure their coherence with these broader principles. In doing so, though, they may not infrequently be confronted with a tension between the specific and general: a rule that works well enough overall in governing injurious interactions may fail to do justice in that area (due to factors specific to that sphere of life). In such cases there will be pressure to modify the rule by developing exceptions. However, a significant point here, with respect to comparing discrete legal systems, is that, since the general rules differ, these pressures will occur in different places.

In the course of this work we have seen various illustrations of this phenomenon. Thus, as noted in chapter three, a defining feature of German medical malpractice law is the elaborate system of secondary rules that allow for proof modifications in various circumstances. The courts have fashioned these as a creative response to the patient's proof difficulties—an upshot of the onerous civil standard of proof in German law. In England, with its lower standard of proof—and a judiciary less inclined to encourage litigation against doctors—there is

wake of the Shipman murder trial (where a GP was found to have murdered dozens of his patients) and the Bristol Royal Infirmary scandal: see M Brazier and J Miola, 'Bye-bye *Bolam*: a medical litigation revolution?' (2000) 8 *Medical Law Review* 85 at 100.

[13] As suggested in n 6 above, this will be the usual variant. Admittedly, the opposite scenario can be imagined where, in the same circumstances, a claim would succeed in England, but fail in Germany—eg where causation can be shown on the balance of probabilities but not to the higher German standard of proof, and no proof modifications or arguments based on non-disclosure apply. However, this is likely to be rare.

nothing comparable. Another example of how general features of private law exert long-range influence on the specific rules of medical malpractice concerns the wrongful non-disclosure of risks. Here, as we saw in chapter four, the common law courts have held the patient's consent to medical treatment to be valid. In doing so they have avoided exposing the doctor to the stigma of a battery action (with its criminal law associations). At the same time, the choice to address non-disclosure claims in negligence has brought in its train further consequences for how such claims are structured (which may also be seen as more consonant with the requirements of corrective justice).

By contrast, in Germany, the different structure of tort liability in the BGB means the issue of stigma does not arise in the same way in non-disclosure cases.[14] There the courts have found consent to be vitiated, an approach that better serves the distinct goal of patient autonomy (and sidesteps the problematic proof rules in treatment malpractice cases). Ultimately, as this suggests, the factors that have influenced the development of the rules within each legal system are a subtle amalgam of outcome-led and doctrinal factors—the first take the form of a disposition (crudely, to be more or less patient-friendly); the latter operate at a systemic level, presenting the courts with antinomies that they have solved according to their underlying disposition.

In the light of this, it remains finally to ask what the English and German systems may learn from one another in this field. In terms of immediate practical consequences, the answer is in fact unclear. It is certainly true that a rule or approach adopted in one country may be suggestive for the other. For example, an English lawyer may be moved by the German rules as to 'fully-masterable risks' to ask how far a similar approach would be feasible in his country. More generally, when a divergent stance has been taken on a doctrinal question, the other system offers a window on how things might otherwise look. Thus, a German lawyer, interested in the implications of the courts there reclassifying the non-disclosure of risks as an injury to the patient's personality right, rather than a *Körperverletzung*, may consider how such claims are dealt with in negligence under common law. Conversely, the English lawyer gains a sense, from the German rules, as to how a battery-based approach might operate.[15]

Nevertheless, the question of whether a given change is actually desirable in terms of its outcome must ultimately be answered from within the relevant system (in the light of the particular social arrangements there). Secondly, as discussed, the individual rules in each jurisdiction draw their colour from their surrounding context, making the prediction of how they will work elsewhere problematic. In this regard, it is telling that the courts have largely eschewed contact with the rules and doctrines of the other country. As noted at the outset of this chapter, to the extent that judicial notice has been taken at all, this has been in respect of the basic

[14] As noted (see text at n 12), it is also not clear that it would matter so much to the German courts if it did.

[15] See further the discussion in ch 4 pt II 1 and 2.

choice whether a given form of injury should qualify for protection, rather than in resolving subsequent, more detailed issues.

Instead, arguably the greatest benefit of a theoretical comparative study of the type pursued here is that it furthers the understanding of one's own system. The legal scholar, in the very act of comparison is propelled beyond the categories and concepts of his particular jurisdiction. This forces a direct engagement with the underlying issues, helping to bring the quirks and pre-suppositions of that system into sharper relief. By the same token, the scholar may emerge with a deeper appreciation of what in the relevant law is more essential.

Deutsche Zusammenfassung (German Summary)

1. Mit dieser Arbeit wurde es unternommen, die Regeln des englischen und des deutschen Arzthaftungsrechts zu vergleichen. Erfasst werden dabei sowohl Fälle, in denen der Patient eine zusätzliche, 'iatrogene' Verletzung durch die Behandlung erleidet, als auch diejenigen, bei denen der erwünschte Heilungserfolg ausgeblieben ist. In beiden Ländern hat die Anzahl von Ansprüchen auf Schadensersatz in solchen Fällen unter dem Einfluss von ähnlichen gesellschaftlichen Faktoren in den letzten Jahrzehnten stark zugenommen: Einerseits werden die Erwartungen einer zunehmend emanzipierten und anspruchsvollen Patientenschaft immer höher; andererseits übt der Arzt seine Tätigkeit als Teil eines Massengesundheitswesens aus, in dem die therapeutische Beziehung zwischen Arzt und Patient, die sich früher hemmend auf die Klagebereitschaft des Patienten ausgewirkt hat, seltener zustande kommt.

Um seine Ansprüche geltend zu machen, ist der Patient in England wie in Deutschland auf die Rechtsinstitute des Privatrechts angewiesen. In beiden Ländern stammen die für die Arzthaftung relevanten Rechtsinstitute aus dem Vertrags- und dem Deliktsrecht, wobei das Arzthaftungsrecht in England seinen Schwerpunkt eher in dem Zweiten, in Deutschland ihn eher in dem Ersten findet. Gleichwohl erweist sich dieser Unterschied in der Praxis als unbedeutend: Die ärztlichen Behandlungspflichten lassen sich nach beiden Instituten konkurrierend begründen, so dass es letzten Endes wenig ausmacht, ob der Patient seine Ansprüche auf Vertrag oder Delikt oder beide zusammen stützt. Ebenso ist der grundsätzliche systematische Unterschied zwischen dem deutschem und dem englischem Rechtssystem, dass das eine ein kodifiziertes, das andere ein fallrechtlich geprägtes 'Common Law'-System darstellt, hier kaum von Bedeutung: Denn das deutsche Arzthaftungsrecht besteht ähnlich wie das englische im wesentlichen aus Richterrecht, das die in diesem Gebiet lückenhaften gesetzlichen Regeln auf eine komplizierte und nuancierte Weise ergänzt hat.

Im deutschen wie im englischen Rechtssystem sind die rechtlich geschützten Interessen des Patienten, deren Verletzung den Ausgangspunkt für einen Anspruch gegen den Arzt bildet, im Grunde gleich. Diese umfassen auf jeden Fall den Schutz seiner körperlichen Integrität, seines Lebens und seiner Gesundheit gegen unmittelbare Eingriffe. Weniger geschützt ist dagegen zumindest in Fällen unbeabsichtigter

Schäden sein reines Vermögensinteresse. Dies ist freilich im Arzthaftungsrecht, wo die meisten Verletzungen ohnehin den Körper betreffen, eher von zweitrangiger Bedeutung. Eine Ausnahme bilden aber die Fälle, in denen Patientinnen die Unterhaltskosten für unerwünschte Kinder fordern, deren Existenz sich auf einen ärztlichen Fehler bei einer Sterilisation oder einem Schwangerschaftsabbruch zurückführen lässt. Hier bieten die englische und die deutsche Lösung vor dem Hintergrund unterschiedlicher rechtlicher Ansätze einen lehrreichen Kontrast. Im ersteren Land ist das House of Lords in den letzten Jahren einer eher restriktiven Linie gefolgt, nach der die Existenz eines gesunden Kindes nicht als Schaden bewertet wird; der Anspruch auf finanzielle Unterstützung wurde grundsätzlich abgelehnt. In Deutschland bleibt der BGH großzügiger in Fällen, in denen es um eine fehlerhafte Sterilisation geht, die der Familienplanung dienen sollte. Sonst ist auch in Deutschland die Tendenz, weitgehend eine Haftung zu verneinen, nicht zuletzt wegen verfassungsrechtlicher Bedenken aufgrund des Schutzes der Menschenwürde und des Persönlichkeitsrechts des Kindes.

2. Das zweite Kapitel befasst sich mit Ansprüchen, die auf einen Behandlungsfehler des Arztes gestützt werden. Hier geht es darum, die weiteren Elemente zu erkunden, die einen Schadensanspruch gegen den Arzt rechtfertigen, wenn der Patient eine Verletzung eines geschützten Rechtsguts erleidet. Wie bereits im ersten Kapitel angedeutet, sind die relevanten Elemente in beiden Rechtssystemen ähnlich, unabhängig davon, ob der Anspruch auf einer vertrags- oder deliktsrechtlichen Basis beruht.

Ausgangspunkt in beiden Systemen ist das Verschuldensprinzip, nach dem der Arzt nicht ohne weiteres für eine vom Patienten erlittene Verletzung haftet. Vielmehr muss feststehen, dass der Arzt bei der Wahl oder bei der Durchführung der Behandlung schuldhaft Leben, Körper oder Gesundheit des Patienten verletzt hat. Im englischen wie im deutschen Recht kommt es in diesem Zusammenhang grundsätzlich darauf an, ob der Arzt fahrlässig gehandelt hat, d.h. nicht diejenige Sorgfalt angewendet hat, die objektiv von einem Arzt in dessen Spezialbereich verlangt werden kann. Der englische und der deutsche Ansatz gehen allerdings bezüglich der Frage auseinander, inwieweit ein beklagter Arzt sich darauf berufen kann, dass er einem Ansatz gefolgt ist, der auch von anderen Ärzten für richtig gehalten wird. In England wurde dieser Umstand von den Gerichten traditionell als entlastend bewertet (der so genannte 'Bolam test'). Damit wurde der Ärzteschaft ein breiter Ermessungsspielraum für ihr Handeln eingeräumt. Auch wenn dieser Ansatz in den letzen Jahren relativiert worden ist, ist das englische Recht in diesem Punkt weiterhin großzügiger in seiner Bereitschaft, den Arzt zu entlasten, als das deutsche Recht: Beim letzteren war es von Anfang an klarer, dass die vom Arzt angewendete übliche Sorgfalt nicht ausreicht, wenn er bei der Behandlung die im Verkehr erforderliche Sorgfalt (§ 276 II BGB) außer Acht lässt.

Was im deutschen Recht zusätzlich dazu führt, dass dem Arzt öfter als im englischen Recht eine fahrlässige Pflichtverletzung zur Last gelegt wird, ist die Figur der 'vollbeherrschbaren Risiken'. Danach ergibt sich in Fällen, in denen sich im Umfeld der Behandlung ein Risiko verwirklicht, eine starke Verschuldensvermutung, die vom Arzt nur schwer zu widerlegen ist. Im Ergebnis kommt dieser Ansatz, der im englischen Recht Seinesgleichen nicht findet, der Gefährdungshaftung nah. In beiden Ländern bleibt es allerdings in jedem Fall Voraussetzung der Haftung, dass der Behandlungsfehler für den vom Patienten geltend gemachten Schaden kausal war. Hier sind die Regeln, die diese Frage bestimmen, einschließlich der Unterteilung in Fragen der äquivalenten Kausalität (factual causation) und adäquaten Kausalität (legal causation) weitgehend gleich.

3. Das dritte Kapitel setzt die Betrachtung von Ansprüchen von Patienten, die auf einem Behandlungsfehler des Arztes basieren, fort. Hier bilden aber nicht wie im Kapitel zwei die dem Anspruch zugrunde liegenden substantiellen Elemente den Schwerpunkt, sondern prozessuale Aspekte. Denn in der Praxis der Arzthaftung nehmen diese eine ebenso bedeutende, oft gar die entscheidende Rolle bei der Rechtsanwendung ein: Dies betrifft vor allem Fragen des Beweisrechtes. Um eine bestimmte Behandlung des Arztes als fahrlässig qualifizieren zu können, muss das Gericht zunächst feststellen, mit welchen konkreten Umständen der Arzt tatsächlich konfrontiert war und wie er auf sie reagiert hat. Ebenfalls von großer Bedeutung ist die für die Kausalität entscheidende hypothetische Frage, ob der Patient den Schaden nicht erlitten hätte, wenn der Arzt richtig gehandelt hätte. Die Lösung dieser Fragen, die den Gegenstand des dritten Kapitels bilden, wirft erhebliche Schwierigkeiten auf: Die Umstände sind auf der tatsächlichen Ebene häufig kompliziert und lassen sich auch von Gutachtern nicht immer befriedigend aufklären. Das gilt insbesondere für die Kausalitätsfrage, bei der es angesichts der Tatsache, dass die Krankheit des Patienten bereits ein Risiko für seinen Gesundheitszustand darstellte, manchmal schlicht unmöglich ist zu sagen, ob das vom Behandlungsfehler ausgehende zusätzliche Risiko sich tatsächlich verwirklicht hat oder ob die Verletzung allein der Krankheit zugeschrieben werden muss.

In diesem Bereich bestehen ausgeprägte Unterschiede zwischen dem englischen und dem deutschen Ansatz. Diese beruhen auf historischen und systematischen Faktoren. Zwar legen beide Systeme grundsätzlich gleichermaßen dem Patienten als Kläger die Beweislast für ihm günstige Tatsachen auf, sie legen dabei aber unterschiedliche Beweismaße zugrunde: In Deutschland gilt das Prinzip der richterlichen Überzeugung, nach dem selbst ein geringfügiger Zweifel am Tatsachenvortrag zu einem Urteil des 'non liquet' führt. Im englischen Privatrecht reicht es dagegen im Normalfall aus, dass eine Tatsachenbehauptung nach Meinung des Richters mit überwiegender Wahrscheinlichkeit der Wahrheit entspricht. Vor diesem Hintergrund haben sich die deutschen Gerichte viel eher bereit gezeigt als die englischen, den besonderen Beweisschwierigkeiten des Patienten Rechnung zu tragen. Dies ist geschehen, indem sie die strenge Ausgangsposition des deutschen Beweisrechts mehrfach aufgelockert haben.

Dieser Sonderansatz der deutschen Gerichte schlägt sich in verschiedenen Regeln nieder, die dem Patienten im Falle der Beweisnot bezüglich dreier

Hauptfragen zu Hilfe kommen: erstens bei der Aufklärung der dem Fall zugrunde liegenden Tatsachen (Dokumentations- und Befundsicherungspflichten des Arztes), zweitens bei der Vermutung eines schuldhaften ärztlichen Handelns in Fällen ungeklärter Verletzungen (Anscheinsbeweis, vollbeherrschbare Risiken) und drittens durch die Erleichterung des Beweises hinsichtlich des Kausalzusammenhangs zwischen dem Behandlungsfehler und dem Schaden des Patienten. Besonders in der letzten Frage ist das deutsche Recht mit der Figur der Umkehr der Beweislast in Fällen von groben Behandlungsfehlern dem Patienten und seinen Interessen an der Rechtsdurchsetzung deutlich entgegengekommen. Im englischen Recht gibt es, abgesehen von der allgemeinen Figur des 'res ipsa loquitur', die im Arzthaftungsprozess jedoch von begrenzter Bedeutung ist, nichts Vergleichbares. Die eher restriktive Linie der englischen Gerichte kommt unter anderem darin zum Ausdruck, dass sie bislang Klagen abgewiesen haben, die Schwierigkeiten bei der Kausalitätsfeststellung nach fehlerhaften Diagnosen auszuweichen versuchten, indem sie auf die statistische Chance eines dadurch vereitelten Heilungserfolges abstellten ('loss of chance'). Im Ergebnis ist das deutsche Recht trotz seiner strengeren Ausgangsposition in Beweisfragen deutlich patientenfreundlicher als das entsprechende englische Recht.

4. Im Gegensatz zu den Kapiteln zwei und drei befasst sich das vierte Kapitel mit einem anderen Ansatz, auf den ein Patient alternativ oder zusätzlich zu einer Behandlungsfehlerklage einen Anspruch gegen den Arzt zu stützen vermag. Hier geht es um die in manchen Fällen vorgetragene Behauptung, der Arzt habe den Patienten vor der Behandlung nicht ausreichend über die damit verbundenen Risiken aufgeklärt. Selbst wenn der Arzt die Behandlung hinterher fehlerfrei ausgeführt hat, stellt die Unterlassung der Aufklärung eine eigenmächtige Handlung des Arztes und eine Verletzung des Selbstbestimmungsrechts des Patienten dar: Wenn der Patient darüber hinaus während der Behandlung einen iatrogenen Schaden erleidet, liegt es nah, dass er den Arzt für denselben in Anspruch nehmen möchte.

In beiden Rechtssystemen wird dem Recht des Patienten, selbst zu entscheiden, ob er sich einer medizinischen Behandlung unterziehen will, eine große Bedeutung beigemessen. Das kommt vor allem darin zum Ausdruck, dass die Behandlung der Einwilligung des Patienten bedarf, um rechtsmäßig zu sein. Dabei setzt die Einwilligung im englischen wie im deutschen Recht ein bestimmtes Maß an Information über die Behandlung voraus. Allerdings gehen die zwei Systeme in anderen Punkten auseinander. Dies betrifft zunächst die Frage, ob das Nichterwähnen von iatrogenen Risiken die Patienteneinwilligung ungültig macht: In Deutschland wird diese Frage bejaht, in England verneint.

Das heißt jedoch nicht, dass der englische Patient ohne Anspruch bleibt: Er kann sich immerhin auf eine Pflichtverletzung des Arztes berufen. Aber diese wird als Teil des Tatbestands für 'negligence' (im Gegensatz zu dem der 'battery') angesehen, genau wie in einem Fall, in dem es um einen Behandlungsfehler geht. Die Folge ist, dass der Patient beweisbelastet bleibt und die gleichen Hürden nehmen muss wie in jenen anderen Fällen: Dies betrifft auch die Kausalitätsfrage, ob der richtig informierte Patient die Behandlung abgelehnt hätte. Der Kontrast, den das deutsche Recht hier gegenüber dem englischen bietet, ist erheblich: Die ganze Behandlung wird als eine rechtwidrige Körperverletzung eingestuft. Folgerichtig ist es dann Sache des Arztes, sich von deren weiteren Folgen, der Haftung für iatrogene Schäden eingeschlossen, zu entlasten. Zwar bleibt ihm in manchen Fällen das Argument, dass der Schaden außerhalb des Schutzzwecks der Norm liegt, sowie der Einwand der hypothetischen Einwilligung des Patienten, aber die Voraussetzungen dafür sind streng.

Weiter fallen beim Vergleich zwischen dem englischen und dem deutschen Recht die unterschiedlichen Anforderungen dafür auf, dass die ärztliche Aufklärung über die Behandlung als fehlerfrei gilt. In diesem Punkt waren die englischen Gerichte traditionell zurückhaltend und haben es weitgehend dem ärztlichen Ermessen überlassen, Risiken der Behandlung preiszugeben oder nicht. Dies hat sich freilich in jüngster Zeit verändert, so dass das englische Recht nun doch dem Ansatz des 'informed consent' entspricht, wie er schon seit mehreren Jahrzehnten in anderen Ländern des Common Law-Rechtskreises praktiziert wird. Danach ist der Arzt verpflichtet, dem Patienten alle Informationen zu geben, die für die Entscheidung eines verständigen Menschen von Belang sind, ob er in die Behandlung einwilligt. In Deutschland bleibt der Standard der erforderlichen Aufklärung diesem Ansatz immerhin um Einiges voraus, so dass auch Risiken, die statistisch betracht kaum wahrnehmbar sind, für aufklärungsbedürftig gehalten werden, wenn sie nur irgendwie von Bedeutung für den individuellen Patienten hätten sein können.

Im Ergebnis sind Ansprüche, die auf einem Aufklärungsfehler basieren, in Deutschland zu einer erheblichen Bedeutung und Popularität gelangt. Das erklärt sich dadurch, dass der von einem iatrogenen Risiko betroffene Patient dadurch eine bessere Chance hat, seinen Anspruch auf Schadensersatz durchzusetzen, als wenn er sich auf eine Klage wegen eines Behandlungsfehlers verlässt. Denn trotz der von den Gerichten geschaffenen Beweiserleichterungen scheitern letztere Klagen oft wegen des hohen Beweismaßes im deutschen Privatrecht. Das entsprechende englische Recht, in dem Aufklärungsfehler nicht konzeptionell von Behandlungsfehlern getrennt werden und in dem das Beweismaß ohnehin geringer ist, hat in dieser Hinsicht nichts dergleichen zu bieten.

5. Im fünften Kapitel geht es im Gegensatz zu den früheren Kapiteln nicht mehr um die aktuell geltenden Regeln, welche die Ansprüche wegen Arzthaftung in England und Deutschland bestimmen. Stattdessen gilt unser Interesse hier den verschiedenen Reforminitiativen, die in den beiden Ländern auf diesem Gebiet zur Diskussion gestellt wurden. Die herkömmliche privatrechtliche Lösung solcher Fälle ist in beiden Ländern zunehmend in die Kritik geraten, zum einen wegen der Belastung des Verhältnisses zwischen Arzt und Patient, zum anderen wegen der hohen Kosten der Prozesse und der Beweisschwierigkeiten, die bei solchen Prozessen auftreten. In dieser Hinsicht haben sich manche Kommentatoren in beiden Ländern gefragt, ob

nicht der bessere Ansatz eine allgemeine Versicherungslösung wäre, bei der es nicht mehr auf das Verschulden des Arztes ankommt; Länder wie Schweden und Neuseeland haben z.T. gute Erfahrungen damit gesammelt. Im Ergebnis wurde diese Alternative aber bislang in England und Deutschland abgelehnt: Das liegt daran, dass in beiden Ländern große Zweifel bestehen, sowohl bezüglich der möglichen Kosten einer solchen dem Grunde nach erweiterten Haftung als auch wegen des Problems, ein solches System so zu gestalten, dass eine gerechte Abgrenzung erreicht wird zwischen Schäden, die auszugleichen sind, und denen, die dem Lebensrisiko des Patienten angehören und von ihm zu tragen sind.

Gleichwohl sind aber Unterschiede in der Reformdynamik in England und Deutschland zu spüren. Im ersteren Land hat sich, der schwierigeren Rechtslage aus Sicht der Patienten entsprechend, mehr Druck in Richtung Reform als im zweiten aufgebaut. Es wird demnächst in England ein neues zentrales System für die Regelung von Ansprüchen in geringer Höhe eingeführt, das, obgleich das ärztliche Verschulden eine Voraussetzung bleibt, entlastend auf die jetzige Prozesslage wirken soll. Hier ergeben sich manche Parallelen mit dem System der Gutachterkommissionen und Schlichtungsstellen der Ärztekammern, die in Deutschland seit etwa dreißig Jahren eine außerrechtliche Alternative zu einer Patientenklage bieten.

6. Wenn man über die aufgeführten Unterschiede zwischen dem englischen und dem deutschen Ansatz in Sachen Arzthaftung insgesamt nachdenkt, um eine mögliche Erklärung für sie zu finden, fällt auf, dass die Differenzen in ihrer Grundgestaltung zwei Kategorien bilden. Zum ersten steht, was das materielle Ergebnis in solchen Fällen angeht, fest, dass das deutsche Recht allgemein eine patientenfreundlichere Tendenz aufweist als das entsprechende englische Recht: Der Arzt wird durch den Patienten in Deutschland häufiger in die Haftung genommen. Dieser Umstand lässt sich plausibel auf die unterschiedliche Struktur und Organisation der Gesundheitswesen in den beiden Ländern zurückführen. Dem englischen Gesundheitssystem fehlen die für die Begleichung von Haftpflichtforderungen in Anspruch genommenen Ressourcen für die Krankenversorgung selbst, während in Deutschland die Haftpflichtforderungen von Haftpflichtversicherungen erfüllt werden und nicht aus dem für die Krankenversorgung zur Verfügung stehenden Etat. Die Auswirkungen von Schadensersatzansprüchen auf die Ressourcen für die Krankenversorgung werden dementsprechend von englischen und deutschen Richtern unterschiedlich beurteilt. Wie im Schlusskapitel dargelegt, lässt sich das Aufeinandertreffen von den gegensätzlichen rechtlich-moralischen Ausgangspunkten der kommutativen und der distributiven Gerechtigkeit hier auf eine lehrreiche Weise beobachten.

Zum zweiten sind die rechtlichen Regeln in den beiden Ländern von grundsätzlichen strukturellen und systematischen Unterschieden geprägt. Dies betrifft z.B. die komplexen Sekundärregeln, die auf beweisrechtlicher Ebene dem deutschen Arzthaftungsrecht seinen distinktiven Charakter verleihen, sowie die ganz unterschiedlichen Ansätze bei Klagen, die sich auf einen angenommenen

Aufklärungsfehler des Arztes stützen. Differenzen dieser Art, die an unterschiedliche historisch bedingte Faktoren des jeweiligen Rechtssystems anknüpfen, sind ebenso allgegenwärtig wie nicht mehr wegzudenken. Während es angesichts dieser Tatsache in einem Rechtsvergleich schwierig wird, eine abschließende Bewertung vorzunehmen, in welchen Punkten das eine System von dem anderen unmittelbar lernen kann, bleibt es, einem unumstrittenen Vorteil einer solchen Forschungsarbeit festzuhalten: Für den rechtsvergleichenden Wissenschaftler selbst kommt das Eigentümliche, aber auch das Wesentliche jedes der Systeme klarer zum Vorschein.

BIBLIOGRAPHY

Materials in English

ATIYAH PS, *Accidents, Compensation and the Law* (London, Weidenfeld & Nicolson, 1970)

BIX B, *Jurisprudence: Theory and Context*, 4th edn (London, Sweet & Maxwell, 2006)

BOHLANDER M, 'The German Advantage Revisited: An Inside View of German Civil Procedure in the Nineties' (1998) 13 *Tulane European and Civil Law Forum* 25

BRAZIER M, 'The Case for a No-Fault Compensation Scheme for Medical Accidents' in SAM McLean (ed), *Compensation for Damage: an international perspective* (Aldershot, Dartmouth Publishing, 1993) 51

—— *Medicine, Patients and the Law*, 3rd edn (London, Penguin Books, 2003)

BRAZIER M and MIOLA J, 'Bye-bye *Bolam*: a medical litigation revolution?' (2000) 8 *Medical Law Review* 85

BRITISH MEDICAL ASSOCIATION, *Report of the BMA Working Party on No Fault Compensation* (London, BMA, 1987)

CANE P, *Atiyah's Accidents, Compensation and the Law*, 6th edn (London, Butterworths, 1999)

CHIEF MEDICAL OFFICER (Sir Liam Donaldson), *Making Amends: A consultation paper setting out proposals for reforming the approach to clinical negligence in the NHS* (London, Department of Health, 2003)

CLERMONT K and SHERWIN E, 'A Comparative View of Standards of Proof' (2002) 50 *American Journal of Comparative Law* 243

DEPARTMENT OF HEALTH, *An Organisation with a Memory: Report of an Expert Group on Learning from Adverse Events in the NHS* (London, DoH Consultation Paper, 2000)

DWORKIN G, *The Theory and Practice of Autonomy* (Cambridge, Cambridge University Press, 1988)

FARRELL A-M and DEVANEY S, 'Making Amends or Making Things Worse? Clinical Negligence Reform and Patient Redress in England' (2007) 27 *Legal Studies* 630

FAURE M and KOZIOL H (eds), *Cases on Medical Malpractice in a Comparative Perspective* (Vienna, Springer, 2001)

FENN P, GRAY A and RICKMAN N, 'The Economics of Clinical Negligence Reform in England' (2004) 114 *The Economic Journal* F272

FLEMING JG, *The Law of Torts*, 8th edn (Sydney, The Law Book Co Ltd, 1992)

GENERAL MEDICAL COUNCIL, *Seeking Patients' Consent: the Ethical Considerations* (London, GMC, 1998)

GIESEN D, *International Medical Malpractice Law* (Tübingen, Mohr, 1988)

GRUBB A, 'Infertility Treatment: Multiple Birth and Damages for the Birth of a Healthy Baby—*Thompson v Sheffield Fertility Clinic*' (2001) 9 *Medical Law Review* 170

—— (ed), *Principles of Medical Law*, 2nd edn (Oxford, Oxford University Press, 2004)

HARRIS J, 'The Injustice of Compensation for Victims of Medical Accidents' (1997) 314 *British Medical Journal* 1821

HART HLA, *The Concept of Law*, 2nd edn (Oxford, Clarendon Press, 1994)
HART HLA and HONORÉ AM, *Causation in the Law*, 2nd edn (Oxford, Clarendon Press, 1985)
HEALY J, *Medical Negligence: Common Law Perspectives* (London, Sweet & Maxwell, 1999)
ISON T, *The Forensic Lottery: a Critique on Tort Liability as a System of Personal Injury Compensation* (London, Staples Press, 1967)
JANSEN N, 'The Idea of a Lost Chance' (1999) 19 *Oxford Journal of Legal Studies* 271
JOLOWICZ JA, *On Civil Procedure* (Cambridge, Cambridge University Press, 2000)
JONES M, *Medical Negligence*, 3rd edn (London, Sweet & Maxwell, 2003)
KENNEDY IM, *Treat me Right: Essays in Medical Law and Ethics* (Oxford, Clarendon Press, 1988)
—— *Report of the Bristol Royal Infirmary Inquiry, Learning from Bristol: the report of the public inquiry into children's heart surgery at the Bristol Royal Infirmary 1984–1995* (Cm 5207) (Chairman: Professor Sir Ian Kennedy)
KENNEDY IM and GRUBB A, *Medical Law: Text, Cases and Materials*, 3rd edn (London, Butterworths, 2000)
KING J, 'Causation, Valuation, and Chance in Personal Injury Torts Involving Pre-existing Conditions and Future Consequences' (1981) 90 *Yale Law Journal* 1353
LEWIS R, MORRIS A and OLIPHANT K, 'Tort Personal Injury Statistics: Is there a Compensation Culture in the United Kingdom?' (2006) *Journal of Personal Injury Law* 87
LUNTZ H, 'Loss of Chance' in I Freckelton and D Mendelson (eds), *Causation in Law and Medicine* (Aldershot, Ashgate, 2002) 152
MACCORMICK DN and SUMMERS R (eds), *Interpreting Precedents: a Comparative Study* (Aldershot, Dartmouth Publishing, 1997)
MAGNUS U, 'Causation in German Tort Law' in J Spier (ed), *Unification of Tort Law: Causation* (The Hague, Kluwer Law International, 2000) 63
MARKESINIS BS (ed), *The Gradual Convergence: Foreign Ideas, Foreign Influences and English Law on the Eve of the 21st Century* (Oxford, Clarendon Press, 1994)
MARKESINIS BS and UNBERATH H, *The German Law of Torts*, 3rd edn (Oxford, Hart Publishing, 2002)
MERRY A and MCCALL SMITH A, *Errors, Medicine and the Law* (Cambridge, Cambridge University Press, 2001)
MORAN M, *Governing the Health Care State: a comparative study of the United Kingdom, the United States, and Germany* (Manchester, Manchester University Press, 1999)
OLIPHANT K, 'Beyond Misadventure: Compensation for Medical Injuries in New Zealand' (2007) 15 *Medical Law Review* 357
PEARSON, *Report of the Royal Commission on Compensation for Personal Injury* (Chairman: Lord Pearson) Cmnd 7054 (3 vols) (London, HMSO, 1978)
ROBERTSON J, 'Informed Consent to Medical Treatment' (1981) 97 *Law Quarterly Review* 102
ROBINSON GO, 'Probabilistic Causation and Compensation for Tortious Risk' (1985) 14 *Journal of Legal Studies* 779
ROGERS WVH, 'Country Report—United Kingdom: England' in M Faure and H Koziol (eds), *Cases on Medical Malpractice in a Comparative Perspective* (Vienna, Springer, 2001) 226
SHAW J, 'Informed Consent: A German Lesson' (1986) 35 *International Comparative Law Quarterly* 865

SPIER J (ed), *Unification of Tort Law: Causation* (The Hague, Kluwer Law International, 2000)
STAPLETON J, 'Occam's Razor Reveals an Orthodox Basis for *Chester v Afshar*' (2006) 122 *Law Quarterly Review* 426
STAUCH M, 'Causation, Risk and Loss of Chance in Medical Negligence' (1997) 17 *Oxford Journal Legal Studies* 205
—— 'Risk and Remoteness of Damage in Negligence' (2001) 64 *Modern Law Review* 191
—— 'Approaches to Fault in German Tort Law' (2005) 13 *Torts Law Journal* 242
TODD S, 'Twenty years of professional negligence in New Zealand' (2005) 21 *Professional Negligence* 257
TREITEL GH, *The Law of Contract*, 11th edn (London, Sweet & Maxwell, 2003)
VAN GERVEN W, LEVER J and LAROUCHE P, *Tort Law: Common Law of Europe Casebooks* (Oxford, Hart Publishing, 2000)
VOGENAUER S, 'An Empire of Light? Learning and Lawmaking in the History of German Law' (2005) 64 *Cambridge Law Journal* 481
—— 'An Empire of Light? II: Learning and Lawmaking in Germany Today' (2006) *Oxford Journal of Legal Studies* 627
WEINRIB EJ, *The Idea of Private Law* (Cambridge MA, Harvard University Press, 1995)
WEIR T, 'Chapter 12: Complex Liabilities' in A Tunc (ed), *International Encyclopaedia of Comparative Law, vol XI, Torts* (Tübingen, Mohr, 1971)
WENDEHORST C, 'Compensation in the German Health Care Sector' in J Dute, M Faure and H Koziol (eds), *No-Fault Compensation in the Health Sector* (Vienna, Springer, 2004) 261
WENDEL L, 'Compensation in the Swedish Health Care Sector' in J Dute, M Faure and H Koziol (eds), *No-Fault Compensation in the Health Sector* (Vienna, Springer, 2004) 367
WITTING C, 'National Health Service Rationing: Implications for the Standard of Care in Negligence' (2001) 21 *Oxford Journal of Legal Studies* 443
WOOLF, *Access to Justice: Final Report to the Lord Chancellor on the Civil Justice System in England and Wales* (Chairman: Lord Woolf MR) (London, HMSO, 1996)
WRIGHT RW, 'Causation in Tort Law' (1985) 73 *California Law Review* 1735
—— 'Right, Justice and Tort Law' in D Owen (ed), *The Philosophical Foundations of Tort Law* (Oxford, Clarendon Press, 1995) 159
ZIMMERMANN R and JANSEN N, '*Quieta Movere*—Interpretative Change in a Codified System' in P Cane and J Stapleton (eds), *The Law of Obligations—Essays in Celebration of John Fleming* (Oxford, Oxford University Press, 1998) 285
ZWEIGERT K and KÖTZ H, *An Introduction to Comparative Law*, 3rd edn (trans T Weir) (Oxford, Clarendon Press, 1998)

Materials in German

BERGMANN K-O, 'Die Reform der Zivilprozessordnung und ihre Auswirkungen auf den Arzthaftungsprozess' in T Ratajczak and C-M Stegers (eds), *Arzthaftungsrecht—Rechtspraxis und Perspektiven* (Berlin, Springer, 2006) 1
BEYERLE B, *Rechtsfragen medizinischer Qualitätskontrolle* (Heidelberg, Müller, 2004)
BUNDESÄRZTEKAMMER, *Statistische Erhebung der Gutachterkommissionen und Schlichtungsstellen* (Berlin, 2006).
DEUTSCH E, 'Anmerkung zu BGH, 20 September 1988' *Neue Juristische Wochenschrift* 1989, 769

DEUTSCH E, 'Schutzbereich und Beweislast der ärztlichen Aufklärungspflicht' *Neue Juristische Wochenschrift* 1984, 1802
—— (ed), *Kommentar zum Arzneimittelgesetz*, 2nd edn (Berlin, Springer, 2007)
DEUTSCH E and GEIGER M, 'Medizinischer Behandlungsvertrag—Empfiehlt sich eine besondere Regelung der zivilrechtlichen Beziehung zwischen dem Patienten und dem Arzt im BGB?' in Bundesminister für Justiz (ed), *Gutachten und Vorschläge zur Überarbeitung des Schuldrechts*, vol II (Cologne, BMJ, 1981) 1049
DEUTSCH E and SPICKHOFF A, *Medizinrecht*, 5th edn (Berlin, Springer, 2003)
EHLERS A and BROGLIE M (eds), *Arzthaftungsrecht*, 3rd edn (Munich, Beck, 2005)
FISCHER G and LILIE H, *Ärztliche Verantwortung im europäischen Rechtsvergleich*, (Cologne, Heymann, 1999)
GEHRLEIN M, *Grundriss der Arzthaftpflicht*, 2nd edn (Munich, Verlag Franz Vahlen, 2006)
GEIß K and GREINER H-P, *Arzthaftpflichtrecht*, 5th edn (Munich, Beck, 2006)
GIESEN D, *Arzthaftung*, 4th edn (Tübingen, Mohr, 1995)
GOTTWALD P, *Schadenszurechnung und Schadensschätzung* (Munich, Beck, 1979)
GRAF U, *Die Beweislast bei Behandlungsfehlern im Arzthaftungsprozess* (Munich, VVF, 2001)
HANAU P, 'Anmerkung zu BGH, 11 June 1968' *Neue Juristische Wochenschrift* 1968, 2291
HART D, 'Ärztliche Leitlinien—Definitionen, Funktionen, rechtliche Beziehung. Gleichzeitig ein Beitrag zum medizinrechtlichen und rechtlichen Standardbegriff' (1998) *Medizinrecht* 8
—— 'Autonomiesicherung im Arzthaftungsrecht. Ein Beitrag zur Entkoppelung von ärztlicher Aufklärungspflicht und Körperverletzung' in A Heldrich (ed), *Festschrift für Helmut Heinrichs* (Munich, Beck, 1998) 291
HAUBERICHS S, *Haftung für neues Leben im deutschen und englischen Recht* (Berlin, Springer, 1998)
HEIDELK S, *Gesundheitsverletzung und Gesundheitsschaden: Ärztliche Verantwortung im Kontext des § 280 Abs. 1 BGB* (Berlin, Duncker & Humblot, 2005)
HELBRON H, *Entwicklungen und Fehlentwicklungen im Arzthaftungsrecht* (Munich, Utz, 2001)
HEMPFING W, *Aufklärungspflichten und Arzthaftung* (Starnberg, Schulz, 2000)
KASCHE M, *Verlust von Heilungschancen—eine rechtsvergleichende Untersuchung* (Frankfurt/Main, Peter Lang, 1999)
KATZENMEIER C, *Arzthaftung* (Tübingen, Mohr Siebeck, 2002)
KÖTZ H and WAGNER G, *Deliktsrecht*, 10th edn (Neuwied, Luchterhand, 2006)
KOZIOL H, 'Rechtmäßiges Alternativverhalten—Auflockerung starrer Lösungsansätze' in H-J Ahrens (ed), *Festschrift für Erwin Deutsch* (Cologne, Heymann, 1999) 179
LANGE H and SCHIEMANN G, *Schadensersatz*, 3rd edn (Tübingen, Mohr Siebeck, 2003)
LAUFS A, 'Die Verletzung der ärztlichen Aufklärungspflicht und ihre deliktische Rechtsfolge' *Neue Juristische Wochenschrift* 1974, 2025
—— (ed), *Die Entwicklung der Arzthaftung* (Berlin, Springer,1997)
—— 'Delikt und Gefährdung—Von der Schadenszurechnung zur Schadensverteilung?' in A Laufs (ed), *Die Entwicklungen der Arzthaftung* (Berlin, Springer, 1997) 1
LAUFS A and UHLENBRUCK W (eds), *Handbuch des Arztrechts*, 3rd edn (Munich, Beck, 2002)
MEDICUS D, *Schuldrecht I, Allgemeiner Teil*, 17th edn (Munich, Beck 2006)
MÜLLER G, 'Beweislast und Beweisführung im Arzthaftungsprozeß' *Neue Juristische Wochenschrift* 1997, 3049

NÜßGENS K, 'Zwei Fragen zur zivilrechtlichen Haftung des Arztes' in E von Caemmerer (ed), *Festschrift für Fritz Hauß* (Karlsruhe, VVW, 1978) 287
PRÜTTING H, 'Gibt es eine ärztliche Pflicht zur Fehleroffenbarung?' in B-R Kern (ed), *Festschrift für Adolf Laufs* (Berlin, Springer, 2006) 1009
RADAU H, *Ersetzung der Arzthaftung durch Versicherungsschutz* (Karlsruhe, VVW, 1993)
RIEDEL U, *Kind als Schaden* (Frankfurt am Main, Mabuse-Verlag, 2003)
SCHLUND GH, 'Bestandaufnahme: Gutachter- und Schlichtungsstellen' in A Laufs (ed), *Die Entwicklung der Arzthaftung* (Berlin, Springer, 1997) 333
SCHREIBER H-L, 'Handlungsbedarf für den Gesetzgeber?' in A Laufs (ed), *Die Entwicklung der Arzthaftung* (Berlin, Springer, 1997) 342
STEFFEN E, 'Haftung des Arztes für Fehler bei der Risikoaufklärung—Zurechnungsbeschränkungen oder *versari in re illicita*?' in V Beuthien (ed), *Festschrift für Dieter Medicus* (Cologne, Heymann, 1999) 637
STEFFEN E and PAUGE B, *Arzthaftungsrecht—neue Entwicklungslinien der BGH-Rechtsprechung*, 10th edn (Cologne, RWS Kommunikationsforum, 2006)
STOLL H, 'Schadensersatz für verlorene Heilungschancen vor englischen Gerichten in rechtsvergleichender Sicht' in E Deutsch (ed), *Festschrift für Erich Steffen* (Berlin, de Gruyter, 1995) 465
THUMANN U, *Reform der Arzthaftung in den Vereinigten Staaten von Amerika* (Cologne, Heymann, 2000)
ULSENHEIMER K, 'Die Entwicklung des Arztstrafrechts in der Praxis der letzten 20 Jahre' in A Laufs (ed), *Die Entwicklung der Arzthaftung* (Berlin, Springer, 1997) 27
VOLL D, *Die Einwilligung im Arztrecht* (Frankfurt am Main, Peter Lang, 1996)
VON CAEMMERER E, 'Das Verschuldensprinzip in rechtsvergleichender Sicht' (1978) 42 *Rabels Zeitschrift* 5
VON GERLACH J, 'Die Haftung des Arztes für Fernwirkungsschäden' in E Deutsch (ed), *Festschrift für Erich Steffen* (Berlin, de Gruyter, 1995) 147
WAGNER G, 'Die Reform der Arzneimittelhaftung im Entwurf eines Zweiten Schadensrechtsänderungsgesetzes' *Versicherungsrecht* 2001, 1334
WEIZEL I, *Gutachterkommissionen und Schlichtungsstellen für Arzthaftpflichtfragen* (Hamburg, Kovaç, 1999)
WENDEHORST C, *Anspruch und Ausgleich: Theorie einer Vorteils- und Nachteils-Ausgleichung im Schuldrecht* (Tübingen, Mohr Siebeck,1999)
—— 'Anmerkung zu BGH, 30 January 2001' *Lindenmaier Möhring Nachschlagewerk des BGB §823 (Dd) (Nr 27)*
—— 'Fragwürdige Verschärfung des Arzthaftungsrisikos bei Aufklärungsfehlern trotz Behandlung lege artis' *Lindenmaier Möhring, Kommentierte BGH-Rechtsprechung 2003–6/2005*, 143
WEYERS H-L, 'Empfiehlt es sich, im Interesse der Patienten und Ärzte ergänzende Regelungen für das ärztliche Vertrags- (Standes-) und Haftungsrecht einzuführen?' *Gutachten zum 52. deutschen Juristentag* (Wiesbaden, DJT, 1978)

INDEX